THE PROBLEM OF PROGRESS

A

THE PROBLEM OF PROGRESS

BY

VINCENT BROME

CASSELL · LONDON

CASSELL & COMPANY LTD
35 Red Lion Square · London WC1

and at

MELBOURNE · SYDNEY · TORONTO · JOHANNESBURG
CAPE TOWN · AUCKLAND

———

Made and Printed in Great Britain by
C. Tinling & Co. Ltd., Liverpool, London and Prescot
F.563

Contents

Acknowledgments

The author wishes to thank the under-mentioned copyright-holders for permission to quote extracts from the publications mentioned:

George Allen & Unwin, Ltd. (H. G. Wells, J. Huxley, etc.: *Re-shaping Man's Heritage* and L. T. Hobhouse: *Social Development*); Cambridge University Press (Sir George Thomson: *The Foreseeable Future*); John Langdon-Davies (*A Short History of Women*); Faber & Faber, Ltd. (Roger Fulford: *Votes for Women*); Hogarth Press, Ltd. (Sigmund Freud: *The Future of an Illusion*); Methuen & Co. Ltd. (Morris Ginsberg: *The Idea of Progress* and G. M. Trevelyan: *England under the Stuarts*); Oxford University Press (J. B. Bury: *A History of Freedom of Thought* and A. J. Toynbee: *Civilization on Trial*); Penguin Books Ltd. (Peter Benenson: *Persecution 1961*); Society of Authors (Christopher Dawson: *Progress and Religion*); and University Tutorial Press, Ltd. (S. J. Curtis: *History of Education in Great Britain*).

THE Predicament of Man is all the rage now that people have sufficient leisure and are sufficiently well-fed to contemplate it and many a tidy little reputation has been built upon exploiting it; anybody nowadays who dared to suggest that the plight of man might not be wholly desperate would get a sharp rap over the knuckles in any literary weekly.

Professor P. B. Medawar,
in *Mind*, January 1961.
Vol. LXX, No. 277.

Preface

IT should be made clear, at the outset, that in this study of progress I am concerned with the Western European tradition and not the world as a whole. The concept of progress in the following chapters is essentially that of Western Man. The thread which runs from Asia Minor through Greece and Rome to Europe is, of course, only one civilization and there are many others, from the ancient Chinese and Indian civilizations to the Maya and Amerindian.

In some cases these civilizations have declined, in others they were disturbed and sometimes destroyed by European infiltration. We have also to remember the vast African continent in some parts of which poverty is possibly worse than it was a thousand years ago. If I repeat that I am concerned with progress in relation to the Western European tradition that is not to emphasize any indifference towards the African or Asian continents. It is simply to define the limits of this study.

I must acknowledge my debt to the late Professor J. B. Bury whose two books, *The Idea of Progress* and *A History of Freedom of Thought*, were invaluable sources of fact and inspiration. Similarly, I found Professor Ginsberg's book, *The Idea of Progress—a Revaluation*, very fertile in suggesting many lines of thought and full of factual enlightenment. I drew on his Frazer lecture—*Moral Progress*—for my chapter Progress and Morals, and made more general use of his later book *Essays in Sociology and Social Philosophy*. Many other sources are given in the select bibliography.

Once more I must acknowledge the help and detailed criticism of Pat Grosskurth, who patiently analysed each chapter of this book. Professor Ginsberg also went to considerable trouble to read the manuscript and gave me his general comments, Michael Young criticized the book, and John Keep read it with an historian's eye. I need hardly add that none of these can be held responsible for anything I say.

For the rest, this volume is loosely connected with my earlier volume, *We Have Come a Long Way*, where I gave a more detailed account of material progress.

CHAPTER ONE

The idea of progress

IT is fashionable among many modern intellectuals to consider what we once thought to be progress as the process by which we energetically go through the motions of moving in a desired direction, only to find ourselves more or less in the same place.

In this never-never-land nothing is really true. A clear-cut advance in one direction is immediately qualified by sad lapses in others. We live in a self-satisfied maze inhabited by hidden monsters who watch us struggle forward towards a land of promise and at precisely the moment when we exclaim that it is within our grasp we are sucked back by forces we do not clearly understand.

Progress is all a malignant deception. Yet the idea of progress has persisted for generations and it is remarkable how many people who protest that it is a complete and dangerous myth cling, with no sign of shame, to their electric light, sanitation, books, music, democracy, vote and—if you are a woman—emancipation.

Equally there are pale and harassed Marxists who insist that progress under Capitalism is a bourgeois delusion while accepting the very point which made eighteenth-century optimism so very sure of itself—that man is a rational being who can interfere with and change his destiny.

What are we to make of these contradictions? Where, to begin with, did the idea of progress originate? Not until the seventeenth century did the modern idea of progress take shape in the written records of European thought. A brilliant young man, Fontenelle, trained in the principles of Descartes, gifted as a writer and given to paradoxical wit, wrote a series of conversations called *Dialogues with the Dead*, which first broke away from the old traditions.

Before we examine these, let us turn back to the beginnings of civilization and see whether the Greeks had any faith at all in progress. The short answer is—no, they did not—but like all short answers it needs qualification. The Introduction to the First Book of Thucydides gives a brief account of the past history of Greece in terms which might have belonged to nineteenth-century England, and it is to Lucretius that we owe the word progress in its old-fashioned sense, but this first flirtation with the idea of progress, does not develop.

Platonic philosophy laid down a clear-cut interpretation of the laws of the universe which admitted the world as the work of the Deity and did not see it as immortal. In Plato's view the mechanism which moved the sun, the stars and the earth in strict rotation contained the seeds of its own decay. The duration of the world was fixed and within the 72,000 solar years of its life the Deity had devised a series of subtle rhythms calculated to confuse any attempt man made to interfere with it. The early period of this 'vast' life-span was a time of happy innocence when the Creator held sway over its uniformity and order, but slowly he relaxed his grip and in the second period, extending for 36,000 years, there would be decay and degeneration. Left to itself earthly organization would continue to decline and collapse into chaos but the Deity now intervenes, gathers together all the disintegrating forces under His direction once more, and restores the original conditions. Earthly life is ready to begin its cyclic process again.

Thus, to the Greeks of the fifth century, the behaviour of the universe was predetermined and any attempt to change the understood rhythms pointless. A Golden Age was followed by a period of degeneration, to be followed in turn by another Golden Age, but wherever your own personal lot was cast on the sinister curve of the circle, there was nothing you could do about it. Thus the principle of gradual change and adaptation to new conditions, the idea that men could work together to interfere with natural processes, was utterly alien to Plato's thinking.

It at once becomes clear that any acceptance of the idea of progress depends upon the way in which men viewed the universe. Back in Babylonian times it was common to see the world as 'an oyster, with water underneath and more water overhead, supported by the solid firmament'. Later, the earth became a rectangular body twice as long as it was wide, surrounded by ocean and placed at the bottom of a universe which had four vertical planes for walls. Either of these views regarded the universe as fixed and unchangeable, and progress, in the modern sense of the term, could not exist.

The early Christian Fathers reaffirmed this view by teaching that every human being born into the world was a victim of original sin and could not, therefore, progress morally. The whole purpose of the universe, in the eyes of St Augustine, was to realize immortality for a small part of the human race selected by God, in a world quite different from this one. As Bury says in his excellent book *The Idea of Progress*, 'For Augustine, as for any medieval believer, the course of history would be satisfactorily complete if the world (as we know it) came to an end in his lifetime.' Human history was, in his view, due to shrivel away, once the select handful destined for immortality had reached their heaven. Meanwhile Providence, not progress, held sway. This might intervene where and when it chose, and if less spiritually minded men preferred to call it Accident, that was their affair. Against the combined forces of original sin, salvation and Providence, progress stood no chance.

For most medieval thinkers the whole idea was ludicrous, but at least the universe had acquired for St Augustine a point and purpose which, to the ancients, it lacked, even if the methods of this world for selecting those spiritually qualified for the next one were not very subtle. The astonishing Roger Bacon rebelled against this philosophy, but his introduction of experimental method into science, and his use of astronomy, physics and chemistry in the study of theology, did not free him from the notion that the *only* world which really mattered was a remote and divine world to which people must aspire. He was prepared to grant celestial bodies rather more influence over people and events on this earth than even our wildest astrological quacks today, and he saw great historic changes brought about by their movements. Life on this earth was, in many ways, determined 'by the stars'. It was not merely that a 'pull' produced a corresponding movement on earth: specific events, like civil wars or revolutions, could be caused by the behaviour of the stars. Moreover, for Bacon, the arrival of Anti-Christ on this earth meant the end of the world and he believed that such a time was not very far removed. Once again, real progress had little place in all this.

The Renaissance broke into the obscurities of medieval thinking with the effect of a revelation but no sooner had men's

3

eyes opened to the rich potential of the world *here and now*, and the possibilities of every individual on this earth, than another cloak ensnared their vision. Everywhere the old gods of Roman and Grecian thinking were disinterred and worshipped. Men spent a lifetime analysing the work and writings of the ancient philosophers, and unquestioning veneration became one of the chief obstacles to further progress. Many discoveries were made and new ideas fermented but most thinkers continued to conform to the classical pattern. The first dazzling glimpse of heaven on earth had suffered serious inhibition.

Not until the sixteenth century did another tide rise when men like Copernicus challenged the authority of Ptolemy, Bruno questioned the infallibility of Aristotle, and Vesalius introduced revolutionary ideas into medical research.

Once again there was not much room for the modern idea of progress in all this, but science was beginning to soften up the defences of antiquity and many contradictions arose.

Optimism about the development of learning enlivened many writers of the late sixteenth century, and if it did not amount to a conviction that they were constantly progressing in a desired direction, it did involve a vague consideration of progress. Once barren ground had been made fertile. Everything was at last ready for the emergence of the idea of progress in the seventeenth century.

Three big prejudices remained to be overcome. First the belief persisted strongly that the Greeks had achieved in Classical antiquity a perfect way of life and it followed that all modern attempts must fall short of this. Men looked romantically over their shoulders at the far distant past as if it were an unquestioned Golden Age, and the habit was to paralyse any attempt to see 'the present' clearly. Second, Christianity had indoctrinated men and women with the belief that Man was a fallen being who could not recover his lost perfection on this earth but must live in the hope of achieving grace in Heaven. Third, there could be no doubt that this solid world, so laboriously going about its business, was approaching Judgement Day, and the last explosion must set a limit to any attempt we made to improve our lot. These forbidding ideas, taken together, simply said—you may expand the limitations of your life on earth, but not very far, and even if you do, it will eventually collapse into dust.

4

The seventeenth century brings us at last to Fontenelle. Fontenelle believed that each man born renewed the youth of the race and Man as a species would not experience old age in the same sense as the individual. Moreoever he wrote: 'The sound views of intellectual man in successive generations will continually add up . . .' Thus an educated person living in Fontenelle's day had inherited the wealth of preceding educated minds and a continuous process of developing education could be traced down the ages. Man, in his infancy, at the beginning of the world, had been absorbed by the struggle to survive, to wrest a living from hostile nature, and later, in his youth, had blossomed into literature and the beginnings of reasoning, until now, in growing maturity, Man reasoned much better and was indeed approaching enlightenment. War remained one of the forces which distracted his attention from the sciences wherein, perhaps, would presently lie his salvation.

For Fontenelle, not only was there a progressive development in knowledge, but such a development had its own necessity. It was a certainty. He did not commit himself to the wider implication that society, too, would progress. Indeed, he strongly resisted it because human nature was, in his view, unchangeable. A man who believed in Epicurean refinement and lived to be a hundred years old in almost undisturbed tranquillity, he yet thought it absurd that we could ever control men's passions. The great majority of men remained at heart, whatever one did, the same. They would continue to quarrel, to hate, to create wars and famines while the web of love and knowledge wove the illusion of civilization about them. The man who conceived the theory of the progress of knowledge could only regard social progress as something on which to exercise his wit.

And yet it was in French intellectual circles of the late seventeenth and early eighteenth centuries that a wider view of progress began to take shape, until the writings of the Abbé de Saint-Pierre gave the whole idea fresh definition. He reaffirmed Fontenelle's view that humanity would not decay as it grew older, but would instead become capable of fresh and vigorous development. He thought that civilization was in its infancy and saw thousands of unrealized years, full of promise, stretching ahead. The forces of superstition and war which had confused the world for so long could be brought under control if only governments would take heed of his enlightened theories and

5

create new Political and Ethical Academies. From being a
vague doctrine which inspired social reformers, progress was
hardening into a self-sufficient principle.

Voltaire played his spectacular part. The peak of his activities
came between the years 1755-1758 when his belief in progress
and hatred of the obstacles to progress fused in the famous work
Candide. He frequently acknowledged that the world was mad,
completely mad, the weight of human folly enormous and some
degree of injustice inescapable, but progress was there waiting
to be realized if we were prepared to fight for it. A man who
felt that all his preaching and wit, all his dash and style, were
wasted on the thin air unless political leaders were prepared to
translate them into reality, he did not turn to revolutionaries
with any hope of the right response, but relied on hereditary
kings and enlightened despots. In the end it was the Jacobin
demagogues, not the enlightened despots, who tried to carry out
Voltaire's instructions, and the recognition of intellectual
freedom as a generally accepted fact, not a benevolent exception,
marked the beginning of the modern intellectual outlook.

By the end of the eighteenth century, the idea of intellectual
enlightenment leading towards greater happiness, justice and
liberty had not only become widely accepted; it was said to be
taking place. Its enthusiasts drew optimistic conclusions from
the French Revolution.

Condorcet, permeated with the spirit of the Encyclopaedists,
had written his *Sketch of a Historical Picture of the Progress of
the Human Mind* and had come to see man as a perfectible
creature: 'The human species can be improved, firstly by new
discoveries in the arts and sciences and, consequently, in the
means of well being and common prosperity, secondly by
progress in the principles of conduct and moral practice and
thirdly by the improvement of human faculty. This may be the
result of improvements in the instruments which increase the
intensity or change the direction of the use of our faculties or
perhaps also of a change in the innate organization itself.'

The mainspring of the march of the human race to Condorcet
was the development of human knowledge. The history of
the growth of civilization would be the story of human enlightenment and as we steadily accumulated more insight into
the mysteries of nature and human behaviour, and pushed back
our boundaries of knowledge, we would become better people.

6

'Men could not,' he wrote, 'become enlightened upon the nature and development of their moral sentiments, upon the principles of morality and their natural motives for conforming their conduct to their interests, either as individuals or as members of society, without making an advance in moral practice not less real than in moral science itself.'

Condorcet also believed in the unity of mankind. In his effort to trace the movement of humanity towards truth and happiness he accepted the proposition that all men of whatever class or creed were rational men and that one day the backward peoples would pull up into line with the advanced peoples.

Consideration of the history of civilization led Condorcet to believe that we could not only establish the fact of progress but that once its direction was determined we could know and accelerate its future course.

All this was optimistically characteristic of that splendid enthusiasm which fired so much of Encyclopaedist thinking in his day. It remained for three other French thinkers to carry the theory of progress into yet more remarkable fields when Fourier, Saint-Simon and Comte claimed that they had 'discovered the secret of social development, and desired to carry theory into practice'. It was typical of speculative philosophers of the eighteenth and nineteenth centuries that they could claim as laws something quite insusceptible of proof, and sometimes rushed in with an enthusiasm which, to modern eyes, seems more suited to sportsmen than thinkers. The tougher reaches of critical reflection may thrive on imaginative leaps of a spontaneous and spectacular kind, but truth today requires the cold water of factual and even experimental verification before modern science considers it respectable.

No such niceties troubled men like Fourier. He thought that he was an original thinker without derivation from any preceding master and if he had contented himself with his interesting scheme for reorganizing society by industrial co-operation he would have been far more sympathetic to readers today. Instead, inspired by Newton's discovery of the law of gravitation, he ignored the fact that Newton dealt with physical matter and set out to discover an equivalent law which would co-ordinate and explain contradictions of moral behaviour. Men's passions were a constant source of distress and misery and if we could unravel the laws which governed them we could adapt ourselves in such a way that pleasure instead of pain ensued. A man granted remarkable insight into the unknowable, he presently claimed that not only had he discovered the all-embracing law of Passional Attraction, but that once this law was translated into action he could give a precise statistical picture of the number of unhappy, very happy and tolerably happy lives which would result. The law of Passional Attraction could be applied to convert human passions to whatever purpose one chose and Fourier laid down the nature of the society in which it would best operate.

The picture he gave of his Utopia is much more interesting and remarkable than his more absurd law of Passional Attraction.

He envisaged an enlargement of the normal family as a social unit until no less than 1,800 people were all brought together in one 'organism' which occupied one vast building surrounded by 'a domain sufficient to produce all they required'. The spirit driving these new social units would be co-operative rather than socialistic and the products of the combined work of rich and poor would be distributed in proportion to the capital, talents and labour of every 'citizen', with the proviso that no one must receive below a certain acknowledged minimum.

In itself non-socialist by conception, this was, none the less, one of the many sources of inspiration which were to lead nineteenth-century socialists to a new development of the idea of progress.

Two other thinkers of the same period whose names are indispensable to any sketch of this kind—the Comte de Saint-Simon and Auguste Comte—sometimes worked together, sometimes in rivalry but Comte, highly derivative from Saint-Simon, added a brilliance and range to his work which created bitter jealousies among Saint-Simon's followers.

Comte is famous, of course, for that brand of philosophy known as positivist and the Law of the Three Stages. In the past, he said, men had sought to explain the irrational behaviour of natural forces by imagining a series of gods, who manipulated the sea, the winds, the earth and human-beings according to divine caprice. This first phase was superseded by an attempt to substitute abstractions for gods but when these proved equally unsatisfactory, men began to practise a primitive form of science based on observation, measurement and experiment. The three stages of development he called the theological, the

8

metaphysical and the positive, and the word positive was in his view linked with the word Science.

In the hey-day of the eighteenth and nineteenth centuries philosophers were not above a certain glow of self-satisfaction and Comte occasionally named his own 'great achievements' in terms which any modern philosopher would regard as embarrassingly immodest. These were robust days when people did not mind enthusiasm, and philosophers were carried away by ideas which explained the movement of the planets, the fall of the sparrow and the purpose of life in one simultaneous sweep. Modern scientific caution was unknown and wholesale interpretations of the universe were deduced on the slightest provocation from ideas which revealed under analysis more imagination than sense.

But Comte undoubtedly made a big contribution to the idea of progress. Every branch of knowledge, he argued, passed through the three categories which he had outlined—theological, metaphysical and positive—but confusions arose because differing branches of knowledge were at different stages of development. Thus investigations of nature, of the earth, of animal life and the behaviour of the stars had reached the scientific level, but the study of social phenomena, of people, government and justice had not. 'The central aim of Comte and his great achievement in his own opinion was to raise the study of social phenomena'[1] from the metaphysical to the positive or scientific stage, where facts could be studied unconfused by the superstitions of the past.

Unlike Condorcet, Comte had no faith whatever in the rationality of man, acknowledged the continuity between men and the animals, and emphasized the dominance of the egoistic, self-regarding instincts over the social or other-regarding instincts. The egoistic impulses drove man to action, to increased knowledge, to commonplace work, and it was only with difficulty that intellectual selfishness and social impulses became reconciled. None the less, Comte believed that the wayward intellect could be subjected to altruistic emotions and looking back over history he found that altruistic tendencies had steadily grown in man and were open to indefinite extension. The big factor which stopped the selfish and benevolent impulses from cohering was the state of 'intellectual anarchy' which prevented any agreement on the underlying principles

9

guiding political action. If we could introduce the positive methods of science into regulating social relations 'the prevailing anarchy would be progressively reduced', but the social sciences had not, unfortunately, in his day, reached the positive stage. Nor, of course, have they today. Comte's enthusiasm swept aside the terrible complications which confront any attempt to create a positive science of human relations.

In Comte's view the driving force of history was man's constant need to 'ameliorate' his lot and to 'develop in all ways the sum of his physical, moral and intellectual life'. The many components of the social scene interacted upon one another and political, moral and intellectual progress were inseparable from material progress. The scene which he set out to interpret was exclusively European and he did not hesitate to give precise dates for different stages of development. The first Theological Stage ran to a close towards A.D. 1400, the second Metaphysical Stage was approaching its collapse in his own day and he saw his own work preparing the way for the third Positive or Scientific Stage.

Whatever the precise characteristics of the Utopia which would follow from Comte's positivist examination of society it was not a place which any modern humanitarian would very much enjoy. As for the average British worker today, clearly the spirit of the whole thing would strike him as crack-brained and illiberal. There was no escaping the logical conclusions of Comte's ideas. If the laws driving society were as certain as scientific laws, then we knew roughly how each individual ought to behave to carry out these laws, and there was no room for such feminine frills as liberty of opinion, and the idea of an industrial strike must be regarded as sabotage of natural processes.

While this ferment of new progressive views enlivened the French philosophic scene British thinkers were not idle. From the days when Locke announced his belief that 'the mind of man at birth is like a sheet of white paper on which any kind of inscription may be stamped' progress and its possibilities had exercised their wits.

Presently the far more definite writings of men like Priestly and Godwin began to appear. 'Perfectibility,' wrote Godwin, 'is one of the most unequivocal characteristics of the human species.' Given the infant undefiled at birth he could be shaped, at will, in the likeness of any chosen image. The idea of evolution from lower to higher forms of life, from simple to complex organisms, from crude and imperfect species to beautiful and adapted ones, did not have to wait on Darwin for its discovery. He, of course, produced the proof, but the idea of evolution was neutral. It could be optimistic or pessimistic. It did not necessarily mean that man was moving towards a desirable goal. For many people, the appearance of the *Origin of Species* in 1859 converted what had been a brilliant guess about progress into a *scientific* possibility. The work of Herbert Spencer now carried the argument in favour of evolution into a theory of social progress. Human nature, Spencer said, was not a 'constant' which did not change, but, like every other living thing 'ever growing to a new development'. Evil, therefore, was not an irrevocable necessity, but a result of failure to adapt properly to the conditions in which Man found himself. Forces were operating in Nature which strove towards a new and more perfect equilibrium and as time went on these would eliminate evil. 'The ultimate development of the ideal man is logically certain—as certain as any conclusion in which we place the most implicit faith; for instance that all men will die. . . . Always towards perfection is the mighty movement—towards a complete development and a more unmixed good.' Inevitably Spencer was far more subtle and complicated than such simplifications imply.

The idea of social and personal progress had now reached a splendid peak but its glittering attraction suddenly suffered a serious shadow in the light of modern scientific knowledge. If we were to become personally more perfect in each succeeding generation it was desirable that we should inherit the good qualities of our fathers, but it was presently agreed that fathers could not pass to their offspring qualities which they had acquired in their lifetime. Thus, the idea of continual *psychical* progress suffered a setback. Again, the idea of *social* progress seemed spurious when we remembered that at least four complete civilizations had developed, achieved great cultural wealth alongside appalling squalor, and slowly decayed.

Into the rhetorical flourishes of many writers of the day, the cold voice of Professor T. H. Huxley now struck a chilly but not contradictory note. 'I warn you,' he said, 'that so far from man finding salvation by uncovering the cosmic processes and

11

collaborating with them, it is clear to me that these cosmic forces are hostile and amoral, and it is only by combating them, by man imposing his own moral order on the tiger-rights of a brutal nature that we shall progress.'

In the upholstered optimism of Victorian England there remained many people who continued to defend the faith of 'natural progress', and others who looked back nostalgically to the past.

None the less, increased wealth, material comfort, developing knowledge and invention did reaffirm the belief that progress, straightforward and unhampered, towards the greatest good of the greatest number, was taking place in Queen Victoria's reign, but another thinker with quite different ideas of progress has to be taken into account—Karl Marx. A man who believed that the patterns of social culture and behaviour were economically determined, he looked forward to the day when the class struggle would break out into the open in all countries and the Rule of the Proletariat would overwhelm the profiteering capitalists who were hopelessly struggling against the forces of historic necessity.

His three great doctrines were the materialist conception of history, the Labour theory of value and 'the class struggle', but too much has been written about these jaded principles to make any summary very useful. He believed that once the proletariat had rebelled and taken over the means of production, exchange and distribution in any society, we could redistribute national wealth in such a way that every man prepared to contribute according to his ability would have his needs met by that society. The more imaginative reaches of his doctrine looked forward to a very special form of progress when man would not merely revolutionize his way of life, but take conscious charge of his future and begin to mould the hostile forces of nature to his own purposes. Progress, in Marxist terms, seemed to imply the realization of the historical mission of the proletariat, but the dialectical principle involved a continuous conflict which, theoretically, would never finally be resolved.

One wave of economic forces carried to power one class which built a state in its own image but implicit in that state was another class antagonistic to the first and working steadily to overwhelm it. The capitalist class would cause the working-class to revolt and the capitalist system contained the seeds of its own decay, but when the working-class at last held supreme dominion over everything would they, in turn, be swept away by another self-created antagonist?

Within these complexities the old theories of progress were impregnated with fresh meaning. The status of the working-man was to develop beyond recognition, economic forces would no longer terrorize the worker with the dual spectres of hunger and unemployment, and the redistribution of power and national wealth would offer undreamt-of opportunities to the son of the miner, the weaver and the milkman.

A man of different temperament and calibre, not to be considered an original thinker in his own right, but a person possessed with the idea of world progress, H. G. Wells wrote scathingly about *Das Kapital*. It was to him a monument of pretentious pedantry, and vast divisions of people into proletariat and *bourgeoisie*, phantom unrealities. He also felt that something called liberty was liable to be seriously jeopardized if Marx's theories were put into practice.

It was the view of Bernard Shaw that H. G. Wells had one unmistakable resemblance to Marx—he could not tolerate the existence of any other pebble on the beach—and certainly Wells had his own vision of the future with which he was prepared to challenge Marx.

In the writings of his middle years Wells became the prophet of the modern idea of progress. A tiny gnome of a man possessed of incredible vitality and torrential talk, he wrote in his lifetime a hundred books but continued, far into life, to cherish the Utopia he had conceived forty years before his death in a book which caused a considerable stir when it was first published.

Disarmingly, *A Modern Utopia* (1905) adopted the widest possible hypothesis, the complete vacuum of a community totally emancipated from tradition and habit. Only within the sweeping ambit of a society completely free from the debris of the past could he work with any real zest. He must begin with a *new* world. It was a world where people were divided into five temperamental classes—the Samurai, the Poietic, the Kinetic, the Dull and the Base. The Samurai appeared to be a self-elected voluntary nobility, a new ruling class taking the place of the old capitalist class, distinguished by that disinterested feeling for people and beliefs of which Wells thought many men capable. The Poietic were the creative class with well-developed mental individuality, capable of constantly exploring new ground; the Kinetic, very intelligent people able to work within accepted formulas. They lived while the Poietic experimented with life. A primary problem of government was to vest all the administrative and executive work in the Kinetic class, while leaving the Poietic an adequate share in suggestion, criticism and legislation, controlling the Base and giving the Dull an incentive to Kinetic effort. Only the Base were forbidden entry into the ranks of the Samurai and by Base, Wells meant 'people who had given evidence of a strong anti-social disposition'. Otherwise the flow from one class to another was largely self-determined and was certainly irrespective of the circumstances to which a child was born, his accent, dress or manners.

Herbert George Wells was the logical outcome of the long curve which ran from the Renaissance through the Encyclopaedists to Fourier, Condorcet, Comte and Huxley. It was a curve sustained by the conviction that man was a rational being and once enlightened education had become universal and scientific techniques widely accepted, the confusions of the social scene, unemployment, hunger, frustration and war would be either removed or controlled.

Nothing if not visionary, Wells reached out to envisage World Government, the final pinnacle of social progress, where racial differences would be resolved and the world was inhabited by a race of Cosmopolitans, all collaborating to enrich the species.

As the certainties of the late Victorian period passed away and the first ominous rumblings of war broke into the early nineteen hundreds, the romantic elements in Wells's Utopia became clear to more sharply thinking men, and then the whole splendid fabrication suddenly shook as the years 1914-18 erupted volcanically. There followed the economic collapse of 1929, widespread unemployment, the brutal appearance of Nazi Germany and another even more destructive war which shattered the last complacencies. Progress, straightforward, unqualified progress had, it seemed, come to pieces in our hands.

*   *   *   *

If we pause now, to look more closely at the word 'progress', it reveals something of the intangibility of the philosopher's stone. There are so many changing facets as you spin the stone in your hand. The first which comes up seems solid enough and leads into comparisons between conditions of work, hours and wages. Material circumstances continue to flash back as the basis of another facet of the stone, and material circumstances are measurable. This facet reflects housing, heat and light, food, clothing and education. Facet number three remains, like the preceding two, observable, but in a different sense, and deals with penal codes. Number four is not so clear-cut but is certainly susceptible to broad comparisons—freedom of expression. The fifth facet is unsubmerged and obvious. It reflects questions of health, medical treatment and expectation of life. Knowledge, the sixth facet, can be related to progress and the question—have we progressed in knowledge?—answered satisfactorily.

There, then, is more than one half of the philosopher's stone open to comparison if not measurement. When we spin the stone again and consider the submerged half, the situation changes. If anyone asks—has this modern, twentieth-century society with its love of abstract art and geometric patterns progressed æsthetically in comparison with the age of Velasquez or the French Impressionists?—we at once set off a score of passionate voices without hope of reconciliation. Æsthetics are intangible. There follow a number of bigger questions which will be answered in later chapters. Can progress be shown in morals or the status of women? Is there such a thing as spiritual progress and where and in what way does this relate to the happiness of the individual? Are we any wiser as a result of material progress? Do we know any more about the arts of government? There remains one other great question which tends to infuse, colour and change much of the nature of the stone as a whole. Have we progressed in the *proper use* of the knowledge which we have so painfully and laboriously acquired?

In this disillusioned age, with heroic pessimism saturating France, Colin Wilson writing his *Age of Defeat* in England, and American beatniks re-echoing gloom and despondency, the answer to the last question should be an emphatic and savagely destructive No. Indeed, in the vast shadow of the H-bomb the whole philosopher's stone of progress once more disintegrates, for many people, into nothingness. Progress becomes a glamorous delusion. It has held its deceptive shape alluringly before our eyes far too long. Now it has dissolved and left the grin of a demon conjuror in its place.

And yet . . . and yet . . . We have still, I believe, come a long way, but before I begin to analyse such a ludicrously old-fashioned idea as progress let me clarify one misconception. In France we still hear the tortured and impressive voices of Sartre and Camus, voices which are sometimes so subtle and complex as to become, on some issues, almost wilfully obscure. One part of their message remains clear. Man is sick and his future without hope. Could it possibly be that this new and modern sickness is in the minds of the French intellectuals and not in the minds of ordinary people? Are they projecting the tortured perversities of their own thinking on to the mind of the Common Man, and does he really feel himself weighed down with the night of all their disillusion, nihilism and torment? On scores of occasions the Common Man is a much more sane and sensible fellow who, rather than give himself up to despair, finds many sides of life still enjoyable despite the threat of cancer and the H-bomb. He knows pain and anxiety, he does not necessarily believe in a glorious future, but life is not to him a black, meaningless tunnel from which there is no escape except in death.

There are times, reading French writers like Sartre, when it seems that thinking has been pushed to such tortured lengths that nothing short of a deliberately contrived intellectual position will satisfy them, and it is just this degree of artificiality in one of the most brilliant writers of the day which drives me back with relief to the common sense of many Common Men.

Of course, common sense is not an infallible guide to conduct, but it has now to be asked whether, in Western Europe today, common sense allows the possibility of a belief in progress.

CHAPTER TWO

Material progress

IF we take the Common Man, at the material level, the answer is
undoubtedly—Yes, we have progressed—but the Common Man
is too vague a concept to make any satisfactory comparison
possible and it is necessary to take certain representative trades
and people. A miner, for instance. Consider the life of the miner
living and working in England today and his counterpart in
ancient Greece. Today, the mine is properly ventilated, controlled by stringent safety regulations and well-lit. Today, a
man at the coal face works shifts which last for eight hours,
earns between £15 and £20 a week, lives in a four-roomed house
with a wife of his own choosing, probably has two children and
is free to vote and travel. He can control the number of children
in his family; they are educated by the state; the whole family
is properly nourished, it has 'free' medical attention and can
stare hypnotized every evening at a magic box which mysteriously carries images from a far-off transmitting station. For
sixteen hours out of every twenty-four, and for two days every
week, he is his own master, disposing of his leisure as he pleases
within certain limits enforced by family responsibility and
income. Of course, the spectre of unemployment still haunts
the scene and the miner knows that a precarious prosperity can
be struck from his hands by economic forces which sometimes
reveal malignant intent, but questions of employment and unemployment are academic niceties which did not trouble his
Grecian counterpart.

He was employed fully, continuously, brutally, without
cessation. The mines at Laureion in Greece were a series of
shafts and galleries sometimes 250 feet below the surface without
any system of ventilation, where men crawled to work on all-
fours. They were branded on the arm or forehead with their
master's stamp, worked naked in clumsy iron chains and ate
underground whatever sparse food the day had to offer. One
ten-hour shift was followed by ten hours' rest, and then came

another ten-hour shift which did not give place to the Sabbath or any complete day of rest at all. Thirty days sometimes elapsed before the miners escaped from the crushing routine, and the extent of the break which then occurred could be less than twenty-four hours. What private life, with what pretence to pleasure was possible, within the iron treadmill of such a routine? It did not allow of leisure in our sense of the term, payment for work was a romantic dream, wives, if they existed, were known under brutal conditions, and serious illness the automatic prelude to death.

There is a sense in which any comparison between the ancient Greek and modern British miner becomes grotesque because we find ourselves dealing with extremes which cease to have any logical connexion. If the man working in the mines of Laureion had found himself miraculously transported to a Yorkshire coal-field, one week working under modern conditions would have convinced him that he had found paradise.

The lot of the average citizen-craftsman in fifth-century Greece was, of course, quite different. Looking back into the streets of Athens as the stonemason, potter and tanner began their work in the early morning, there was something romantic about the sheer individuality of each of these men, working in limited groups in small workshops, fashioning a herm, a vase or a pair of shoes with infinite care. Conditions of work and payment varied considerably, but there were periods when many citizen-craftsmen extracted deep satisfaction and a reasonable standard of living from their work.

Of course, the citizen-craftsman's children received no state education, medical attention, when it occurred, was dangerously makeshift, his house entirely lacked sanitation, windows or adequate heating in the winter, *paid* holidays in our sense of the word did not exist, unemployment compensation had not been conceived and whenever a plague struck the city the chances of survival were not very good. There were no letters waiting for him in the mornings because a postal system did not exist, there was no watch to tell him the time, he remained in ignorance of important events for days, weeks and even months at a time because there were no newspapers, and when he went out into the narrow, unlit streets at night, they were full of dangers unchecked by any police force.

The position of the common labourer was far less happy. We

have no equivalent today of the labourer who receives only his food and no pay for his work, and if we argue that it is better to have food rather than money guaranteed, the answer is that in several periods there was no such guarantee in Athens. Unemployment troubled Hellenistic Greece no less than it troubled England in the 'thirties and the provisions for it were far less adequate.

If it can be shown that the citizen-craftsman in fifth-century Athens enjoyed an æsthetic awareness which is far less evident today, we must remember that he represented a privileged minority whose numbers were overwhelmed by labourers and slaves. Moreover the slaves, from time to time, seriously undermined the position of the citizen workers.

The slaves . . . It does not need saying that a man who has no political rights, who cannot marry without the permission of his master, whose children are liable to be sold, who can be whipped at the whim of his employer and hired out to any passing stranger for any job determined by his owner, without payment of any kind, bears no comparison with even the poorest and most dependent product of this sadly abused and sometimes evilly misrepresented twentieth century.

If we ask the question—have we progressed in relation to fifth-century Athens, the answer is that at the *material levels* of hours and conditions of work, wages, houses, medical and sanitary services, the working-classes today, compared with the working-classes then, live in luxury. Political privileges, too, are better distributed, the vote is much more representative and the penal code less subject to metaphysical nonsense about the gods. Æsthetically it would be interesting to know whether many slaves appreciated the beauties of a culture which could, on occasion, so sadly abuse them. Moreover a culture which believed that the majority of men were born to be slaves and should be happy to accept that condition, can hardly compare with the democratic subtleties of our day. Opportunity? Yes, there the Common Man today scores once more. If the value of a culture is to be measured by the opportunities it offers the majority of Commen Men to realize whatever potential they possess, the twentieth century is preferable to the fifth B.C.

On the other hand, æsthetically, the case in favour of Greece seems clear-cut, and but for the fact that we are concerned for the moment with the Common Man, the tale of the brilliant minority of thinkers, sculptors, craftsmen, poets, writers and playwrights would have to be taken into account, and would, for many people, completely redress the balance.

Turn now to Rome. If we transfer the Common Man from his worker's flat on the tenth floor of a towering block in London, to an apartment house in Rome, we find his sleep broken into before the dawn. It is dark and he reaches out his hand to switch on the light, but there is no switch. The room is pitch black, the air stale and very still. He fumbles his way across to the wooden shutters and when he has exerted his strength to unbar and fling these wide, the cold morning air flows in and he finds himself in a sparsely furnished room without running water and with a nasty smell from the jar in one corner. He looks for the lavatory and there isn't one. He wants to light the gas stove— but there is no gas stove. He fumbles into his clothes in darkness, shivering from the chill air, and becomes aware that half of Rome is already awake and creating such a noise as would only disturb him at eight in the morning in a main London thorough-fare.

His breakfast is a draught of cold water, which he drinks hurriedly because he must borrow from a neighbour the toga which has to grace his shoulders before he will be given audience by his patron. He walks sleepily through the narrow streets, stumbling over a pile of rubbish on the way. He is surprised to find a group of people already gathered in reverence at the rich patron's solidly furnished house. His surprise becomes dismay when he realizes that he, an honest working-man, who has been taught that charity and integrity are irreconcilable, is expected to flatter his patron in order to receive a sum of money which will help him pay his bills. It does nothing to reassure him when he learns that every second person in second-century Imperial Rome is receiving public assistance in some form.

By the time he has carried through his rôle at the morning reception, and set out through the lightening streets in the direction of the tanneries, he is already beginning to wish himself back in twentieth-century London. At the tanneries, he learns that he is late for work and should have arrived half an hour before, but nobody is very disturbed. The smell from the workshops is rich and heady, the 'rooms' themselves are badly lit and the windows admit strong draughts unchecked by a solitary pane of glass.

He works for five hours, until eleven o'clock, with a single break of half an hour, and eats a lunch of bread and cheese and cheap wine. When he returns to the tannery he finds it almost empty and is told that everyone has gone to the Colosseum where six wild bears are to be set loose to fight twenty criminals. He makes his way to the Colosseum and sees the crowd thrown into a frenzy as a bear tears open a man's stomach and twists off his head. The sight and the smell of blood and entrails so sickens him that he has to hurry away from the packed arena, make his way through the streets of Rome, searching for the magic password which will carry him swiftly back to modern London. In his distress he cannot recollect it and, suddenly feeling ill, he collides with a Roman soldier who mutters something at him and brushes past.

A doctor? Yes, where in this terrible confusion of streets, so narrow as to seem suffocating, would one find a doctor? Gifted momentarily with the Roman tongue he stops and asks a passer-by who says—yes, turn left and right, cross the Via Nova and next to the Argiletum there lives a doctor—a very expensive one—but they are all expensive, and he will probably ask for cash.

If our Londoner spends a whole week in Rome he will be worried to discover that he is half dependent on charity for survival, that there is only sufficient work in the tannery to occupy him three days a week and that his living is precarious and impoverished. Of course, the baths are beautiful, the rich variety of Roman life stimulating and idleness for three days a week, in a sense, luxury; but it is a dearly bought luxury too much dominated by anxiety, toadying, patronage and barbarism. He is tremendously relieved on the seventh morning, as he stares at a group of slaves being driven back to their barracks by whip-cracking overseers, to remember the magic formula. He slips silently down the centuries, back through the broad clean streets of Holborn, up in the lift to the tenth floor, and bursts in on the commonplace sitting-room, with its badly designed but comfortable furniture, its windows and central heating, its too insistent television set and a sense of peace, ease and security.

One enormous qualification follows. His Roman opposite number probably did not suffer strain and distress to the same degree. It may be possible, imaginatively, to step down into another century, another civilization and city; it may be within our powers to reoccupy the shoes of a tanner dead these seventeen hundred years, and by sheer imaginative force to undergo the experiences which made up his everyday life, but there remains that mysterious element—the spirit of the times—which often eludes the finest insights. Unless we penetrate into the spirit of the times we cannot accurately translate what everyday life *meant* to the tanner in Rome. Possibly it did not mean anxiety and dissatisfaction. Possibly, as a man of much tougher fibre imbued with the coarse vitality of his day, he would have found the flat in Holborn anæmic and have yearned to recover the barbaric life of Rome. There is no certain answer. Certainly it is very dangerous to project our own values into the past with any certainty because the past so often has its own justifications.

Move swiftly across the centuries to fourteenth-century England. The lot of the agricultural worker then was very different from today. He lived in a hovel without a chimney and slept, sometimes five in a bed made up of bags of flock or straw. The floor of the cottage was beaten earth, the smoke from the fire hung about the room and food was of the simplest. He went to church but could not understand the service, he believed in the Devil as a living incarnation, but he could not read or write, and if he was caught stealing a sheep he knew that death by inexpert strangulation on the gallows would follow. During the harvest period the seneschal expected him to abandon his own crops for four or maybe five days, in order to work on the land of the Lord of the Manor, and throughout the year his struggle to tear a living from the soil was continually interrupted by similar demands. If he fell ill he would be treated more by superstition than science, a serious injury requiring surgical attention almost certainly proved fatal, and always in the background, if he was unlucky enough to be born in the early part of the century, the Black Death hovered—waiting to strike down indiscriminately whomsoever it touched.

The advantages of his modern counterpart hardly need description. He has a settled eight-hour working day, he lives in a three- or four-roomed cottage with running water, windows, a proper fireplace, a chimney, and probably at least two well-sprung beds. He can read and write, and in the Church of England every word of the service is intelligible to him. The Devil has ceased to be a grinning fire-spitting reality, the labourer does not have to serve his master unpaid two or three days a week and if some moment of avarice drives him to steal a sheep he may be sent to gaol. Medical service of the most skilled kind is freely available, the threat of plague has diminished to vanishing point and he is not confined by lack of transport or money to the thirty miles immediately surrounding the farm on which he works, or the companionship of some fifty people living in a small area.

Consider next some comparisons with the sixteenth century. Elementary education then rested in the hands of dame schools and a boy left school at a very early age to be absorbed into a working-day of terrifying extent. The whole family, in many cases, had to work to live in reasonable comfort, and sometimes city workers in the lower income groups dropped below the subsistence level. The death rate was very high and in Tudor times a man or woman could expect to live only until the age of forty. There were no real police, the ordinary citizens who fell into serious debt would be imprisoned, operations were performed without anæsthetics and midwifery was in such a parlous state that half the children born would probably die. As for the penal code: it still practised brutalities which sent a man to the gallows for stealing a sheep, and had not quite abandoned torture. None the less, your Elizabethan lived in a time when people had a tremendous zest for life, a great upsurge of creative energy had broken loose, and the city of London presented a vivid, animated, many-coloured face to the world.

Today elementary education is prolonged and taught by skilled teachers, working hours have been reduced from thirteen hours a day to eight, and a skilled worker can keep a family on his wages. He can expect to live to sixty-five or seventy, anæsthetics protect him against the worst outrages of pain, the police render the streets safe at night, and opportunities to realize whatever potential the Common Man may possess are multiple.

To confuse the apparent line of development through the centuries, in the middle eighteenth century the lot of the Common Man dropped back and seems to have been rather worse, in the lower-income groups, than it was in the sixteenth. Social machinery had not learnt how to contain and deploy an increased population and the East End of London created areas where vice, dirt, hunger and gin vied with one another to debauch and destroy the inhabitants. Houses not infrequently

C

fell down; there were no licensing laws to prevent anyone distributing cheap gin to rot the guts of young and old; distilling at one period, was officially encouraged by the government itself; and men and women still went to the gallows for stealing a few shillings from their employers. It was common in the middle of the century to find 'handicraft trades' working from six in the morning until eight in the evening, shops very often stayed open from seven in the morning until ten at night, a clerk's wages did not support his family, and child labour was officially encouraged. Before a poor patient gained admission to hospital he had to indemnify the authorities against his burial costs, and too often health institutions bred as much disease as they cured.

Comparatively, it was far better for the Common Man to live out his days in fifth-century Athens than in eighteenth-century London. Sixteenth-century London, too, was preferable, but if material satisfactions are what one needs, then quite clearly there is no time like the much-maligned, materialistically-minded twentieth century. Nor must we be too glib in dismissing material satisfactions as the main preoccupation of twentieth-century man, because material satisfactions cannot be isolated from more subtle enrichments which will presently emerge.

Tracing our steps from Greece to Rome, from thirteenth-century France to fourteenth, sixteenth and eighteenth-century England, one comment is inescapable. There is no clear outline of material progress. The line falls back from Greece to Rome, comes forward somewhat in thirteenth-century France, develops in sixteenth-century England, wavers and falls back again in eighteenth-century London, but reaches an unmistakable peak in the twentieth century in the West.

H. G. Wells has written:

Let me turn now to the horrible and tragic waste of human lives that has been going on since, five hundred generations ago, war and subjugation broke upon mankind. This period of five hundred generations, a mere yesterday in the long history of this globe, was spent for the great majority of human beings in abjection and frustration. Winwood Reade in his immortal book has called these twelve or fifteen thousand years the Martyrdom of Man, and maybe it was a necessary schooling for our species. . . . Our human heritage indeed is a devastated estate of undeveloped or distorted possibilities. One can only guess what proportion of human-beings in the past missed the slightest chance of self-development, how many mute, inglorious Miltons died in silence, how many potential Newtons never learnt to read . . .[1]

Yes, indeed. In more specific, less spectacular terms, time and again the potential of the ordinary human-being was crippled in the past by a score of forces, mysterious and unpredictable then, but understood and controlled now. They were forces which could so easily bring his life to an abrupt and unfulfilled end at the age of thirty or forty. He had to grow up rapidly, crowd what he could into his short life and find some solace in primitive religions for the threats brought against him by every agency which nature could muster. A hundred years ago 'out of every 100 male babies born alive in England and Wales roughly 65 survived to the age of 20, and 53 to the age of 40; of 100 girl babies 67 lived to the age of 20 and 55 to the age of 40'.[2] Today, in some countries the expectation of life has been extended from forty to sixty years, in others from forty-five to seventy years, and however gloomily the pessimist may regard man's tragic lot as something to be cut short at the earliest possible moment, common sense would suggest that an extension of years increases his chances of finding happiness.

Modern medicine has loaded the dice in his favour in a way which would have been regarded as sheer magic by the fumbling, superstitious, ill-informed and sometimes malignant medicine-men of the past. Until the year 1675 no one knew that the water they drank or the air they breathed was charged with multitudinous organisms which could choke, strangle and destroy in certain favourable circumstances with a savagery and certainty beyond the might of most military dictators. It was a Dutchman —Leeuwenhoek—who first discovered, with the aid of a primitive microscope, a number of 'little animals' in a rain-water jar, but whole generations of men, women and children were decimated by these unseen hosts until comparatively recent times. 'At the height of an epidemic when it is flushed with victory the meningococcus can kill a strong man in twelve hours . . . Or it may produce a lingering illness which leaves a child deaf and dumb and crippled. Today the meningococcus has lost its sting. It is no longer allowed to kill or cripple. The new sulphonamide drugs have put an end to all that . . .'[3]

It was customary, in the past, to combat illness in some cases by fasting, in others by praying, and doctors were shamelessly ready to apply the blood of a newt, the spawn of a frog, or fumes from some unbelievable brew, to any part of the human anatomy. In the thirteenth century elegantly dressed physicians with fur-trimmed caps and richly embroidered mantles talked learnedly of 'febrifuges' and 'humours' and kept repeating with oracular awe 'thus says A Vincenna, the prince of Spanish physicians'.[4]

When in doubt about the precise nature of a disease, a fairly common predicament, doctors would release a cloud of technical words intended to intimidate the patient to silence and remind him of the gulf between the doctor's profound knowledge and the patient's abysmal ignorance.

The devastating contrast between medicine in the twelfth and nineteenth centuries was perfectly crystallized by Macaulay in the House of Commons: 'Does the honourable gentleman know from what cruel sufferings the improvement in surgical science has rescued our own species? I will tell one story, the first that comes into my head: You may have heard of Leopold, Duke of Austria, the same who imprisoned our Richard Coeur de Lion. Leopold's horse fell under him and crushed his leg. The surgeons said that the limb must be amputated, but none of them knew how to amputate it. Leopold, in his agony, laid a hatchet on his thigh and ordered his servant to strike with a mallet. The leg was cut off, and the Duke died of the gush of blood. Such was the end of that powerful prince. Why, there is not now a bricklayer who falls from a ladder in England, who cannot obtain surgical assistance infinitely superior to that which the sovereign of Austria could command in the twelfth century.'

Until a very advanced stage in the history of medicine, if a patient developed appendicitis or pneumonia, underwent a difficult child-birth or serious haemorrhage, picked up any of a wide number of germs or was injured in an accident, the chances were that he or she would die. Hippocrates, the father of Greek medicine, 'knew little of anatomy or physiology and possessed neither clinical thermometer nor stethoscope.' He has left a record of forty-two cases in his book *Epidemics* and no less than sixty per cent died. It is not difficult to imagine what the popular newspapers of our day would do with the story of a G.P. who had even a fifty per cent death-rate among his patients.

It passes the powers of even the most heightened imagination to visualize the tortures suffered by men and women who had legs sawn off, or a hand removed, without anæsthetics of any kind, and the very smell of the ferocious concoctions brewed by wise women to cure children of diphtheria would have horrified the modern child. Speed was everything in the operations of the past. 'There were records for operations as there are for the half mile or the Derby. When Mr X the famous surgeon of early Victorian days took the leg off right through the thigh in under three minutes, the whole hospital buzzed with the news. You could not do good work under those conditions. To remove a tumour of the brain, for example, takes infinite care and skill . . . A brain operation today often lasts seven or eight hours.'[5]

The whole story of material progress is wide and complex and only the most impressionistic picture is possible in one short chapter. Medicine apart, technology requires a separate book to do it justice. Looking back into the past, the imagination boggles at the time, blood and sweat required in ancient Greece to transport a single block of stone by oxen, along the almost non-existent roads, or the laborious monotony of drawing endless small buckets from unreliable wells, and nothing can quite recapture the buffeting exhaustion and dangers of travelling a hundred miles by unsprung bullock cart in a land where caravans extended their journeys over a whole year travelling between one town and another.

Imagine a world without the wheel. Imagine a world where books were written on parchment and if you required a second copy it was necessary to re-write the whole book yourself. What could it have meant when only a minority of people communicated with one another by letter and those letters were entrusted to a fleet-footed runner, whose chances of reaching the intended recipient 200 miles away involved at least a week's travelling across country where he was open to every hazard from simple robbery to savage murder? Visualize the long, slow process of personally weaving the suit or dress you wear and the multiplicity of tools and gear which must have cluttered every home. Consider the grey, resistant earth in the soggy mass of spring sowing, with no plough—or only a wooden, hand-managed one—to break open its sullen flesh, and only the hand to scatter the seed from a rough sack. Imagine the sense of suffocation which would trouble the modern mind if it knew that short of a marathon journey of thirty miles every day on foot or by horse, it could not communicate with any new people, fresh spirits or ideas, but must continue all its life to know the same thirty people, because there was no bus available, and the idea of a railway train had never entered men's consciousness.

The wheel, the plough, the loom, the printing press, the blast furnace, the steam engine, the generator, the internal combustion engine, the aeroplane have continued over the years to liberate men's energies from drudgery and tasks which were lower in the scale of material preoccupation than anything we know today. Mechanical invention has raised men's eyes from the earth and set him looking at the distances. The work mechanically performed by the elaborate machinery of a modern city from its sewerage, roads, water supply, electrical illumination, food services and transport would have obliterated the complete working life of hundreds of thousands of men and women in the past.

At its higher levels education is concerned with cultural and spiritual matters and falls outside the limits of this chapter. At its lower levels it is concerned with common literacy and comes much closer to material matters. In elementary education, progress has been revolutionary. In fourteenth-century England large parts of the population could not read or write and the peasants were entirely without any education worth the name. As for the sixteenth century, as S. J. Curtis wrote in his *History of Education in Great Britain*:

> The real blow fell in 1547 when an . . . Act of Edward VI completely abolished the chantries . . . This meant the closure of a large number of schools, both grammar and other types. Even those which were permitted to remain were very badly hit . . . Elementary schools maintained by chantries were unable to continue. The Government threw the responsibility for elementary education upon the clergy. Gradually, elementary education fell into the hands of private individuals who were often, in character and attainments, unfit for the job. It was not until the eighteenth century when the efforts of individuals and the philanthropic societies were turned to the education of the masses, that elementary education revived.[6]

The qualifications prescribed for a schoolmaster in the six-teenth century varied from 'a pious, learned and sober man', or a 'learned and painful schoolmaster' to a 'true member of the Church of England as by law established, a good grammar scholar, and an expert writer and arithmetician'. Many lesser schools had only one master and an assistant master, neither of them properly equipped, in modern terms, to teach. School hours were much longer and holidays much shorter than today.

As Curtis wrote: '. . . in every town and in many large vil-lages there existed one or more persons who gave instruction in reading and writing. In what cases this instruction was given privately and in what cases it was provided in a school are questions we have no means of answering accurately.'[7]

Another authority on educational history, A. F. Leach, gives some precise examples of teachers in the middle of the sixteenth century, describing a bellringer teaching the children of the poor in Falmouth and 'an aged man', selected by the mayor, fulfill-ing the same rôle in Launceston.

Curtis points out that whereas the seventeenth century witnessed the decline of the grammar schools, secondary educa-tion reached a new low ebb in the eighteenth century. As for the public schools in the eighteenth century, their condition was almost as deplorable as the grammar schools and their curricu-lum just as restricted.

Most schools were grossly understaffed, the food badly cooked and scarce, and the administration chaotic. 'Flogging was not the only form of punishment at Christ's. Lamb's descriptions of solitary confinement in fetters and public scourging fill the modern reader with horror. An age which began with the use of the pillory and stocks for minor offences and hanged the small pilferer, which later sanctioned transportation to Botany Bay and suffered the sight of the bodies of criminals hanging on gibbets, was not likely to be unduly disturbed by the flogging of school-boys.'[8]

As Paul Johnson wrote, Lord Brougham 'not only created Britain's first modern university, he virtually invented State education by persuading the government to devote public funds to a purpose, which until then, had been left to charity or private enterprise. As Dr Arnold told Brougham: "Upon the general subject of popular education you are the founder and leader of us all." '[9] This was in the late eighteenth and early nineteenth

The problem of progress

centuries, and it does not do to dwell on the widespread
ignorance and illiteracy which was the fate of any low-born,
poor or not very well-off person in preceding centuries, or the
concomitant sense of inferiority and fear which so often marked
the uneducated person.

The field of economic progress is much too wide and complex
to analyse in any detail in a short chapter of this kind, but it is
crystallized in one sense in the growth of real wages down the
ages. Any attempt to isolate and compare the payments made to
different kinds of worker is foredoomed to failure because past
statistics are not only unreliable; the needs of individuals vary
so widely from age to age that the purchasing power of Greek,
Roman or European currencies cannot accurately be reduced to
modern equivalents.

The picture presented by Western Europe over the last
century is also subject to wide fluctuations and there have
certainly been periods of acute unemployment when the lot of
millions of average workers was not much different from the
poorest paid labourers of other days. If they escaped the
starvation which sometimes overtook their historical counterparts, the threat remained like a spectre in the background.

The complexities of the picture, even in recent times, is
clearly shown by Willian Ashworth in his excellent book *An
Economic History of England, 1870-1939*:

Before 1880 wage statistics were hardly sufficient to be very
reliable when reduced to general averages, but it is probable
that most wage rates were rather higher in 1880 than in 1870,
despite widespread cuts in the late seventies. Between 1880
and 1900, for the industrial worker who stayed in the same
occupation, money wages increased on the average by fifteen
to twenty per cent, while retail prices fell by about fifteen per
cent, a state of affairs which must have done much to reconcile
the mass of the people to current changes in living and
working conditions. After 1900 average money wage-rates
changed little for a decade and in 1914 were only about eight
per cent higher than in 1900, an increase more than offset by
the rise in retail prices.[10]

The proportion of workers who moved into better paid
occupations made the figures for the second half of the nine-

teenth century in Western Europe very subtle reading, because the eighty per cent rise in average real wages in England was reduced by this movement to roughly fifty per cent. Even so, a fifty per cent rise was spectacular and when allowance is made for this redistribution of workers the average real wage in 1914 was between seventy and a hundred per cent higher than in 1860 and forty-five per cent higher than in 1880.

If real wages certainly rose in this period, another equally important factor also underwent considerable variation in Western Europe; the intervals at which wages were paid. Some employers paid their workers every fortnight; some every month and at Wanlockhead (England), in the second half of the nineteenth century, the lead mine workers were paid once a year, but this was extreme. More common were pay days which, in the iron industry of South Wales, occurred every three to twelve weeks. In the past, this system of delayed payment had the effect of encouraging a spendthrift outburst when the accumulated wages at last arrived, followed by a period of living in debt or hardship. By the end of the nineteenth century the Webbs were at last referring to the commonplace phenomenon of men 'dependent on weekly wages', and the sheer regularity of payments introduced a much more evenly distributed security of income.

In recent years the average worker's share in the increased national income is probably better than it has been ever. A very small percentage of people still receive too high a proportion, but anyone who masters the jugglery of statistical analysis must emerge—breathlessly perhaps—with the triumphant conclusion that the ordinary person is better off.

*   *   *   *

There, then, are many facets where material progress in Western Europe seems a reasonable assumption, but it has to be emphasized that it has not been achieved straightforwardly. From far back, when Neanderthal Man first struggled to fit a skin round his body until elegant salons swathed beautiful women in impossibly expensive garments, the line of development has twisted back upon itself, given every sign of confusing its own ends, but has at last, in the present age, come through with some certainty.

Anyone interested in a much more detailed account of material progress will find it in my earlier volume *We Have*

Come a Long Way, but I must now turn to a related consequence. It is commonplace among people beautifully equipped with fine houses, cars, television and every mechanical device a modern age can offer to consider material progress a negligible matter, the achievement of which does not represent real advancement, but this is the natural consequence of not knowing the true nature of their own good fortune. Material progress not only makes people more comfortable; it opens the frontiers of other experiences, it makes possible the freedom required for a greater variety of intellectual and artistic life, and it can, at such simple levels as health, make or break happiness. We are far too prone, in the sickness of intellectual subtlety, to assume that the conditions which allow an organism its proper biological harmony are not, very often, the prerequisites for further growth. Excluding the saints of this world, the Common Man flourishes better when his 'material appetites' are rhythmically satisfied. A man utterly absorbed in the grapple to extract a living from nature is not normally given to philosophic flights. The submerged self very often waits on the relief of material pressures before it breaks surface. Artists may flourish in terrible conflicts and creative neurotics embrace every variety of pain, but the Common Man, without brilliant talents, frequently requires material liberation before his submerged self comes into play.

A series of subtle interactions make it difficult, sometimes, to distinguish where material satisfactions end and—for want of a more exact word—spiritual satisfactions begin. It is commonplace that technology has provided swift and beautiful machines to transport the newly liberated worker to parts of the world which, to his ancestors, remained remote and forbidden mysteries. The ordinary worker now has the leisure and the means to travel, but whether such travel widens and enriches his mind or merely leaves him horror-struck that—as Dickens wrote—'foreigners do as they do do' no one yet clearly knows. This duality runs through the whole situation. The worker now has much greater leisure than he had in the past, but does the way in which he uses his leisure enrich him or does it reduce him to a standardized unit in the mass-produced values of a television world?

The problem is not simple. Certainly there are many psychological and emotional satisfactions which spring from the most solidly material roots. The pressure for increased wages and better working conditions led to the trade unions which, in turn, forced the community to recognize the vital part played by the ordinary worker, and he has now achieved a respect which he never knew before. Raising the worker's status in a society gives him emotional and psychological satisfactions which are not purely material. Similarly, the need for workers who were literate enough to understand the machines they were expected to control played no small part in driving through the Education Act of 1870 and from that Act whole new worlds of mind, body, spirit, art, were opened to the blinkered eyes of a stunted generation. The fact that a miner's son can now pass through the democratic sieve and scholarship by scholarship reach out to those remote places of the intellect where the pursuit of truth carries a kind of intoxication which never entered his father's ken, really had its beginnings when a handful of men decided to agitate for better material conditions in the mines. The very fact of full employment transforms an anxiety-ridden worker from cringing dependence on his job into someone with a virile independence who can afford to search for the place in society which best suits him. The even simpler fact that a man arrives home from his job in a far less exhausted condition when his hours are comparatively short, means that he is left with energy enough to pursue adult education, sport, music, dancing, or even to get drunk at his own whim, a freedom of time and choice which elevates him into a self-directed, mature human-being who can make or break his own leisure.

There is no doubt about it—material liberations have lifted the Common Man's eyes from the sodden earth to new and infinitely rich prospects.

CHAPTER THREE

Penal progress

IT is customary for anyone unfamiliar with ancient Roman Law to pay it the reverence which seems due to a system capable of reaching out to the furthermost corners of Europe and deciding the fate of many a criminal who had never come within reach of Italy, much less Rome. It needs only the scantiest survey of the famous Twelve Tables of Roman Law to realize that civilized susceptibilities, as represented by modern man, would be outraged by half the penalties here prescribed, but the Tables still carry for some the sanctity of the Tablets which Moses brought down from the mountain.

The Twelve Tables have been reconstructed by various authors and no one interpretation is quite free from imaginative bias, but Sir James F. Stephen accepts M. Ortolan's reproduction of what he numbers as the eighth table.[1] It makes the most instructive reading:

1. Libels and insulting songs to be punished by death.
2. Breaking a limb, unless settled for, to be punished by retaliation.
3. Breaking the tooth or bone of a free man, three hundred asses: of a slave, fifteen asses.
4. For insulting another, twenty-five asses.
5. For damage to property caused unjustly . . . If it is accidental it must be repaired.
6. For damage caused by a quadruped, repair the damage or give up the animal.

There follow some mild offences for which the penalties remain obscure and then come these:

9. Whoever by night furtively cuts or causes to be grazed crops raised by ploughing, shall be devoted to Ceres and put to death if he is an adult, or if he is under the age of

puberty shall be flogged at the discretion of the praetor and made to pay double value or damages.

10. Whoever burns a house or a stack of corn near a house knowingly and maliciously, shall be bound, beaten and burnt. If by accident he must pay damages. If he is too poor he must be slightly flogged.

11. A man who wrongfully cuts another's trees must pay twenty-five asses for each tree.

12. If a man is killed while committing theft by night he is lawfully killed.

13. If a thief is taken by day he may not be killed unless he resists with a weapon.

14. A thief taken in the fact must be beaten with rods and adjudged (as a slave) to the person robbed. If he is a slave he must be beaten with rods and thrown from the Tarpeian rock. Youths are only to be beaten with rods at the discretion of the magistrate, and condemned to repair the damage.

There are, in the eighth Table, twenty-six items of this kind, all so curtly expressed as to make it quite clear that whoever administers the law can interpret each statute according to personal persuasion. As Sir James Stephen wrote in his classic study: 'We know . . . from other sources that in ancient Rome the courts and the magistrates practically made their own laws to a great extent.'[2]

There are penalties in the Twelve Tables which seem more just than their equivalents today, as for instance that concerning money lending: 'Interest on money is $8\frac{1}{3}$ per cent and whoever lends at a higher rate forfeits four times the amount lent.' There are others which seem to us little short of exercises in sheer sadism—'If a man kills his parent, veil his head, sew him up in a sack and throw him into the river.'

Item 21 reads: 'A patron who cheats his client is devoted to the gods and may be killed by anyone.' Item 23: 'Whoever gives false evidence must be thrown from the Tarpeian rock.' The fact that a man could be bound, beaten and burnt alive for setting fire to a cornstack may seem a brutal burlesque of justice in modern eyes but it must be remembered that cornstacks were probably ten times as valuable in those days, and the malicious destruction of food a criminal attack on the very life-blood of the community. Food apart, property and its violation plays a big part in ancient Rome as it does in modern law, but the value given to food, clothing, horses or household possessions varies so widely down the ages that any comparison is difficult. It has to be remembered that the term Roman Law covers a vast period of thirteen centuries which elapsed between the foundation of Rome until the fall of the Western Empire in the fifth century A.D. and beyond that into the Eastern Empire. Evidence in the early years is unreliable and the picture of later years very complex.

In the time of Constantine (A.D. 288-237) the Roman Empire was divided into four praetorian praefects, one in the east covering Africa, Syria and Asia Minor, another called Illyricum taking in south-east Europe, a third for Italy and a fourth for the Gauls including Britain. The praefectures were subdivided into thirteen dioceses and the dioceses divided again into 116 provinces. Each province included a number of cities with their *territoria*. The 'policemen' of each territory were under military control, each group having a centurion or superintendent and over him a man known as *princeps pacis*, a title which as Sir James Stephen wrote 'it is impossible not to translate by—justice of the peace'.

Prosecutions in these areas were of two kinds—public and private. It is possible to piece together a fairly detailed picture of what happened under the Roman Empire when a crime was committed and a public prosecution followed. The actual procedure of Roman Law at this stage had much to commend it, but this chapter is more concerned with penalties than procedure. However, there are resemblances to criminal procedure today and it would be prejudiced not to acknowledge the extraordinary power which the Romans had to devise a framework likely to yield justice, only, in our eyes, to confuse it in practice.

Marcian—Emperor of the East, 450-457—has left this fascinating picture of the checks and balances which, theoretically at least, brought Roman criminal procedure within reach of modern civilized standards.

. . . A chapter of an order is still extant by which Antonius Pius when President of Asia, enacted in the form of an edict, that the [magistrates] when they apprehended robbers, should

36

question them about their accomplices and receivers, and
send their examination enclosed in a sealed letter for the
information of the President. Persons sent up with a letter
are to have a full trial. . . . So, too, both Pius and other
princes ordered that even those who were reported for
punishment are to be tried, not as if they were convicted,
but from the beginning, if there is any one to accuse them.
Therefore, who ever tries them ought to send for the
magistrate and require him to prove the extent of his report.
If he has done it diligently and faithfully he must be com-
mended; if he has acted hastily and without careful enquiry
it must be officially noted . . . but if it appears that he
questioned the defendant maliciously, or reported what was
not said as if it had been said, the magistrate is to be punished
for the sake of example. . . .[3]

Thus the offender was arrested by the equivalent of the
modern policeman, a preliminary investigation followed, the
man was then committed to prison and later came up for trial
before the *praeses* 'who, like the Indian Commissioners of
Divisions in some parts of India . . . exercised the powers of a
judge of assize and made a circuit to the different [areas]—
The *praeses* . . . had before him the [magistrate's] report and
copies of the depositions just as an English judge of assize has
the depositions taken before a magistrate.'[4]
The general parallels are deceptively similar: the working
details sometimes very different. The question of witnesses
introduces complications where the actual facts are not quite
clear. In the course of a trial, an understood time was allowed
for the production of witnesses and documents, and witnesses
were examined, as modern lawyers say, 'in chief on facts' and
cross-examined, but whether defence and prosecution could
call witnesses under similar conditions remains obscure.
According to Pothier, the French jurist, both sides could call
witnesses, but only the prosecution was able to compel their
attendance, and in a society where guilt by association frequently
occurred and private citizens were not the most punctilious
people, there was a danger that witnesses simply might not turn
up. Certainly the accused was allowed to call witnesses as to
his character, but as to the facts of the case he might be forced
to stand alone as his own sole witness.

In itself, the privilege of calling witnesses on equal terms remained a luxury far into criminal history, but the first impulse to admire the attempt to establish an atmosphere of judicial detachment, where truth could be examined in classical calm, collapses when we learn that torture was freely used to extort evidence. Torture formed an essential part of criminal procedure under the Roman Empire and if it was usually reserved for slaves the very multiplicity of their numbers made it commonplace to have slave-witnesses in many cases. Even worse, the slaves were sometimes tortured not because of complicity in the crime or any offence on their part but simply because their masters had come under suspicion. True, the accused, if the evidence was strong enough, might also undergo torture, but nothing in our eyes could justify prolonged floggings, brutal mutilations and a wide variety of brandings in the service of discovering 'the truth'. Of course, the sophisticated Roman lawyer, steeped in the iniquities of colonial peoples and completely familiar with every art of Roman subterfuge, no more believed in the facts elicited from a man whose back had become a mass of agonized pulp than in a divine hereafter. Cynicism had its place in legal as in religious ritual. Indeed, in one sense, it was written into the law. Evidence extracted by torture was to be received with caution; but torture remained a principal weapon in the legal armoury.

There was an enormous span of years—roughly a thousand—between the first formulation of the Twelve Tables and the much more complex and interesting 'code' of Justinian. Roman lawyers in the days of Justinian divided crimes into three classes, Publica Judicia, Extraordinaria Crimina and Private Delicta. Under the first class came a number of sexual offences which followed a course monotonously familiar today, from adultery and fornication to incest and unnatural offences. In whatever else we have progressed there seems to have been no great development in the nature of sexual offences. The position of women as chattels in some classes of Roman society was closely reflected by laws which made adultery a crime on the part of the wife but not the husband. The liberties given to men and the restraints put upon women seem, in these days of greater sexual equality, unfair, but as in all sophisticated societies, a minority of Roman women, at different periods, succeeded in living their own rich, individual and sometimes debauched lives.

There was a period in Roman history when husbands were permitted to take the law into their own hands in a manner which would never be tolerated today. If a man persistently pursued the wife of another, the husband could warn him three times in writing or in the presence of three witnesses, and later, if he came upon the man again in his wife's company, he was legally permitted to kill him. In practice, on one occasion at least, the husband of a Roman beauty, a woman of easy virtue, was confronted with a lover physically much more powerful than he was. The lover laughed uproariously when threatened with death, but adultery could be a very dangerous indulgence even for the most massively built offender. The law regarded the slaying of an adulterer in far less harsh terms than normal murder and in an age when secret poisons were easily available the possibilities of private vengeance were considerable. Moreover, a father had the right to kill both his married daughter and her accomplice if she was taken in adultery either at his house or in her husband's.

There were, of course, special laws against the straightforward poisoning of an enemy and the penalties were severe for a form of destruction which had become too fashionable to be ignored. As for commonplace murder, under the Republic it was punished by confiscation of goods and imprisonment on an island, and under the Antonines by death.[5]

Class distinctions introduced privileges and prejudices into the law which were far more extreme than anything we know today and it was quite normal for the common murderer who had no distinction of rank or wealth to be dragged off and thrown to the wild beasts with no more compunction than one might feel at crushing a fly. If '. . . the person killed was a father or mother . . . the offender was burnt, that punishment having been substituted for the ancient one of drowning with a cock, snake and dog. Burning was also the punishment of incendiaries.'[6]

Within the complicated religious observances, superstitious rites and occult practices of the day, it was possible in some periods to fall into the crime of sacrilege on very unexpected grounds, but the most common definition was to steal something at once public and sacred. Punishment took three forms: the offender was put to death by the sword, burnt alive or simply thrown to the wild beasts.

Under the Empire the widespread practice of throwing criminals to wild beasts served the double purpose of providing diabolically satisfying spectacles to keep the idle plebs in a state of happy subservience and warning the populace of the horrible fate awaiting the next offender.

An interesting passage in Sir James Stephen's book records the complicated subtleties of the law and punishments relating to certain kinds of theft: 'It seems that the crime [of stealing animals] could not be committed on less than four pigs or ten sheep. They need not however all be taken together. In such a state of the law one would expect thefts of three pigs or eight sheep to become abnormally common. By a law of Hadrian this offence was punished by the mines, or, if the thieves were armed [with death].'⁷

The influence of Roman law and procedure can be traced all over Western Europe today, but it does not follow that Roman penalties had any very direct effect on the modern British penal code. If we took a modern citizen accused of stealing a horse, or committing adultery or libelling a neighbour, through the machinery of the Roman law courts he would be lucky to emerge alive, partly out of horror that such extreme and savage laws could exist and partly because death was the automatic penalty for so many crimes.

*   *   *   *

Leaving Rome and sweeping across Europe to Anglo-Saxon England we find that the principles behind the laws and penalties laid down in the time of Cnut are more Christian than Roman in spirit, and occasionally achieve poetic expression: 'Though any one sin, and deeply foredo himself, let the correction be regulated so that it be becoming before God and tolerable before the world. . . . And we command that Christian men be not on any account for altogether too little condemned to death: but rather let gentle punishments be decreed for the benefit of the people; and let not be destroyed for little God's handywork and His own purchase which he so dearly bought.'⁸

For lesser crimes a whole system of compensation, fines and payments according to rank operated in Cnut's day, and much of the legal wrangling concerned what fines and compensation were relevant to what kind of person. There seems to have been little appeal against arbitrarily imposed verdicts and the penalty for repeating many offences was a straightforward and brutal beheading. Brutality, in fact, quickly broke in on all sides to confuse our poetically sensitive preamble. The lofty protestations of Christian tolerance suffer a rude shock when we read some of the penalties imposed for quite commonplace crimes. 'That his hands be cut off, or his feet, or both, according as the deed may be. And if he have wrought yet greater wrong, then let his eyes be put out, and his nose and his ears and his upper lip be cut off, or let him be scalped; whichever of these those shall counsel whose duty it is to counsel thereupon, so that punishment be inflicted and also the soul be preserved.'[9]

In very early days the threat of private vengeance was the main check upon crime and violence, and private war between one group and another, or bloody feuds between two families, established a crude, uneasy resolution of what was generally regarded as a criminal act. In William the Conqueror's day trial by combat between two representative men was introduced as a refined form of the old private wars, but they were not representative in any exact sense.

The *right* of one person summarily to kill another was really an early attempt to give social sanction to what had been arbitrary practice before. The power to kill a fellow human-being for certain understood crimes makes many appearances in early Saxon laws. One law lays it down that 'if a thief be seized let him perish by death, or let his life be redeemed according to his captor'. 'He who slays a thief must declare on oath that he slew him offending.' Another code states 'that no thief be spared over twelve pence, and no person over twelve years whom we learn according to folkright that he is guilty and make no denial; that we slay him and take all he has'.

We come next to Magna Carta, issued by King John in June 1215 under compulsion from his barons, and subsequently misunderstood by seventeenth-century lawyers and enthusiastically misinterpreted by some nineteenth-century historians. Trial by jury, and the principle of *habeas corpus*, were thought to have been secured by Magna Carta but considerable qualifications arose. Writs of *habeas corpus* were issued before Magna Carta and enabled persons of less sanguinary persuasions to substitute a rough and ready trial by jury for the bloodthirsty and frequently lethal trial by battle. Magna Carta refined the process and enabled a judge to issue a writ of *habeas corpus* commanding anyone holding a person in illegal confinement to bring 'the body of such a person' before a court of law. It was a tremendous step towards establishing the right of the common felon, or for that matter of a high-born aristocrat to a fair trial, but it did nothing to modify the appalling penalties still in common use.

I described in *We Have Come a Long Way* what became of men accused of robbery in thirteenth-century baronial France. One particular case concerned two soldiers charged with attacking and robbing the wife of a castle falconer and each soldier directly accused the other of the actual crime, claiming the half-innocent rôle of accomplice.

The two men were allowed to argue with one another in the Great Hall of the castle for a time, until, at a certain arbitrarily determined point, the provost—a castle official—saw fit to intervene. Disagreement between the prisoner-witnesses had caused sufficient confusion for him to ask the baron whether he required what was known as preparatory torture to establish the facts of the case. The baron agreed but the two mercenaries fell on their knees begging for mercy. It was useless. Surrounded by guards the mercenaries were escorted to the torture tower, a room whose walls were six feet thick and fitted with a number of devices capable of extorting confessions true or false with a horrible inevitability. The provost in full ceremonial dress and the executioner in his yellow cloak, accompanied the prisoners. First the lesser thumbscrew was applied. This had the effect of redoubling the victims' accusations against one another and left them pale, screaming wretches incapable of logical thought, their whole spirit bent to the one purpose of escaping further torture. The executioner next tried the second thumbscrew which slowly reduced both thumbs to a bloody mess of crushed flesh, bone and nail.

Any qualms which the court may have about the barbarity of such methods are quelled by the underlying principle common to legal thinking of the day; so long as it uncovers 'the truth' any method is justified. The agonized outpourings of the accused are at last assumed to have made some sort of sense and both men are judged equally guilty. Half carried, half dragged back to the Great Hall of the castle, as they still writhe in agony from their torture, the Baron talks over their 'confession' with his two assessors. There is only one possible verdict—

death, summary death after the usual rituals have been duly satisfied.

Of course, the two mercenaries are, in one sense, fortunate people. They have merely committed robbery with violence and undergone inexpert strangulation. The man or woman convicted of gross blasphemy has a far worse fate to face. It begins when the executioner burns off certain carefully prescribed areas of flesh (in the case of a woman it may be part of one of her breasts) with red-hot irons, and ends with four fiery stallions each one attached to an arm or leg being savagely whipped off in different directions.

Modern sensibilities prickle with horror at the number and variety of agonizing punishments devised by the medieval mind, but these gradually diminished as time went on, although the belief persisted that violations of sex or property were the final outrages for which no penalty could be too extreme.

It was a big step in the direction of enlightened justice when the old principles which regarded criminals as animals to be hunted down and put to death, began to undergo refinements which defined, if with elaborate obscurity, the precise circumstances of an arrest for felony. The many confusions which arose between the powers of zealous citizens and what became known as constables and justices forced 'the authorities' to attempt to re-clarify the code.

Where a felon fled, tried to resist 'lawful arrest', or could not be apprehended without force, it was still possible to kill him in the process, and such killing was held to be lawful. Under early English law a constable who joined a hue and cry after a criminal and killed the suspect, even though it was subsequently shown that the man was quite innocent, could not be held guilty of murder, manslaughter or indeed of any charge brought against him in connexion with the death.

As for witnesses, their place and powers in any given trial varied widely from county to county and country to country. All over Europe the civil law was administered in such a way that the prosecutor alone could call witnesses and it was not until the reign of Queen Anne that an English prisoner had the right to call witnesses upon equal terms with the Crown. In the reign of Henry VIII torture continued to be used to extract information from witnesses, although it was no longer recognized as part of the legal code. According to Margery Fry the last time a man died, unconvicted, under torture in England, was in 1686. 'In 1726 a prisoner yielded under it, and consented to plead; our law was not cleansed of it until 1772.'[10]

It is difficult to imagine a worse penalty than that inflicted in the reign of Henry VIII on the cook who, convicted of attempted poisoning, was boiled to death by Act of Parliament, some perverted sense of poetic justice insisting that a man who spent his life cooking should undergo the torment of his trade. The imagination retreats from what this must have meant in fact, and it is better not to probe too much into those moments when a half-suffocating, half-drowning man felt the water scalding the skin from his body.

In Queen Elizabeth's day, court procedure had refined away many crudities and if penalties remained harsh they were not quite so sadistically preoccupied with causing the utmost pain. Sir Thomas Smith, Secretary of State to Queen Elizabeth, has left this fascinating description of a trial at the Assizes:

> In the town house or in some open common place there is a tribunal or place of judgment made aloft. Upon the highest bench there sit the judges which be sent down in commission. . . . Next them on each side [sit] the justices of the peace. . . . Before these judges and justices there is a table set beneath, at which [sits] the . . . keeper of the writs . . . the under sheriff and such clerks as do write.
> At the end of that table there is a bar made with a space . . . [for] twelve men to come in when they are called, behind that space another bar, and there stand the prisoners which be brought thither by the gaoler all chained together. . . .[11]

There follows a ritual remarkably close to our court proceedings today with the 'taking of pleas', the swearing of the jury and the first prisoner pleading not guilty. Take a case of commonplace robbery, of two men accused of stealing a horse and a purse. Already, before it reaches 'the Assize' the case has been examined by a local magistrate whose evidence is presently produced in court.

> If they which be bound to give evidence come in, first is read the examination which the justice of the peace doth give . . . then is heard the man who has been robbed . . .

44

being first sworn to say the truth and [afterwards] the constable and as many as were at the apprehension of the [robber]. . . .

These be set in such a place as they may see the judges and the justices, the inquest and the prisoner. . . .

The judge, after they [all] be sworn asketh first the party robbed if he know the prisoner and biddeth him look upon him. . . .[11]

Then the robbed man gives evidence '. . . thou [robbed] me in such a place, thou [beat] me, thou tookest my horse from me and a purse. Already, before it reaches 'the Assize' the case has thy company. The thief will say—No—and so they stand a while in altercation. . . .'[11] The accused man is, it seems, expected to produce no small part of his defence in argument with the plaintiff. There follows an outline of the evidence against the prisoner by the prosecutor, and a number of witnesses are called to support his case.

'When the judge hath heard them say enough, he [asks] if they can say any more. If they say No, then he [turns] his speech to the [Jury]. "Goodmen ye of the inqueste ye have heard what these men say against the prisoner. You have also heard what the prisoner can say for himself. Have an eye to your oath and to your duty, and do that which God shall put in your minds to the discharge of your consciences". . . .'[11]

It is customary to confront one jury with two or three prisoners on different charges at the same time, and it requires a considerable feat of memory to prevent the confusion which puts each prisoner in danger of suffering for another's crime. Sometimes the jury protests that it is 'overweighted' with too many cases, but the example given by Sir Thomas Smith is more straightforward. The jury, in this case, finally retires to consider its verdict and is encouraged to 'make this speedy by being denied bread, drink, meat or fire'.

Anyone found guilty of stealing a horse and purse, in our day and age, might go to prison for a few weeks, but under Queen Elizabeth, many penalties remained savage, and when the judge came to pass sentence he said: '. . . thou shalt return to the place from whence thou camest: from thence thou shalt go to the place of execution. There thou shalt hang till thou be dead. . . .'[11]

45

In the seventeenth century, according to Sir Matthew Hale's *History of the Pleas of the Crown*, it was laid down that:

1. Any person may arrest any person who is actually committing or has committed a felony.
2. Any person may arrest any person whom he suspects on reasonable grounds to have committed any felony, if a felony has been committed.
3. Any constable may arrest any person whom he suspects on reasonable grounds of having committed a felony, whether in fact any such felony has been committed or not.

The laws governing the behaviour of witnesses remained so primitive and dangerous in the seventeenth century that it needed only the sworn word of two men to convict another of treason, a crime of appalling proportions in those days which certainly sent him to the gallows, if not a far worse death. Corroboration was regarded as an unnecessary refinement of truth and any honest man might well go in fear of conspiracy from two unscrupulous enemies who decided to exploit the law to bring him down. The evidence of an accomplice in any crime was accepted at its face value without any attempt at verification. Today, uncorroborated evidence of accomplices is held in the highest suspicion and never 'acted upon'.

Rich in many devilish conspiracies, the seventeenth century was famous for the Popish plots when Titus Oates engineered the conviction of fourteen innocent people and there were six 'memorable failures of justice'. The whole story of Titus Oates becomes much more alarming when we remember that the trials were 'held before the highest courts of judicature under a procedure closely resembling that still in force in some states of late nineteenth-century America'.

As Sir James Stephen says: 'A criminal trial in those days was not unlike a race between the King and the prisoner in which the King had a long start and the prisoner was heavily weighted.'[12] A person committed for trial was kept in confinement under the most unpleasant circumstances, and it was a rare favour if the court allowed him either counsel or solicitors. He had absolutely no knowledge of the evidence which had been given against him, and in court, none of the witnesses ever confronted him in person. He simply had thrown at him, without any preparation on his part, the evidence which they had recorded. 'That an uneducated man,' says Sir James Stephen, 'whose life is at stake and who has no warning of what is to be said against him should do himself justice on such an occasion is a moral impossibility.'[13]

Criminal justice under the Stuarts after the Restoration continued to create fertile tracts of misery where scores of innocent people were penalized as felons, and false witnesses like Titus Oates sent many a man to the gallows. Scores of people must have suffered from a less primitive, more obscure form of witch-hunting when the machinery of arrest, prosecution and penalty allowed so many abuses to creep in and the mere asseveration of six men was still sufficient to convict a man of terrible crimes.

Yet it was from the scandals and confusions of the second half of the seventeenth century that penal progress stemmed into the nineteenth century. As Sir James Stephen puts it: 'There was . . . considerable improvement in the methods of trial during the seventeenth century. Prisoners were not tortured (as they were in every other part of Europe): witnesses were produced face to face, the prisoner could cross-examine, the rules of evidence were beginning to be, though to a small extent, recognized and understood, and the horrors of party warfare carried on by reciprocal prosecutions for treason alternately instituted against each other. . . [reduced].'[14]

One aspect of punishment still lagged behind. John Howard, in his famous book *The State of the Prisons*, drew attention to gaols where 'debtors crowd with their wives and children', and 'there are often by this means ten or twelve people in a middle-sized room, increasing the danger of infection and corrupting the morals of children. . . .' He came to the conclusion that 'the number of men in the same room and of lewd women admitted under the name of wives proves that this affair needs some regulation'. Some of the gaols were privately owned and before 1786 the warders of Ely Gaol, owned by the Bishop of Ely, devised a remarkably effective method of stopping escapes, which makes the blood run cold today. 'This was by chaining them down on their backs upon a floor across which are several iron bars; with an iron collar with spikes about their necks and a heavy iron bar over their legs.' Loading prisoners with heavy irons, even women prisoners, was fairly commonplace and lunatics were very often confined with normal prisoners 'although it is probable that by medicines and proper regimen some of them might be restored to their senses'.

Bishop Joseph Butler was the first outspoken advocate of solitary confinement in England and his Hospital Sermon in 1740 recommended 'the discipline of labour and confinement' to 'exclude all sorts of revel—mirth from places where offenders are confined, to separate the young from the old, and to force them both, in solitude with labour and low diet, to make the experiment how far their natural strength of mind can support them under guilt or shame and poverty'.[15]

As for methods of execution, it was a long time before any civilized attempt was made to reduce prolonged suffering and Samuel Richardson in the eighteenth century gave a brilliant description of a public execution which mixed bloodlust and carnival, sadism and commerce: '. . . as soon as the poor creatures were half dead I was much surprised . . . to see the populace fall to pulling the carcases. . . . These, I was told, were Friends of the Persons executed . . . and some Persons sent by private Surgeons to obtain Bodies for Dissection. The contests between these were fierce and bloody and frightful to look at. . . .'

Not very many years before Richardson wrote this, a woman was 'chained to a stake, first strangled and then burnt'. When a group of weavers working under terrible conditions in Bethnal Green decided to smash their silk-looms they were promptly sent to the gallows. Charged with stealing a few pieces of worked muslin from a draper's shop on Ludgate Hill in 1771, Mary Jones was carried by cart to Tyburn where they tore her suckling child from her breast and hoisted her up on the gallows. 'I do not believe,' Sir William Meredith later wrote, 'that a fouler murder was ever committed against the law, than the murder of this woman by law.' In the same period a girl of fourteen sentenced to be burnt to death for 'hiding at her master's bidding some whitewashed farthings', had the faggots already laid around her body and the torches lit before her reprieve came through. As late as 1804 this notice appeared in the *London Observer*: 'Wednesday morning Ann Hurle for forgery and M. Spalding for an unnatural offence were executed in the Old Bailey.' In other words anyone convicted of homosexuality in those days could go to the gallows.

It is possible to extend this recital indefinitely but perhaps enough has been said to illustrate, in some detail, what may have been self-evident to anyone familiar with legal history. Certainly it is difficult to associate the long and twisted history of penal codes which sometimes seemed more designed to satisfy the revenge fantasies of the public than common justice, with the subtleties of the modern approach to what we no longer think of simply as crime and punishment. Today, we carefully divide prisoners into different classes, we take into account mental instability, we put some guilty men on probation, allow judge and magistrate wide penal licence, have more or less abolished flogging, and no longer permit primitive ideas of tribal retribution to dominate our thinking. Death, flogging, or physical mutilation as a penalty for minor crimes have become repugnant to the modern mind and the whole idea of retribution has given place to the principles of reform and prevention.

As Max Gruenhut says in his book, *Penal Reform*, the *process* of reform can be traced in the nineteenth and twentieth centuries all over Europe reaching up into modern times: 'In many countries numerous consecutive draft codes and counter proposals raised a lively academic discussion; in some countries they led to the promulgation of new criminal codes. . . .' Development was not by any means in a straight unhampered line and the great emotional issues of flogging and capital punishment released contradictory surges through different nations as the timeless factions of reform and reaction battled to achieve a compromise, one helped by war and new political trends, the other by peace and the growing rule of reason. The conflict was sharply crystallized in Italy where the Draft Code of 1921, the work of Enrico Fierri, was an outstanding achievement, but after the rise of Fascism it was superseded by the Draft Rocco of 1927, which reverted to stern retribution.[16]

England, with her traditional system of non-codified law, 'has been spared the cumbersome method of total reform', and introduced many enlightened measures by special statute. The right to trial by jury if any person has committed an offence punishable by more than three months' imprisonment, has become inalienable. The Probation of Offenders Act (1907) allowed convicted persons to be given a period of probation in which they could prove themselves of good conduct and escape the stigma and the psychological damage which might result from a prison sentence. The year 1908 brought the Prevention of Crime Act which once again substituted Borstal sentences and preventive detention for actual prison sentences. These were further refined by the 1908 Children's Act which established special juvenile courts for young people and kept children from contact with adult criminals and old lags. The Infanticide Act of 1922 distinguished between murder and infanticide in cases where a mother, suffering from the appalling stress of childbirth, had killed her newly born child. By 1931 it was no longer possible to pass a sentence of death on an expectant mother.

Many anachronisms remained and still remain. Violent prejudices in some countries do not admit the rule of reason on certain highly emotional issues. Nothing arouses blind passion so much in certain sections of British society today as homosexuality, and the law still penalizes consenting homosexual adults for an 'indulgence' which Greek law accepted as normal and straightforward. Many European and American states are more enlightened. They do not set out to pursue and victimize the homosexual.

Homosexuality apart, the general line of development of British and American criminal legislation over the past fifty years has had one common tendency. As Gruenhut says, it has 'aimed at prevention of crime by a differential treatment of criminals'. In England this power was developed by abolishing the minimum statutory punishment and allowing great discretion to judges and magistrates in fixing terms of imprisonment, fines and similar penalties, except in the case of capital punishment for murder which, until very recent times, remained obligatory.

How incomprehensible all this would have sounded to those revered Roman lawyers who sometimes gave advice to their rich clients on the best means of guaranteeing the required penalty for an illiterate and not very responsible member of their household, or to the Greeks who happily condemned a man to certain death in the mines by overwork, starvation and disease on the strength of half a dozen casual rumours.

It is commonplace, at this point, for those with a romantic belief in the past to remark that penal progress is thrown into confusion by the appearance of Nazi concentration camps, by well-authenticated Russian atrocities and a hundred brutalities which still characterize the modern scene. Of course, no one disputes that the line of penal progress is confused or that the forces of reaction are continually trying to check and smother what they regard as dangerous relaxations, but there is one distinguishing feature of Nazi brutality. Political parties in Germany and Italy have used force and brutal measures to suppress political opposition, but it was not written into the law for everyday civil offences. It belonged to a special category of political offences and when we remember what happened to those who challenged the voice of Church or King with heresy or treason in the past, even modern Nazi methods were no improvement on them.

There remains one class of persecution where the distinction between civil and political offences did not apply—the persecution of the Jews. Here the Nazi atrocities were different in kind because the deliberate classification of certain groups of citizen as *hors de loi* rendered them liable to extermination simply because they were born to a certain ethnic group. It has to be said that the persecution of the Jews became far worse under the Nazis, not better.

However, the re-barbarization of specific areas of Europe did not occur among those nation states which had prolonged experience of democracy and when it did occur the surrounding states—in the case of Germany—refused to sanction and approve the new barbarity. Very swiftly, in historical terms, re-barbarization was challenged and overwhelmed. Today we have become highly sensitive about inflicting physical violence by legal means on anyone and even the principle of an eye for an eye and a tooth for a tooth has disappeared in the red mists of the past.

Imagine a world where everyone went in fear of his neighbour as an informer. Imagine a world where the frail individual, unsupported by solicitor, counsel or legal protection, was liable to face charges which could send him to a prolonged and painful death. In so many periods it must have created an atmosphere of anxiety and suspicion which was as persistent as the air people breathed. It must have led to painful humiliations of personality when a man was driven to lie, evade or conceal many activities for fear they might be misunderstood and any attempt at integrity was frustrated by the need to escape the widespread net of legal suspicion.

In modern America there was a period under the sinister 'rule of MacCarthy' when civilized modern men knew just how crippling and demeaning this could become, but it was a temporary throw-back to primitive conditions which the cannon-pulse of American democracy eventually destroyed. It was concerned, in any case, with political behaviour once more and did not extend into general offences.

It is no part of my purpose to examine the penal code of Russia today, but a brief glance will point the sharp difference in approach between East and West. There has been much less unfair and malicious prosecution in the Soviet Union since 1955 and the number of occasions when some unfortunate Westerner is said to have pleaded guilty to espionage against the Soviet Union has diminished. It remains characteristic of all major Russian spy trials that the main evidence advanced to prove the guilt of the accused is a confession. It is at the pre-trial period that such an accused person is at a serious disadvantage compared with anyone charged with a similar offence in Britain or America. Article 22 of the Russian basic legal code makes no provision for defence counsel until the trial has more or less begun and under such conditions the prosecution has the advantage of a 'thorough investigation' of all the facts.

In other cases, procedure has improved considerably since 1955 but still does not come within reach of Western ideals. The preliminary investigation of charges has now been placed in the hands of the Procurators where, before, it was handled by non-legal security forces. The Procurators must all be members of the Communist Party and are subject to instructions by the Party. In general cases, the Defending Counsel are now allowed access to their clients and to the documents, after the Procurator's Department has carried out its investigations. Pressure has also been brought to bear since 1957 to extend Defending Counsel's 'privilege' to include playing a part in the investigation itself. The Russians insist that the Soviet Union came into being in revolutionary circumstances and claim that it would be romantic to expect any widespread legal liberalization until the régime is fully mature.

In Britain and America the whole basis of legal procedure remains different and progress in the penal code can be shown to have liberated more than material forces. Those sides of the personality liable to be stunted by fear of brutal and capricious punishment are able to express themselves. Each individual can speak his mind, secure in the rule of law. Each person accused of an offence has a ninety-nine per cent chance of acquittal, if he is innocent, and a whole machinery is at his disposal to convert him from a cringing, presupposed criminal, into a dignified human-being, able to face and outface with assurance any false charge.

If we define human progress as those conditions which move towards the fullest and richest expression of the best potentials in each human being, then the development of the modern penal code is progress in this higher sense, but the definition of what is meant by progress needs greater elaboration and presently we shall have to discover more exactly what that highly elusive proposition—a rich, diversified, happy human-being—reveals under close examination.

CHAPTER FOUR

Progress and freedom
of expression

IT is commonly supposed that fifth-century Athens encouraged its poets, thinkers and writers to live in an atmosphere
constantly refreshed by the winds of critical reflection. The
picture of Socrates wandering through sunlit groves, followed
by students, disciples and friends, slowly undermining the
validity of the gods and half the precepts by which aristocratic
Athens lived is qualified by his sudden and untimely death from
hemlock, but the death of Socrates is remembered as a romantic
anomaly in an otherwise liberal society where freedom of
expression was as natural as the air the Athenians breathed.

Of course, one must pay tribute to so many astonishing
achievements in Greek civilization that any quibble about the
true nature of freedom of thought might seem ungracious
carping. Certainly as J. B. Bury has said, 'even if they had not
achieved the wonderful things they did in most of the realms of
human activity, their assertion of the principle of liberty would
place them in the highest rank among the benefactors of the
race, for it was one of the greatest steps in human progress'.[1]

The splendour of the Homeric legends persisted into sixth-
century Athens where Homer was regarded as the highest
authority on mythology, yet it was possible for Xenophanes to go
from city to city pouring scorn on his interpretation of the gods.
Indeed Xenophanes would have been most acceptable in
modern rationalist circles when he complained bitterly of the
absurdity of personifying the gods and criticized half of what
they did on the grounds that such acts committed by men
would be considered quite disgraceful. Homer was not, as is
sometimes asserted, the Bible of the Greeks, there was no
sense in which Xenophanes' attacks could be described as
blasphemous, and so far as we know, no one attempted to
silence him in the course of his widespread travels. It can be
argued that the Greeks distinguished sharply in his case be-

tween ridicule and criticism and the element of entertainment in one subdued the possible dangers of the other.

It was very different with Anaxagoras. At a time when the subtleties of Athenian democracy had reached their finest flower and Athens was enriched by writers, thinkers, poets and artists of immense diversity and power, not even the free-thinking Pericles who was 'in touch with all the subversive speculations of the day'[2] could entirely protect the philosopher Anaxagoras. A man who scorned the popular interpretation of the gods, a semi-scientific thinker who dismissed the notion that the sun was one of several divinities to be worshipped morning and night, he taught that on all the available evidence it was absurd to personify what amounted to a mass of flaming, not to say indifferent, matter.

Anaxagoras and Pericles were close friends and that was the philosopher's undoing. Pericles had many political enemies and they decided to strike at him by attacking Anaxagoras. 'They introduced and carried a blasphemy law to the effect that unbelievers and those who taught theories about the celestial world might be impeached.'[3] They demanded a death sentence but Pericles intervened and Anaxagoras was heavily fined and exiled to Lampsacus.

It is chastening to reflect that two thousand years later in modern Russia the author of *Dr Zhivago* suffered similar humiliations for an oblique attack upon secular gods and there have been many political counterparts in modern life who knew a far worse fate.

In the vast interval of time between ancient Greece and modern Russia, freedom of expression has been suppressed, distorted, disguised, masked, and subjected to every kind of persecution which the human mind could devise, but it survives today, stunted in some countries, undiminished in others.

The question—has there been progress in freedom of expression—involves a multiplicity of evidence and is not easily answered, but one distinction has to be made clear at the outset. The capacity of the individual to think in privacy his own thoughts is a natural safeguard against the enslavement of the human mind, but it yields no real satisfaction to many active minds merely to reflect in silence on the state of the world. Freedom of thought becomes highly significant only when linked to freedom of expression and it is this freedom which needs exploration. The soured and inbred reflections of the cynic bear little relation to the expressed thoughts of a person who in the cut and thrust of intellectual debate or publication, seeks to modify, improve or even uncover the truth about the outer world.

Let us turn back for the moment to the past. All analysis of life among the ancient Greeks is chastened by the reflection that only a small minority achieved the full, gracious, satisfying way of life by which we remember them. It was, in the case of intellectual freedom, a matter of a small minority practising the arts of thought and argument which yielded such astonishing results. In the background an amorphous mass of people was held in perpetual thrall to the darkest superstitions and the occasional persecution of intellectuals reflected either a surge of popular superstition when the gods were thought to have been outraged or political manœuvring of a machiavellian kind. To defy or defame the gods was to endanger the safety of Greek cities in the eyes of the mass of the population. Hence the case of Protagoras, a leading sophist, whose book *On the Gods* rejected logic as a means of apprehending the divinities. It opened with the statement: 'Concerning the gods, I cannot say that they exist nor yet that they do not exist. There are more reasons than one why we cannot know. . . .'

It was not merely primitive superstition which roused a storm of criticism against the book. Through the ages from the earliest historical records until the time when Jesus was persecuted and crucified, men had been driven to repress freedom of expression on religious grounds perhaps more than any other. As we have seen, in fifth-century Athens, citizens were properly concerned with the safety and prosperity of the state and these, it seemed, could be wrecked by a glancing blow from a disgruntled god no less than defeat in open battle on good solid earth.

Thus Protagoras was charged with that conveniently unanswerable crime of blasphemy and as public opinion mounted against him he at last decided that it would be better to leave Athens. In the event he not merely left but fled with threats of vengeance echoing in his ears. Yet here was the paradox. While copies of all his works were collected and ostentatiously burned, the heretical volume which had driven Anaxagoras from Athens could casually be bought on any bookstall of the city without restriction of any kind. Nor did the strictures of one city necessarily hold good for another. Dismissed from Athens, Anaxagoras was received with honour in Lampsacus.

Similarly, the prosecution and death of Socrates was not a straightforward matter of corrupting youth and avowing atheism. A long struggle had led to the emergence of Greek democracy in 403 B.C. and Socrates was a man who believed that the will of the ignorant majority should not be the guiding force of an enlightened state. When democracy reached its full flower in fifth-century Athens, its advocates bitterly remembered those who had fought to limit the franchise, and Socrates was probably selected as a representative victim on grounds which were largely political.

The sporadic nature of these prosecutions was typically Greek. There was no organized persecution comparable with that extraordinary outburst of modern witch-hunting which occurred when Senator MacCarthy impugned his fellow-citizens in America and they were even condemned for guilt-by-association. In ancient Greece there was no guilt-by-association, but we cannot overlook the fact that some Greek philosophers were not themselves immune from the joint charges of preaching intolerance and suppression of thought. None other than Plato envisaged a society in his Republic where religious belief became compulsory on pain of imprisonment or death.

The deeper issues of intellectual freedom crystallized in Greece around the trial of Socrates, a man who could have escaped the death sentence with ease, if he had given the required undertaking to abandon spreading his heretical views amongst the young. The authorities would certainly have spared him, but he was adamant and his martyrdom epitomized for all time the priceless gift of freedom of speech, even if the factual basis of the whole story has aroused sardonic comment from some French scholars.

Posterity was not a notion very familiar to Greek thinking because it saw the world as of limited duration, but it is feasible that Socrates died in the illusion that his death would help to preserve one of the higher principles of intellectual integrity. Certainly Plato, in his Apology of Socrates, gave an account of his defence which reaffirmed his belief in freedom of discussion and made a wonderful plea for that free exchange of

ideas which must always remain at the root of creative intellectual life. There was in those days a romantic belief in an
absolute reality called Truth which has since turned out to be
the most illusive mirage, but there was no mistaking the lofty
intent of Socrates' speeches:

'In me you have a stimulating critic, persistently urging you
with persuasion and reproaches, persistently testing your
opinions and trying to show you that you are really ignorant of
what you suppose you know. Daily discussion of the matters
about which you hear me conversing is the highest good for
man. Life that is not tested by such discussion is not worth
living.' And later: 'If you propose to acquit me on condition
that I abandon my search for truth I will say: I thank you, O
Athenians, but I will obey God, who, as I believe, set me this
task, rather than you, and so long as I have breath and strength
I will never cease from my occupation with philosophy. I will
continue the practice of accosting whomever I meet and saying
to him, "Are you not ashamed of setting your heart on wealth
and honours while you have no care for wisdom and truth to
make your soul better?" I know not what death is—it may be a
good thing, and I am not afraid of it. But I do know that it is a
bad thing to desert one's post and I prefer what may be good
to what I know to be bad.'

As Bury says in his excellent book, *A History of Freedom of
Thought*, Socrates outlines the two great principles of freedom
of thought: the 'social importance of discussion and criticism'
and the 'indefensible right of the conscience of the individual'.[4]

Turning to Rome of the late Republic and early Empire we
find a sophisticated attitude to freedom of expression which not
merely attempted for generations to tolerate all opinions and
religions, but expressed itself with a wry smile in the maxim of
the Emperor Tiberius, 'If the gods are insulted let them see to
it themselves'.

Inevitably, Roman law found itself troubled by nice distinctions between opinion and slander, libel and criticism, but where
personalities were not concerned it gave wide freedoms.
Blasphemy was held to be something very different from sacrilege, the one concerned with maligning the gods the other with—
in many cases—stealing something at once public and sacred.
Stealing, robbery, misappropriation, all these matters concerned
with property were, as we have seen, punishable under several

Emperors by extreme penalties which inflicted death as lightly as flogging, but opinions. . . Here there was wide licence.

In the long history of satirical literature the works of Lucian, who wrote in second-century Rome, stand high, and he freely ridiculed the Roman equivalent of the Holy Trinity, giving special attention to the 'absurdities of anthropomorphism'. This did not mean that writers were free to say what they pleased in Lucian's day. It was easily possible to rouse the ire of powerful political figures who might bring down fire on any author's head, but there was no organized attempt to restrict opinion and Lucian certainly ridiculed popular mythologies in a way which would never be tolerated in modern Russia.

Of course, the persecution of Christian opinion is regarded as the classic Roman exception but this had a much more complicated history than is generally appreciated. In the beginning it was Roman policy not to interfere with the new Jewish sect although some members revealed a fanaticism which did not recommend itself to those ruling Romans who thought the cultivation of superstition among the masses wise, but an intolerant new creed dangerous. When the Christians began widespread dissemination of their new ideas an entirely different situation arose. In the interests of what he regarded as the security of the Empire, the Emperor Domitian took severe steps to prevent the new religion from penetrating Roman, as opposed to Jewish, society. These measures reached their extremity under the Emperor Trajan when it became an offence punishable by death to be a Christian.

Although Bury claims that the more savage penalties were not vigorously or logically applied, there is no doubting the evidence which saw Christians casually thrown to wild beasts in the Colosseum, or the callousness with which they were offered as a bloody and brutal sop to the plebs. If various emperors desired, as Bury says, to crush Christianity without shedding blood, at certain periods they made an uncommonly bad mess of it. 'Trajan laid it down,' Bury says, 'that Christians were not to be sought out, that no anonymous charges were to be noticed, and that an informer who failed to make good his charge should be liable to be punished under the laws against calumny. Christians themselves recognized that this edict practically protected them. There were some executions in the second century—not many that are well attested—and

Christians courted the pain and glory of martyrdom. There is evidence to show that when they were arrested their escape was often connived at.' This revealing sentence follows: 'In general, the persecution of the Christians was rather provoked by the populace than desired by the authorities.'[5]

Exactly. In the end the people triumphed. Brutal persecution had its way. Freedom of religious opinion went up in a burst of public rage as superstitious and ill-informed as it was ruthless.

Bury later acknowledges that the Emperor Diocletian tried to infuse new life into the official Roman religion by organizing a long, cruel and bloody persecution, which became 'the most whole-hearted, general and systematic effort to crush the forbidden faith. It was a failure: the Christians were now too numerous to be crushed.'[6]

Another reaction presently set in which led to the famous toleration edicts, one of which read: 'The edicts we have published to enforce the worship of the gods, having exposed many Christians to danger and distress, many having suffered death and many more who still persist in their folly, being left destitute of *any* public exercise of religion, we are disposed to extend to those unhappy men the effects of our wanted clemency. We permit them, therefore, freely to profess their private opinions, and to assemble in their conventicles, without fear or molestation, provided always that they preserve a due respect to the established laws and government.'[7]

Whatever temporary excesses were practised from time to time in Greek and Roman civilizations, the attempts to force opinions into pre-ordained channels were not very successful and there were centuries in classical antiquity when freedom of expression was accepted and practised as a natural right. For educated men in fifth-century Athens it had to be so. Reason was sovereign; argument the sole arbiter of opinion.

When the Middle Ages came everything changed. From the time when Constantine the Great adopted Christianity, the Christian outlook underwent a dramatic revolution. Where before it had claimed that religious belief was a personal matter over which no one should exercise coercion, it quickly reversed this view and presently set out to persuade every man, woman and child that the one true and only God was the Christian God.

Under the influence of the Old Testament the early Christian

Fathers found absolute sanctions for conduct which today would seem savagely irrational, if not criminal, but the Bible itself, born of a low state of civilization, seemed to justify the worst forms of coercion. Had not Christ himself said, 'Compel them to come in'? St Augustine, among others, set about organizing the compulsion with a ruthlessness which, if it did not in his case approve the death penalty for heresy, certainly formulated principles of persecution. Under Pope Innocent III, in the twelfth century, it led to a highly organized attempt to sweep away all heretics. In France during the same century it brought about the famous crusade against the Count of Toulouse.

When Pope Innocent called upon the Count to drive out those who refused to accept the Christian faith, the Count raised objections and the Pope summoned a huge crusade against him, promising every volunteer absolution for all his sins. There followed appalling scenes of bloody war, of pillage and the pitiless execution of heretics by hanging, and burning, even down to women and children.

This was not merely a war to subdue the Count of Toulouse and convert his subjects. It put all European sovereigns in terror of the Pope. From now on he could insist that heretics should be driven from any domain he chose to name. 'The Popes thus established a theocratic system in which all other interests were to be subordinated to the grand duty of maintaining the purity of the faith.'[8]

Quite clearly, in the Middle Ages, when a long line of Popes distorted religious intent and lofty principles were put to debased ends, not only freedom of religious belief vanished, but the free air of critical reflection became so permeated with the poison of persecution that many other kinds of opinion were equally liable to be misunderstood.

Throughout history there has been no finer instrument of repression than that sick, sadistic and malignantly spreading entity which presently came to be known as the Inquisition. Established by a Bull of Pope Innocent IV in 1252, it developed over the whole of Western Christendom, and such were the intricacies of its meshes that a heretic could be hounded from country to country by a hidden system of intelligence which, before the century was out, developed a chain of tribunals throughout continental Europe. It is useless to dwell on the iniquities which followed. Every man was expected to be an informer against his neighbour or even against his own family; fearful penalties were imposed on those who were discovered to have sheltered or concealed a heretic; the judge of each tribunal became in effect the prosecutor and the prisoner was assumed guilty and expected to prove his innocence. Since the Church itself must not be directly responsible for condemning a prisoner to death, when 'immutably proved' to be a heretic he was handed over to secular magistrates, who, by an ingenious twist of inquisition logic, either condemned the prisoner to be burnt at the stake or themselves risked the charge of promoting heresy.

It has to be understood that many of these men acted with an integrity born of the total conviction that one heretic escaping the cruel net of the Inquisition was worse than ten innocent victims burnt at the stake. As Bury says: 'The Greek king, Agamemnon, who immolated his daughter Iphigenia to obtain favourable winds from the gods was perhaps a most affectionate father, and the seer who advised him to do so may have been a man of high integrity. They acted according to their beliefs. And so with the Middle Ages and afterwards men of kindly temper and the purest zeal for morality were absolutely devoid of mercy where heresy was suspected. Hatred of heresy was a sort of infectious germ, generated by the doctrine of exclusive salvation. . . .'[9]

I have recalled already the modern equivalent. Remove the dramatically masked men, abandon the instruments of torture, replace the savage religious principles with equally primitive political beliefs, allow guilt-by-association to substitute the informer and permit a more elaborate legal machine to defend the accused, and we have something not dissimilar in the great MacCarthy witch-hunts in America and certain 'trials' in modern Russia.

In the Middle Ages it was not only that rabid persecution took the place of justice in these matters, and innocent men were swept away in zealous bursts of savagery intended to purify mankind on its painful journey to paradise; by prohibiting public speculation into the nature of God and the universe, by preventing one scientific mind from communicating with another, knowledge was irreparably blocked for—well, centuries. The great boulders of gospel truth came crashing down the paths of speculation, obliterating everything. The biblical explanation of the Creation and the Fall of Man, the belief that the sun revolved around the earth and the conviction that man sprang from privileged beginnings quite different from those of the animals, carried the authority of divine inspiration and whole fields of anthropological and geological enquiry were automatically paralysed. Medicine remained in thrall to sorcery for centuries. Free medical speculation was savagely resisted by Luther, who believed that diseases were the work of an evil spirit called Satan, and by St Augustine, who had it on divine authority that demons were responsible for the broken health of many a wayward Christian. As late as 1484, Pope Innocent VIII announced that plagues and storms were the work of witches and released a fresh wave of brutal witch-hunting which time and again condemned some poor, broken, illiterate crone to the horrible death of burning at the stake.

A dismaying span of time ran its course before this obscurantist world began to fumble out of its choking confines and men were once more allowed to experiment, to express opinions, and to argue about 'the eternal verities'. Many great men went down in the interval.

There is no need to repeat at any length the stories of men like Giordano Bruno or Galileo: Bruno who, because he accepted the recent discovery of Copernicus that the earth revolved around the sun, was finally seized by order of the Inquisition and burnt at the stake in 1600; Galileo, who demonstrated the truth of Copernicus' statement by following sun-spots in his telescope and was immediately told by Cardinal Bellarmin to abandon such heresies on pain of death. Momentarily withdrawing his conclusions, Galileo later republished them in double form, setting out the new and the old theories side by side and 'pretending not to judge'. Pope Urban VIII, much too perceptive to be taken in by this, commanded Galileo to appear before the Inquisition. No story is more ironically tragic, perhaps pathetic, than that of the old and sick Galileo carefully recanting his opinions once more rather than face torture, until that final humiliation of the inquiring human spirit when he was driven to write to a friend: 'The falsity of the Copernican system cannot be doubted especially by us Catholics.'

These men were martyrs in the terrible struggle of the human mind to escape the shrouds of superstition, the naïve

idiocies and primitive fears which were woven into the very
stuff of the thought of the Middle Ages.

Not until that extraordinary lifting of the human spirit
which came with the Renaissance did the individual begin to
feel 'his separate individuality, to be conscious of his own value
as a person apart from his race or country . . . and the world
around him began to emerge from the mists of medieval
dreams'.[10]

Emerge, yes. Emerge once more into an atmosphere where
freedom of thought was encouraged, speculation ran rife, the
first beginnings of serious scientific enquiry were established
and a whole new upsurge of curiosity brought colour, zest and
intellectual audacity, back into life. Modern scholarship has
recently exhumed and interpreted many new complexities in
the life of the Renaissance and it is now clear that instead of
establishing the foundations of modern science this period
largely rediscovered ancient science, but a fine new breeze was
at last blowing through Western Europe. Not unexpectedly,
free-thinking spirits now looked back with exaggerated veneration to those wonderful pre-Christian days in Greece when
Hippocrates could logically analyse illness and nothing was
protected from the solvent of speculation. But the air was by
no means clear.

In the year 1601 there appeared a book *Of Wisdom*, written by
a man called Charron who was a friend of Montaigne, the
essayist. This book and its reception was symbolic of the
change which had begun to permeate European thought.
Charron believed that true morality need not be based on
Christian virtues and he now said so without equivocation. He
also threw doubt on the doctrine of immortality which he
thought the least well-documented part of the Christian creed.
In the days of the Inquisition he would undoubtedly have gone
to the stake for these opinions and even now, but for the
sympathy of Henri IV, the book might have been suppressed.
As it was, a number of Jesuits stirred up sufficient resistance to
force Charron to modify certain passages in the second edition.

But it survived. There were many reasons why Charron
could now, in a guarded way, speak his mind, why reason itself
was at last breaking through the shrouds and knowledge
beginning to advance again. In part, the discovery of new and
totally unexpected areas of the world confronted the old

theologies with some insuperable problems, but it was the decline in the power of the Pope and the growth of national sovereignty which really called in question all the old beliefs. As the Holy Roman Empire decayed and sovereign states developed, secular interests began to determine ecclesiastical policy and the threatening monsters of the Inquisition, excommunication and eternal torment lost something of their terror. The Reformation was not merely the result of such active reformers as Luther, but of widespread revulsion against the corruption of the Church which commercialized spiritual life to the point where a sinner could literally buy himself off by purchasing indulgences. All these forces combined to break down the ruthless authority of fanatical religious leaders, even if, in some cases, as with Luther, it merely substituted a lesser tyranny for a greater one.

Within these changes the invention of the printing press also put into the hands of thinking men the power to disseminate new doctrines far and wide and the creation of the Roman Catholic Index revealed the fear with which the Church viewed its revolutionary possibilities. All over Europe the authorities set out to contain if not paralyse this new means of widening horizons and questioning dogmas. 'Pope Alexander VI inaugurated censorship of the press by his Bull against unlicensed printing (1501). In France King Henri II made printing without official permission punishable by death. In Germany censorship was introduced in 1529. In England under Elizabeth, books could not be printed without licence and printing presses were not allowed except in London, Oxford and Cambridge.'[11]

It is astonishing to remember that in the long and tortured struggle to achieve freedom of the printed word the vacillations of authority, now liberal, now tyrannical, did not reach any real equilibrium until the nineteenth century, and even today in many parts of Europe oppression remains—but I leap too far ahead.

Famous among the statements which justify the freedom of the printed word is Milton's 'Areopagitica—A Speech for the Liberty of Unlicensed Printing', published in 1644. In 1689 came John Locke's *Letter Concerning Toleration* which distinguished between the civil rights of government and those of religious persuasion, the first a proper preoccupation of authority, the second something exclusively the concern of a person's 'inward mind'. It was absurd, Locke argued, for the State to make laws about religion, a process concerned with the intangible soul and not susceptible to magistrates' rulings.

Taking Europe as a whole, once again, the recovery of freedom of thought, opinion and expression was, in secular terms, a very uncertain business in the sixteenth and seventeenth centuries as one government relaxed and another tightened its restrictions. Any chart of freedom of expression covering Europe would be a maze of confusing lines in which no master line of development would come clearly through. The most powerful force challenging the old ideas about the Universe as represented by the Bible and theological dogma was, of course, modern science, which really began in the seventeenth century and saw in quick succession the discovery that the earth moved around the sun, the Newtonian law of gravitation, the circulation of the blood and the existence of continents and animal species until then undreamt of. Each new qualification of biblical history set off fresh conflicts as orthodoxy tried to suppress inconvenient facts or quickly absorbed them in slightly adjusted interpretations. Each time the question of freedom of expression underwent fresh examination. As yet, the modifications required were not fundamental to the very existence of the Scriptures and it was easy to make the sacred texts fit the new discoveries. Thus the strong taboos which still underlay the urbane surface remained undisturbed and nothing occurred which seriously shattered the embalmed correctness of respectable theology. In secular matters things were not much different but the Enlightenment and the French Revolution became a watershed in the process of developing free institutions.

It was in the eighteenth century that Thomas Paine challenged some of the remaining restrictions on freedom of speech in England and brought down on his head fire of an intensity which revealed the true nature of the opposition. In 1791 he published *The Rights of Man* which was a plea for a representative democracy in place of a monarchy and contained some highly inflammable passages: 'The time is not very distant when England will laugh at itself for sending to Holland, Hanover, Zell or Brunswick for men [meaning candidates like George I] . . . who understood neither her laws, her language nor her interest, and whose capacities would scarcely have fitted them for the office of a parish constable. . . .'

It is instructive to pause a moment and think how such a passage would be received today if published in England about Queen Elizabeth II. A public outcry would inevitably follow. Anyone guilty of such an appalling piece of 'bad taste' would certainly be the subject of scurrilous headlines in every popular newspaper and attack from every quarter. Bishop and archbishop would express the strongest distaste and if the culprit held any public office he would certainly be removed from it; the exclusive clubs would ban him, a clamour in the House of Commons would express astonishment that he should be permitted to traduce the Crown in such disgustingly guttersnipe terms; and if, as in the case of Malcolm Muggeridge, the culprit expressed opinions about Royalty so far removed in mildness as to be of a different order he would still be hounded by hooligans wanting to smash his windows and break in his front door.

Progress? Yes there is still progress, but once again of a qualified kind. In Tom Paine's day he not merely risked the scorn and abuse of his fellows: he risked and in fact experienced a trial for high treason. Although Paine's counsel, Erskine, made a fine plea for freedom of speech, Paine was convicted and outlawed from England. In the eyes of the authorities he was much more dangerous than the normal literary hack because he wrote his books in such eloquent English that they were not merely read by but carried the ordinary reader away on waves of moral indignation. If any person could shake the conventional beliefs of the Common Man and win him over to rebellious causes that man was Paine and clearly, while at large in England, he remained a menace. So Paine was outlawed.

It did not stop him producing further and even more heretical books. *The Age of Reason* (1794) which he began to write in a Paris prison, was a blunt and undisguised attack upon the Christian mythology. A deist himself, Paine felt that those who encumbered the divine presence with the trivial stories which occurred in the Old Testament and spoke of these as the Word of God made the whole concept of God ridiculous. It was commonplace in those days for the ruling aristocracy to reject Christianity as represented in the Old Testament but they simultaneously believed that the masses must be kept in ignorance of any such heresies or they would lose all sense of discipline and responsibility. On this occasion, they decided to prosecute not Paine but his publisher. In a remarkably prejudiced trial, with the judge constantly creating difficulties for the defence, Eaton the publisher was sent to prison for a year, a sentence with far more horrible implications than we can appreciate today.

In 1811, the third part of the *Age of Reason* appeared, the publisher was again charged and the judge, Lord Ellenborough, announced that 'to deny the truths of the book which is the foundation of our faith has never been permitted'. This was a sudden and terrible collapse of the forces which were moving towards real freedom of the printed word and Shelley, incensed by what he regarded as a throw-back to the primitive past, wrote at once an impassioned letter to Lord Ellenborough: 'Do you think to convert Mr Eaton to your religion by embittering his existence? You might force him by torture to profess your tenets, but he could not believe them except you should make them credible, which perhaps exceeds your power.'

Shelley notwithstanding, Eaton was sentenced to stand in the pillory once a month and to eighteen months' imprisonment, but the forces of enlightenment were seeping up again everywhere and as the rationalist movement gathered force in the eighteenth century, one restriction after another was challenged and broken down.

Men like Comte, Strauss and Renan were powerful contributors to the scientific spirit on the one hand and a quite new appraisal of religion on the other. Comte thought all theological attempts to explain the universe were not only obsolete but positively banal and he was equally unhappy with Hegel's metaphysical flights. Metaphysics and theology were to be substituted by a view of the world which accepted the positive data of experience as the only genuine evidence. The supernatural was dismissed as an article of belief and scientific observation substituted for God and the Bible, but the assumption remained that somewhere behind natural phenomena there might lurk another form of reality which had one characteristic seldom before acknowledged—it was unknowable. These ideas swept across the Channel to England and were taken up by men like Frederic Harrison. Herbert Spencer followed a similar school of thought and produced many remarkable books in which the idea of progressive evolution was developed to include social organization and human thought.

It was, in a very powerful sense, the gathering momentum of the modern idea of progress and its inevitable questioning of the fossilized dogmas of the past which gave a tremendous impetus to freedom of thought and expression since by its very nature progress demanded a *changing world*. Thus, the appearance of Darwin's *Origin of Species* in 1859, spectacular revolution though it was to any orthodox churchman, did not result in Darwin being impeached for blasphemy or charged with corrupting the faithful. There was an outcry. Different factions took forceful exception to the book, and Gladstone achieved a massive irony characteristic of his best House of Commons utterance: 'Upon the grounds of what is called evolution God is relieved of the labour of creation and in the name of unchangeable laws is discharged from governing the world.' An intellectual upheaval which, in medieval days, would have led to arrests, torture, trials and wholesale slaughter, now set off tremendous debates and much bad feeling but reason was beginning to prevail and physical violence had ceased in England to be a valid method of enforcing conformity.

Matters were very different for David Strauss, whose *Life of Jesus* (1835) rejected the supernatural origins of the Messiah, and brought such a frenzy of attack, counter-attack, venom and bitterness down upon his head that before very long Strauss was deprived of his professorship at Tübingen and his career ruined. Renan, whose biography of Christ followed a similar interpretation, became involved in a series of savage exchanges which led the authorities of the Collège de France to indicate that perhaps it might be better for a man holding such heretical views to abandon his professorship. These were two of many cases where refinements of physical force were employed in an attempt to check the chaos threatening religious thought as science revealed one contradiction after another and professional assassination took the place of the stake as a disciplinary power. At this stage, despite the French Revolution, and the work of men like Voltaire and Comte, highly organized religious orthodoxies frequently succeeded in stifling scientific speculation about the true nature of God and left France struggling with a considerable oppression where England had, in this sense, almost broken free.

In secular matters the growth and dissemination of newspapers, periodicals and pamphlets had set by the ears, in many

European countries, all the old dogmas of repression. From the eighteenth century onwards a ferment of printed matter released on the world ideas which varied from the mad to the brilliant, from the superstitious to the rational, the mystical to the scientific, until freedom of expression burst its banks and ran over in eighteenth-century England where highly personal abuse in print became an everyday event.

In earlier years it was perfectly possible for a baron to abuse and defame a serf who had no right of redress, and in medieval England, where everyone knew and if he had any sense kept his place, it was commonplace for one class scathingly to denounce another. The right of every man not to have his reputation assailed by false and defamatory statements had its roots right back in early Roman law but the subtle definitions which really protected a man's reputation were of comparatively modern origin.

In the long and tortured development of freedom of speech it quickly became evident that certain restrictions had to be placed on opinion if wild accusations were not to create grave injustice and, indeed, chaos in social life. Thus John Wilkes, in his famous attacks in the *North Briton* (1762), was able to print virulent criticisms of Lord Bute, the Tory favourite of the King, which would be quite impossible under the libel laws today. Nothing if not audacious, the witty, Rabelaisian Wilkes, then M.P. for Aylesbury, went even further when he made devastating attacks on George III's Royal Speech and even the King's complacency was shaken. Wilkes had prefaced his remarks with the phrase 'The King's speech has always been considered by the legislature and by the public at large as the Speech of the Minister', in the hope of deflecting his invective to a less sensitive spot, but the King took the whole article as a personal insult. Wilkes was arrested and imprisoned in the Tower. Extraordinarily, and to the public's great delight, the arbitrary powers of the King were challenged, and Lord Chief Justice Pratt had Wilkes released within a week on the grounds that his arrest was a breach of privilege.

A second and more carefully prepared attack was now launched. This was to involve a side issue of freedom of speech and publication which, in the refinements of modern society, has become one of the major struggles of our day; the question of obscene publications. Wilkes had written a brilliant but to the conventional mind obscene, parody of Pope's *Essay on Man* called an *Essay on Woman*, and printed privately a number of copies, some of which fell into the hands of his one-time friend, but now enemy, Lord Sandwich. The poem was presently read aloud with considerable relish to the House of Lords, which at once voted it a breach of privilege and an obscene libel. Simultaneously, the House of Commons, after prolonged scrutiny of Wilkes's attack upon the King's speech, concluded that it constituted a seditious libel and Wilkes was suddenly confronted with a double charge of the utmost gravity. Conviction would have meant public disgrace and imprisonment and Wilkes, already in ill-health from a wound received during a duel, decided to leave England and 'disappear in Paris', the laws of extradition having no power to recall him in those days.

The eighteenth century was alive with examples of scurrilous invective of living persons which our present laws would never permit but whereas whatever Wilkes wrote or said had a steady social purpose, there were times when writers like Junius seemed driven by nothing but malignant malice.

'Junius began by a general attack on the Ministry for their personal immorality or meanness. He then went on to pour acrimonious abuse on Grafton, on the Duke of Bedford, on King George III himself in the letter of Dec. 19, 1769, and ended with a most malignant and ignorant assault on Lord Chief Justice Mansfield. . . . He sinned indeed in a large company. The employment of personal abuse had been habitual in English political controversy for generations. . . . The white heat of his malignity animates the whole. . . .'[12]

As one government after another relaxed its restrictions on religious and secular controversy and it became possible to criticize freely the implications of biblical and scientific teaching, the need for some check on unrestrained personal abuse grew. The licence to describe a politician—with nothing more than rumour to substantiate it—as 'a debased monster who uses his political cloak to cover the seduction of virgin girls of 13, who deliberately mixes poisonous concoctions which rob his victims of their senses and persuades young girls, with his wealth, to give indecent performances to satisfy his base and low appetites . . .' was clearly carrying freedom too far. As the laws of libel and slander slowly took shape and form to protect the innocent individual from smearing attacks, other and less personal restrictions began to dissolve.

The nineteenth century saw the growth of that liberal atmosphere where it was possible to question the divinity of Christ and the inviolability of the Bible with comparative impunity, but as late as 1907 the Catholic Church was still resisting, with all its powers, the invasion of modernist church-men. The Abbé Loisy was one daring spirit who set out to reinterpret Christian teaching in the light of modern science, in the belief that unless Catholicism developed in step with modern knowledge, it might atrophy and die. As a result, in 1907, he underwent a spectacular excommunication.

*   *   *   *

We are now at last in that fine free air of twentieth-century modern Europe only to discover that very large tracts of it are dominated by a political philosophy which admits of no alternative government and appears on the surface to make a travesty of political freedom. Today the whole question of freedom of opinion and expression has moved away from religion into the political arena and invoked that law which allows progress in one field to be confounded by new restrictions in another.

In Western Europe the whole question of freedom of expression has become very subtle and if a man can freely walk the streets of London, New York and Paris, and say just what he pleases within the laws of libel and treason, the distribution of the new machinery for expressing opinion has introduced fresh complications. Any man or woman can now scathingly criticize in public the political leaders of a Western democracy and he or she can embrace rabid atheism and deny the divinity of Christ without fear of physical restraint or reprisal. Clearly this is progress of the widest possible kind, but the development of mass media of communication, the press, radio and television, has introduced a means of imposing, subtly or bluntly, one man's opinions on millions of his fellows. There are whole chains of newspapers which can continuously pour out the views, prejudices and tastes of one Olympian owner and take the place of thinking for six million people at a single stroke. They are free to think and talk—yes—but subject to continuous permeation by the writings of highly skilled journalists and propagandists, and if they themselves desire to have a voice in this machine the way is mysteriously blocked by lack of capital, lack of skill or influence. In the past, the printed word had a limited appeal when sales of books and pamphlets did not exceed a few hundred copies. Now one man is invested with the megaphone voice of millions. As for the Common Man, having achieved a voice of his own and a quite new freedom of expression, he too often finds that he cannot make himself heard in the giant clamour of press and television, or that no one takes much notice when he does.

One huge qualification arises. The vote has given every adult a means of expressing his political preferences and in Western Europe public opinion can and does carry enormous weight during elections. Perhaps the refinements of restriction which have taken place in Western democracies are nothing beside the gigantic liberation given to individual opinion by the modern system of franchise, and it would be absurd not to acknowledge that the average medieval man transported into twentieth-century Europe would consider himself a person of such privileged freedoms as he had never dreamt possible on this earth. All hail then, to the fine free air which modern democracies have engendered, but we represent perhaps one-half of the present world and in the other, ruthlessly efficient means have been found to iron out and perfect a conformity whereby one newspaper, one voice, one state, prevails to the exclusion of any other.

At once a vast question arises: Is the human mind in process of a new political and scientific enslavement? Are we witnessing the steady spread of a philosophy which does not tolerate heresy, a philosophy equipped with means of mass persuasion unknown to the Inquisition, which can blast the words and will of one man or one party simultaneously into the ears and minds of a hundred million people? In the interests of a material millenium have all manner of powers been usurped and abused? Under pretext of realizing the potential of the common people, is their precious faculty of critical reflection undergoing a new repression? Intellectually, is a new dark age with its new Inquisition, its demand of total subservience in politics and science, taking the place of the brutal repressions which crushed out progress with the voice of God in the past? Every sentence in this paragraph can, of course, be shown by any competent Marxist to reflect the unscrupulousness of a decadent Western political propagandist knowing nothing whatever about the inner workings of the Russian State. It has to be admitted that too little is known, especially about the precise results of the relaxations introduced by Khrushchev and their effect upon critical minorities. Has the old Stalinite dictatorship been liberalized to the point where many of these questions are invalidated? Certainly, under Stalin, brutal suppression was widespread, but I am in sympathy with the view that something very remarkable is happening today in Russia.

Even in Western Europe the old volcanoes, the old gods are by no means dead. A sudden eruption of authority breaks into the new freedoms with all the arrogance and violence of the past and continues to disturb what too many people regard as extinct craters. We saw it in Nazi Germany. More subtly the spread of militarism, the curious acceptance of generals with their authoritarian outlook, as national leaders, bodes ill for the future. The names have multiplied—General de Gaulle, General Nasser, General Franco—and so many lesser military juntas continue to manipulate the South American scene.

As for that home of individualism and cradle of revolution, France, the most remarkable censorship of the press was tolerated during the Algerian troubles and a new move to take action against pornographic publications seems to conceal, as it has traditionally, political motives.

The long story of martyrs to freedom of thought continues into modern history and it is disturbing to find that the tragedy of Boris Pasternak in Russia has a counterpart in Maurice Audin in France, that a man like Patrick Duncan can suffer continuous reimprisonment for fighting the forces of Apartheid in South Africa and Ashton Jones be 'thrown to the mob' and beaten into senselessness in the Southern United States because he believes in racial integration.

In his book, *Persecution 1961*, which told the stories of nine people who had suffered savage treatment for their ideals, Peter Benenson wrote: 'They show what can happen to men who put forward views which are unacceptable to their government or unpopular with their neighbours. Despite the inhumanity and in some cases cruelty, these are not extreme examples. . . . Far more horrible cases exist where people have died or killed themselves and where the torturer's instruments have scarred for life. . . . The selection of lives in this book is designed simply to show that there is no area of the world where people are not suffering for their beliefs, and no ideology which is blameless.'[13]

It was in 1957 that two officers of the 1st Regiment of Chasseurs Parachutistes visited Maurice Audin's flat in Algiers and arrested him. Normally, under the French Criminal Code, an arrested person must be brought before a magistrate within twenty-four hours, but during the emergency in Algeria, the authorities had power to detain administratively. Maurice Audin, while a student, had joined the Algerian Communist Party because he believed that the Algerian Moslems had the right to self-determination and long after his disappearance this right was in fact granted the Moslems by General de Gaulle. Meanwhile, the Algerian Communist Party was declared illegal and one member helping another was said to constitute an unlawful conspiracy against the State. Audin's crime consisted in 'sheltering' a man wanted for interrogation by the police, and when the parachutists arrested him they told his wife, 'If he is reasonable, he will be back within an hour'. As Benenson comments, 'He never came back, and Mme Audin never saw her husband again'.

It is claimed by those sympathetic to Audin that he subsequently underwent brutal interrogation and torture by electric shocks which leave no mark upon the body, but since no body or trace of him was ever found the truth is still unknown.

According to the officer commanding the 1st Parachute Regiment, Lt-Col Mayer, Maurice Audin made a dash for freedom on 21 June 1957 and this is what happened: 'The prisoner considered to be not dangerous, was put on a seat at the back of the vehicle, a sergeant sitting on the front seat next to the driver.' To negotiate a sharp bend 'the driver had slowed down when the detained man jumped from the vehicle and threw himself into a hollow trench. . . . The sergeant . . . jumped off the jeep and fired some bursts on his machine-gun in the direction taken by Audin. . . . The dark night prevented any trace being found of the fugitive, nor was any sign of blood noticed. . . .'[14]

His wife has never heard from Audin since.

The story of Boris Pasternak is too familiar to need repetition in detail. Everyone knows that his book *Dr Zhivago* was regarded as subversive literature by the Russian authorities and the editors of Novy Mir, who refused to publish the manuscript in its original form. 'He was asked to re-write it, omitting the critical passages. When he refused to do this Olga [Ivinskaya], who was an employee of the State Publishing House, was sent for. She was asked to use her influence on him; and when she demurred, she was once more threatened with return to Siberia.'[15] Meanwhile Pasternak had sent a copy of the manuscript to an Italian publisher Feltrinelli, a man of the purest political ancestry in the eyes of the Soviet Union since he was a member of the Italian Communist Party. Pasternak expected his book to be published in Russia and the copy sent to Feltrinelli was a precaution against the possibility of an unscrupulous Western publisher printing a text which emphasized the criticism and either modified or simply removed other passages. A leading Soviet writer was sent post-haste to Italy to visit Feltrinelli and explained to him that publication of the manuscript would damage the reputation of the Communist Party. In the event Feltrinelli, a man of considerable literary discrimination, thought it better to leave the Communist Party than to suppress what he had come to regard as one of the masterpieces of modern Russian writing. The book, as everyone knows, was translated and published, highly praised by Western critics and swept across Europe.

Whether or not part of the reason for its elevation to the highest place in literature was the result of criticism which, coming from the heart of the Russian state, the West not merely welcomed but positively embraced, the effect of its Western European success on Boris Pasternak and Olga Ivinskaya was catastrophic. Pasternak suffered immediate expulsion from the Soviet Writers' Union and was thus deprived of his income. Yet as Benenson wrote, 'Pasternak refused the offer of the Nobel Prize. His intention had never been to attack his own country from abroad. He had only wanted to draw attention at home to the state of affairs which had lasted under Stalin, hoping that this would lead to an improvement under Khrushchev.'[16]

Pasternak died ignominiously and alone one day in May 1960 in his wooden house at Peredelkino, and his last message, asking Olga to call and see him, was never delivered to her. She and her daughter Irina were subsequently charged, among other indictments, with receiving royalties from foreign sources, and today they are still in prison.

Now that Stalin's body has been disembalmed and removed from its sacred place on the Red Square plinth; now that Khrushchev has publicly reviled the late Russian master and dictator in terms far more abusive than anything written by Pasternak, it would seem logical that the name of Pasternak should be raised from the mud again and Olga Ivinskaya released from her imprisonment, but there is no sign of this happening.

It is a sad reflection on modern intolerance that a country which speaks proudly of its uncompromising democracy should have produced the story of the Rev Ashton Jones, but the northern states of the U.S.A. profess a liberalism which cannot be found in certain southern states and it would be absurd to judge one by the other. The Rev Ashton Jones broke down the colour bar in Dallas, Texas, for one splendid and disastrous day by eating with Negroes in a white restaurant and from that day in 1960 he became a marked man. A person dedicated to overcoming racial prejudice, his methods were straightforward to the point of bluntness and there are those, even among his friends, who believe that a more subtle approach might have left him unscathed. As it was, he drove through Texas in a motor van painted with slogans proclaiming his mission and the police quickly intervened. Many contradictory accounts are given of what followed but at one point, while under arrest, he was dragged into a sweat-box 4 ft by 4 ft and left lying there, unable to stand up, until the Sheriff arrived: 'I was limp, and he snatched me out and shoved me down a flight of steel stairs towards the ground floor. Some of the deputies stepped in and kicked me and shoved with their feet until I was at the bottom of the stairs.' For the man who became known as 'that dirty nigger-lover' this was only a mild beginning.

Later, he drove on to another town, where the police were waiting for him, and he was 'thrown into a big cage with about thirty other prisoners. One of the gaolers passed round a newspaper cutting showing him shaking hands with some Negroes. This was the signal for the extreme anti-Negroes to start up. . . . They set upon him, not one but several of them. And they hit him unmercifully . . . while the police stood around watching. When he was lying on the floor senseless, the officials intervened and carried him out of the cage to hospital. He had to have four stiches sewn into his jaw before he could leave.'[17]

The end of the story was very different. Justice in fact, to some extent, prevailed. A charge of vagrancy was brought against the Rev Ashton Jones but defence counsel rose to submit that the prisoner had no case to answer and the Judge finally agreed and dismissed the prisoner. Retribution, it seems, did not overtake those who had violated him, but at least his name was cleared and he left the court with the sound of applause in his ears.

Far more dangerous was the era of the great MacCarthy witch-hunt in America when the Committee of Un-American Activities assumed the rôle of the Inquisition, substituting for torture and death, disgrace, professional dismissal and imprisonment. Communists, ex-Communists, those contaminated by knowing Communists, those related to Communists, those who could be shown to have attended a conference at which a single Communist lay hidden beneath another political label; all these were threatened with professional death, loss of income or public disgrace and imprisonment. An insidious spread of smear tactics left men continuously in fear of the informer and even the hallowed precincts of the universities felt tremors of hate and persecution as free-thinking intellectuals came under suspicion. Proportionately to the size and population of America the persecution affected small areas and an even smaller number of people, but the climate of opinion was an explosive cloud hovering over the minds of thinking men.

It has gone now. Its life was short. The cannon-pulse of American democracy could not long allow such a monstrous growth in its midst, but the incident reaffirmed the necessity for eternal vigilance if some accidental coincidence of time, place, person and malicious power were not to undermine a whole way of life.

One consoling factor remains in this sad recital of intolerance in such widely separated parts of the world today; it is a very powerful factor: looked at statistically, the number of cases in Western Europe is infinitesimally small in proportion to the population, and when compared with the wholesale detention, torture, maiming and destruction of people for avowing heretical principles in the past, it dwindles away into insignificance.

Since the collapse of Nazi Germany, the record of Western Europe is far better than anything we have known for seven hundred years and even a Roman or Greek citizen would be astonished to find how freely he could talk and write in a modern

Western European city where the power to vote and a multiplicity of democratic devices protect him against personal or public abuse. In a word, freedom of opinion and expression in Western Europe has, in my belief, for the moment achieved a new and progressive point.

CHAPTER FIVE

Progress and women

In the documents which have come down to us from Babylonia three thousand years ago, we find married women transacting business deals, selling their own property, conducting law-suits, entering into trade partnerships, lending money and buying and selling slaves. Wealth in Babylonia meant power and since the dowry system gave a woman rights over her own property she was, in many cases, an independent agent in business affairs. 'In fact,' wrote Emil Reich, 'in all matters of business rights there would appear to be no difference between the man and the woman in the eyes of the law.'[1]

Remarkable similarities to the double rôle of the modern woman become even sharper when we remember that many Babylonian women continued to cook, bake, grind corn, spin and weave although high-born aristocrats were freed from such domestic responsibilities. Of course, there were many grades of women. The élite had little contact with everyday life and only emerged from their homes surrounded by slaves, but the majority of women moved freely in the outer world.

At first glance it would be easy to conclude that after three thousand years of struggle and bitterness, women have merely regained in the Married Woman's Property Act of modern times the rights which were natural to Babylonians and the myth of progress is once more exposed for what it is worth. In fact, the total Babylonian picture throws a very different light on any comparison between past and present.

Whatever property rights she could claim, the Chaldean wife was subject to a series of divorce regulations which would undermine her status in our eyes. The husband held unrivalled power as supreme head of the household and it was within his rights merely to turn to his wife and say 'Thou art not my wife' to end the marriage. Some check on the wanton use of this privilege arose when the husband was forced, in dismissing her, to return his wife's dowry; if the dowry was large, he did not easily abandon it. The possibility of paying a fine for divorcing a wife also arose, but these penalties bore no comparison with what the wife was called upon to endure if she desired to divorce her husband. She, too, had the power to round on him and say, 'Thou art not my husband', but in her case it meant that she would, in due course, if she did not relent, simply be strangled or flung into the river to drown if she could not swim. What Reich refers to ambiguously as 'an erring wife' was either 'put to death with the sword, or, after being stripped of her clothing with the exception of a loin cloth . . . was cast adrift into the streets to lead a life of infamy.'[2]

Sweeping away once more to the Greek civilization, the status of women changes radically, and the most marked difference in her relationship with men is the abandonment of oriental polygamy for the more austere principle of monogamy. In Homer's day there were very small kingdoms—later to become city states—where individual families played a powerful rôle and women occupied a position and were treated with a respect which, very much later, caused surprise and adverse criticism among the Athenians of the fifth century. According to the redoubtable William Ewart Gladstone, who delivered many sonorous pronouncements on the Homeric Age, 'There is not, in the whole of [Homer's] poems an instance of rude or abusive manners towards women . . . or of liberties taken with them in the course of daily life. . . . The conduct of the Ithacan suitors to Penelope, as it is represented in the *Odyssey*, affords the strongest evidence of the respect in which women were held.'[3]

Gladstone had such a romantic view of anything to do with ancient Greece that it is as well to remember the primitive marriage customs in Homer's day when marriage was an arrangement between the bridegroom and the father of the bride which had many of the characteristics of purchasing a commodity. The bridegroom might pay the father for his bride either in goods or money and the precise market value of a wife-to-be was a matter of nice calculation and hard bargaining. The bride had undergone a rudimentary education by example rather than precept, listening to the freely given advice of her elders and betters. She would henceforth spend her days spinning, weaving, washing clothes and looking after her children, which might number ten in as many years though sickness or war could strike down three-quarters of them. Granted special accommodation in the house, she was not prevented from penetrating the common rooms where the men circulated, and she was free to move about the streets, but legally her position was little better than that of a slave. She was the 'possession' of her husband, a bought 'chattel', and he exercised extreme rights over her. The threat of actual slavery was never far removed from any woman because war frequently broke into her life and once made prisoner she automatically became a slave, the absolute property of her captors who could inflict whatever indignity or cruelty they chose from rape to torture.

The slow development of the City States and the growth of colonization brought about a change in the lot of women which, surprisingly, was not, in some respects, for the better. More settled conditions made the chances of piratical raids, war and slavery less pressing than they were in Homeric days but women were slowly excluded from the main interests of men and the cleavage between the sexes became marked.

The precise position of Athenian women, young and old, married and unmarried, is still in dispute among classical scholars. 'The Athenian girl,' wrote Reich, 'was, till seven years old, brought up at home with her brothers under her mother's supervision. This was, in fact, the period of her greatest freedom and closest intercourse with others. After attaining to that age she was kept in the closest confinement; in the house itself she had to remain in the women's quarters. She was only permitted to leave the house on rare occasions and then only to be a spectator at, or participator in, a religious procession. . . . Or again she might be chosen to take part in one of the choral dances which played so important a part in the religious rites of Greece. Her education consisted in learning to read and write . . . but for all this she was entirely dependent upon her mother, and it is probable that very few women possessed any literary culture.'[4]

According to Thucydides, she was enjoined to silence in or out of the house and was expected to conduct herself in such a way that people would not speak or talk about her.[5] According to Reich, marriage lost any intimately personal character it might have had, and became more and more a social institution. The nearest male relative had the option of the disposal of a woman in marriage, she was expected to bring a dowry and she had little or no influence on what went on outside the house.

'The wife was expected to live at home and keep house; she controlled a large establishment of slaves and had the custody of all the household stores. But her principal duty consisted in being the mother of citizens.' Her quarters were usually confined to the upper story of the house and this was intended to prevent the women escaping for some illicit liaison without being seen by the husbands. Greek thinking believed that it was natural for woman to love and that some women were powerless before its more irresistible appeals. Women were forbidden to be present at banquets and 'in order to defy all possibility of temptation [they] must wrap up every part of their bodies'.

Xenophon tells the story of Ischomachus whose wife was fifteen at the time he married her and 'had been most carefully brought up to see and hear as little as possible, and to ask the fewest questions'.[6] It was, as usual, a marriage of convenience arranged by the parents, and his wife, at first, was appalled at her own ignorance, but gradually he won her confidence and outlined to her the characteristics of an ideal wife. These conversations are, of course, fictitious, but Xenophon was an Athenian and if he tended to idealize the Ischomachus marriage it does at least reveal a relationship where some elements of the modern partnership in marriage were evident.

Divorce was much easier than in modern times. Infidelity, on the other hand, was treated, according to James Donaldson, with something approaching savagery. 'Her husband was compelled to send her away: No man could marry her again . . . if anyone ventured on such a course he was thereby disfranchised. She was practically expelled from society and excommunicated. If she appeared in a temple, anyone could tear her dress off, and maltreat her to any extent with impunity, provided he stopped short of killing her.'[7]

Romantic love, as we know it, played little part in Athenian marriages and there are no love scenes whatever in the plays of Aeschylus. Like Aeschylus, Sophocles took his subjects from the legends of old and his *Electra* and *Antigone* are Homeric in conception. Not until we come to the plays of Euripides do we find women playing an important rôle, but Euripides was regarded, in his day, as cheapening the high tenets of tragedy by giving his characters more human interest than the masked effigies so commonplace in Greek drama.

A movement toward female emancipation had grown under

the impact of imperialism and the scenes in Aristophanes' *Lysistrata*, where the women refuse to sleep with their husbands until they see political sense and abandon war-like intentions, reflects a rebellious impulse which would have been impossible in earlier years. The reaction of men like Euripides to Athenian women who threaten to abandon their traditionally submissive rôle is roughly equivalent to the mass reaction of nineteenth-century people towards the modern suffragettes in England. 'Euripides pours out the vials of his scorn and contempt.' The *Lysistrata* is a comedy and its implications revolutionary. Nothing like the scenes depicted here ever disturbed the normal life of the ordinary women of Athens. Indeed Reich believes that 'the effect of Imperialism upon the *ordinary* Athenian woman was to push her into the background and to compel her to lead a life of restricted freedom and virtual inactivity'.

Later scholarship has seriously questioned this picture. Professor Kitto, in his book *The Greeks*, ridicules the idea that 'Athenian women were kept in a state of almost oriental seclusion' and shows, decisively, that they attended theatrical performances, some of which contained dialogues capable of blanching the cheek of many a modern woman. Dr Charles Seltman has written: 'Romantic nineteenth-century pedants had their own private concepts of fifth-century Athens. . . . They imagined Attic society as made up of clever gentlemen who—though given to nightly symposium feats (and occasional lapses with little flute girls) maintained an august aloofness and never discussed anything unrefined with the "little woman" at home. Professor This and Herr Doktor That always sheltered his "little woman" and the girls from the rough facts of life. What these cloistered scholars did not realize was that, while they were mentally no better than learned adolescents, unspotted by the world, Athenian men and women were adult. Only adults could compose and hear the works of Aeschylus, Sophocles and Euripides and stomach the strong meat of Aristophanes. Only adults could create and understand the characters of Clytaemnestra and Electra, Antigone and Ismene . . . because there were living Athenian women of whom these characters were types.'[8]

Seltman goes on to stress the fact that Athenian women were not merely frank about sex but that the guardian Herm standing outside many homes was 'a stone pillar, square in section, topped with a bearded head of Hermes . . . and having an erect phallus carved on the front. Such a figure stood outside every public building and private house in Athens.' He describes typical scenes from public female life painted on vases which have survived today. They show 'girls going to the public well-house to fetch water, visits to the shoe-maker, weddings and funerals'. Unfortunately, many of the details which Seltman summons to his aid concern the small-scale necessary freedoms—apart from theatre-going—for any woman in a civilized community where she shares the burden of everyday work.

That some discussion about emancipating women did occur in fifth-century Athens is evident from Book V of the Platonic dialogues where Socrates addresses Glaukon:

'If then we are to employ women in the same duties as the men, we must give them the same instructions.'

'Yes.'

'To the men we gave music and gymnastics.'

'Yes.'

'Then we must train the women also in the same two arts, giving them besides a military education, and treating them in the same way as men.'

'It follows naturally from what you say.'

'Perhaps many of the details of the question before us might appear unusually ridiculous if carried out in the manner proposed.'

'No doubt they would.'

'Which of them do you find the most ridiculous: Is it not obviously the notion of the women exercising naked in the schools with the men and not only the young women, but even those of an advanced age. . . . '

'Yes indeed.'

'Well then, as we have started the subject we must not be afraid of the numerous jests which worthy men may make upon the notion. . . .'

If we can believe the picture which emerges by the technique of piecing together fragments of literature, then the legal position of women in Athens was not very happy. 'Women were not enfranchised: that is, they could not attend the

Assembly, still less hold office. They could not own property; they could not conduct legal business. Every female from the day of her birth to the day of her death, had to be the ward, so to speak, of her nearest male relative or her husband and only through him did she enjoy any legal protection.'[9]

However, as Kitto says, the literary evidence is too scanty to give a satisfactory picture which is in any way complete. Indeed, Kitto succeeds in putting much of the evidence in quite different perspective. While Jebb quotes Aristophanes—'It is difficult for women to get out'—and draws the implication that 'married women too were carefully kept indoors', Kitto quotes the full passage in which a married woman is speaking: 'It's difficult for women to get out, *what with dancing attendance on one's husband, keeping the servant-girl awake, bathing the baby, feeding it . . .*' The implication becomes quite different. Such harassing limitations might just as easily trouble a modern woman.

We know, from Theophrastus, that men did the family shopping and at least one of his descriptions implies considerable respect for a wife. As for the women not going out, the common dangers of the street, Kitto says, may have explained the careful escort of women, as when the Coarse Buffoon, in Theophrastus' characters, tells the world at large that he will get drunk 'stand by the door of the barber's shop . . . and when he sees a lady coming he will raise his dress to show his privy parts'.

So much of the evidence is open to qualification but one thing at least seems clear. The life of the average Athenian woman was more restricted than her British or American counterparts today, her legal rights bore no comparison, her marriage was a far less certain affair, her political rights non-existent, and the respect in which she was held of a different and lower order.

Sparta presents a more definite picture than Athens. Here women were given much greater licence and in girlhood they were taught, not merely to wrestle, to throw the javelin and to box but were encouraged to run races with men as well as women in the nude. This freedom had nothing to do with philosophic ideas of emancipation but was reckoned to be the kind of upbringing best suited to producing ideal mothers for tough Spartan sons. Surrounded on all sides by large and hostile states Sparta needed an endless supply of strapping young

warriors who were strong, brave and ready to sacrifice everything to the state. Under the illusion that sons tended to
inherit the characteristics of the mother rather than the father,
Sparta deliberately framed a constitution which subjected
women to a strict military régime where sickly girl children
were not tolerated and had to be destroyed. According to Emil
Reich, 'For a long time marriage retained the form of a forcible
seizure which has always characterized it among primitive
peoples. The young couple could, at first, only meet in secret
and many must have been the shifts to which they resorted to
conceal the relationship. But when once the marriage was
recognized the wife assumed a position of high honour and
respect.'[10]

Thus, all the physical freedoms granted the Spartan women,
all the disregard for false modesties and feminine weaknesses,
served no higher aim than to make them better breeding cows
for warriors whose expectation of life in time of war was very
low.

There remained, in Athens, the *hetaerae*, a high class of courtesan women who achieved a position and respect in society only
matched by the leading women of our day. Broadly, the word
hetaera simply means—companion. Mostly, these women
were drawn from foreign elements or 'strangers' in the city.
Inevitably Athens attracted innumerable foreigners to its
brilliant dramatic performances, schools of philosophy, political
life and works of art, but the authorities came to believe that any
intermarriage between native citizens and foreign settlers
'would corrupt the pure citizen blood'. When such marriages
were prohibited by law, the foreign women formed liaisons
with Greek citizens without marriage and, in time, many men
developed a double life which did not need the furtive cloaks
characteristic of its modern equivalent, since it became socially
acceptable.

Citizen women were restricted to some extent for large parts
of the day but, as Donaldson wrote, 'The men refused to limit
their associations with women to the house. They wished to
have women with them in their walks, in their banquets, in
their military expeditions. The wives could not be with them
then but there was no constraint on the stranger-women.'[11]
Thus arose a division of function between the two classes of
women. 'The citizen-women had to be mothers and house-

wives—nothing more; the stranger-women had to discharge the duties of companions but remain outside the pale of the privileged and marriageable class.'[12]

The *hetaerae* were sometimes women of high intelligence who could talk about politics and art on equal terms with men, and it was reckoned a distinction rather than a disgrace that they had a number of lovers and could attract to their 'salons' statesmen, philosophers and poets of the same brilliance and variety which later made the visitors to Ninon de l'Enclos' salon so formidable. Undoubtedly, the career of some of the best *hetaerae* in the Ionian cities could be a rich and satisfying experience which was better in many ways than the life of the nineteenth-century French courtesan because their morals were socially acceptable to everyone and they were not regarded, in any way, as decadent.

*   *   *   *

In its early years, Roman society had three social divisions similar to the Greek—the full citizen, the alien and the slave. A Roman citizen was expected to marry the daughter of a Roman citizen and none other. Once more the authorities were concerned to produce pure-blooded citizens of Roman origin and they did not concern themselves with the offspring of foreigners or slaves. A female slave was 'treated simply as a cow or sheep. If she produced healthy offspring, it was so much gain to her master, and he did not care who was the father. Of course, she could not marry, and all her children were the property of her owner. Sometimes a male slave and a female slave were allowed or compelled to live together, and there was something like a marriage. But they had no right to their own children and no obligations towards them except such as were imposed upon them by their proprietors.'[13] Reich comes to the conclusion that 'the early Roman woman was legally little better than a slave'.

The story of the Vestal Virgins is too well known to need repetition at length, but it shows the high premium set by ancient Rome on chastity and reveals one tiny group of women as little less revered than emperors. As everyone knows, the Vestal Virgins belonged to a college of priestesses which exempted them from the authority of their fathers and the fasces of the highest officials of State were lowered in their honour, but the fate meted out to anyone who violated her vows of chastity was indicative of the violence which threatened womankind at the time. The Vestal Virgin who became unchaste was, in fact, buried alive near the Colline Gate.

According to Otto Kiefer, the comparative dullness of the Roman matron's life in ancient Rome had its compensations.

> The Roman matron was well enough off in her home: she did no cooking and no menial tasks. Her only occupation was spinning and weaving with the maidservants, the management of the entire household and the education of the young children. There was [no] woman's apartment where she remained concealed from the eyes of all except other women and a few male relations. . . . In those early times she was not expected to make any effort to acquire culture, and her only intellectual stimulus came from her husband. Her education was chiefly directed to practical ends. If she left the house (which she could not do without her husband's knowledge or without a companion) she wore the long . . . matron's dress. Still, she could appear at the theatre, at a law court, or at a religious ceremony; and everyone had to make way for her in in the street. It was absolutely forbidden to touch or molest her.'[14]

A prolonged series of struggles gradually broke into the divisions between patricians and plebeians and the Lex Canuleia in 442 B.C. 'conferred the conubium, or right of intermarriage on the plebeians'. Slowly this right was extended until in A.D. 212 Caracalla conferred citizenship on all the inhabitants of the Roman Empire and afterwards 'any man might marry any woman'.

The idea that the early Roman matrons were solidly submissive creatures who constantly accepted man-made laws without question is qualified to some extent by Livy's account of a rebellion which broke out among them after the proposed law of Oppius in 215 B.C. which would have prevented women from possessing more than half an ounce of gold, stopped them wearing multi-coloured garments or riding in chariots within the city of Rome, except for religious purposes. When two tribunes of the people suggested the equivalent of a modern civil disobedience campaign against the Oppian law, matters came to a head. Slowly the campaign spread throughout the whole city. As Livy wrote:

'. . . the matrons could not be kept indoors either by the authority of the magistrates or the orders of their husbands or their own sense of propriety. They filled all the streets and blocked the approaches to the Forum; they implored the men who were on their way thither to allow the women to resume their former adornments now that the commonwealth was flourishing and private fortunes increasing every day. Their numbers were daily augmented by those who came up from the country towns. At last they ventured to approach the consuls and praetors and other magistrates with their demands.'[15]

The tough red-haired Cato delivered a passionate speech against the matrons:

'If matrons were kept by their natural modesty within the limits of their rights it would be most unbecoming for you to trouble yourselves even at home about the laws which may be passed or repealed here. Our ancestors would have no woman transact even private business except through her guardian . . . they placed them under the tutelage of parents or brothers or husbands. We suffer them now to dabble in politics and mix themselves up with the business of the Forum and public debates and election contests. . . . What they really want is unrestricted freedom, or to speak the truth, licence, and if they win on this occasion what is there that they will not attempt?'[16]

L. Valerius then spoke, far less effectively, in support of the matrons. As Livy concluded:

'After these speeches in support of and against the law, the women poured out into the streets the next day in much greater force and went in a body to the house of the two Brutuses, who were vetoing their colleagues' proposal, and beset all the doors, nor would they desist till the tribunes had abandoned their opposition. There was no doubt now that the tribes would be unanimous in rescinding the law. . . .'[17] In a word, the women had won the day.

All this, of course, was not devoted to any such elevated purpose as establishing female franchise. Women could not hold public offices, follow professions, enter the priesthood or 'gain triumphs'. No, this rebellion was designed to win a few simple privileges which the modern woman would consider her automatic right, but such public demonstrations by women were almost unheard-of in Rome. The Oppius affair did show that Roman matrons were full of spirit when roused to fight for purely feminine and limited rights.

As with the Athenian woman, legally, the Roman woman was a minor factor in the family, and the law placed supreme authority in the hands of the father who could, at one period, 'exercise a power of life and death over his children'.

Roman girls received the rudiments of an education in reading, writing and arithmetic, and schooling could be harsh, beginning before dawn when it was necessary to have slaves carry a lamp to light the way. Young girls did not, like their brothers, proceed to a secondary school and gain some proficiency in history, geography and a subject ambiguously known as ethics. In Roman eyes it was sufficient that they should read, write and count.

Gradually, the increase of wealth released women from some household duties and as slaves took over many of the menial tasks, women tended to become more independent. In the years which followed the conquest of Greece, Rome was 'inundated by women from the East whose grace of wit, added to their easy morals, was not slow in captivating Roman youth'. These essentially feminine women from abroad were a serious challenge to the average Roman matron who was quite without the 'mystery of the east', a person usually mannish in her bearing and lacking the subtlety which 'so many Oriental and semi-oriental creatures seemed able to command'. One distinguished and ruthless woman of this period was the elder Agrippina of whom Tacitus wrote: 'Her masculine preoccupation left no place for . . . feminine frailties in [her] domineering and ambitious soul.'

No wonder, then, that Roman women reacted against the feminine strangers from abroad and stirred themselves to learn new arts to retain what little control they had over husbands and brothers and lovers. It took the form, at one stage, with some women of concentrating on higher education and reached such a pitch under the Empire 'that the main idea of these women who posed as intellectuals was to be thought witty, brilliant and good company'. By slow stages, during the Empire, thousands of women abandoned the rigid rulings of the past and presently—as if neglected by men despite their desperate attempts to hold them—their growing independence turned in upon itself, and they began the wild orgies of Bacchanalia which, at first, were exclusively female and given up to every kind of frenzied abandon and indecency. All the old moral sanctions broke down. 'These mysterious rites were first imparted to a few,' wrote Livy, 'but were afterwards communicated to great numbers of both men and women. . . . When wine, lascivious discourse, night and the mingling of the sexes had extinguished every modesty, then debaucheries of every kind began to be practised as every person found at hand that sort of enjoyment to which he was disposed by the passion most prevalent in his nature.'

From the restricted, closely guarded and highly respected person of the Roman matron, many women of Rome had progressed into ladies of easy virtue who reckoned two husbands in a lifetime sexual impoverishment, and gloated over the worst spectacles of brutality which the Colosseum had to offer.

In his pompous Victorian way, Emil Reich—whose book is otherwise an interesting storehouse of fact and legend—puts the responsibility for this breakdown partly on the complicated Roman marriage system. 'Marriages *cum conventione* could be solemnized under three different forms,' he writes, '*confarreatio, coemptio* and *usus.*'

The solemn ceremony of *confarreatio* was confined to patricians and had to be performed by the Pontifex Maximus in the presence of at least ten witnesses. This gradually fell into disuse. Unlike *confarreatio*, the ceremony known as *coemptio* had no religious significance but was 'a purely legal bargain, a formal conveyance by purchase of the woman to the man such as might be executed in respect of any other property'. The third form *usus*, constituted marriage in those cases where two people had simply cohabited for at least a year.

It made a sharp and, for the woman, sometimes devastating difference whether she was married under the principle of *sine conventione* or *cum conventione*. In the case of *cum conventione* 'a woman passed absolutely into the power of her husband'. She came to occupy a position which made her a member of his family while she remained legally the daughter of her father and thus became 'the sister of her own children'. Anything she possessed automatically passed into her husband's hands and short of selling her into slavery he could rule her life in considerable detail, even to the point of passing her on to another husband, for a consideration, providing she herself was agreeable.

A woman married *sine conventione* was in the even more curious position of being free from her husband's control and remaining subject to the will of her father. Thus her father retained the right to chastise her and could, if he felt the marriage a failure, separate her, even against her will, from her husband. In these circumstances she was a wife in name and bore her husband's children but she was not, in our sense of the word, of the same family. She still 'belonged' to her father, and this had certain advantages because a husband could not exercise brutal despotism over a wife whose father had the power to remove her from his household. Moreover, any property she might inherit from her father did not automatically pass to the husband.

Slowly, among the higher classes marriage *sine conventione* superseded other forms of marriage, the father ceased by custom to exercise his more extreme rights and women became more independent. As a result the divorce rate rose. 'The State did not interfere in the matter; marriage was regarded as a private relationship which might be dissolved in a private manner without the intervention or sanction of any public authority. Under this fatal facility divorces became rife and were made upon the flimsiest pretexts. Marriage meant little or nothing; it was little more than regulated free love.'[18] Seneca cynically declared in his day: 'The ladies do not reckon the years by the number of the consuls, but by the number of their husbands.'

As in all civilizations, the social position, privileges and duties of women varied widely in Roman days according to period and Emperor, but wherever we turn in the rich, confused, sometimes ignorant, sometimes brutal story it is difficult to find among the common run of women, the equivalent of the modern British or American woman with her independence, legal rights, equality and privileges.

*　　*　　*　　*

The status of women in what are regarded today as primitive societies was generally thought to be low but this is open to qualification. Certainly, the habit long accepted among the Indians of Panama, of making their women beasts of burden, was not resented by the women themselves who agreed that the man must be free to fight and protect the 'caravan' unhampered by baggage. As Westermarck said: 'in such communities, it was a common belief that if a man does a woman's work he will himself become effeminate; besides, he will be laughed at and called a woman. Among the Beni Ahsen tribe in Morocco, the women of the village where I was staying were quite horrified when one of my men was going to fetch water: they said they could not allow him to do so because the fetching of water was a woman's business. . . . It is obvious that this division of labour in savage communities is apt to mislead the travelling stranger. He sees the women hard at work and the men idly looking on. . . . What is largely due to custom is taken to be sheer tyranny on the part of the stronger sex and the wife is pronounced an abject slave of her husband destitute of all rights.'[19]

According to Mr Grinnell, who travelled widely among the North American Indians, the Indian woman was not the submissive drudge she at first appeared to be in European eyes. She did all the hard domestic work, but she was highly respected for it and her sphere of influence did not stop there. She was consulted on many matters, sometimes admitted to the tribal councils 'and spoke there, giving advice. In ordinary *family* conversation women did not hesitate to interrupt and correct their husbands when the latter made statements with which they did not agree, and the man listened with respectful attention.' Among the Navahoes, the women 'exert a great deal of influence', and they 'are very independent of menial duties, and leave their husbands upon the slightest pretext of dislike'. The Omahas were remarkable because their women had equal standing in society with men, husband and wife being joint heads of the family, and their possessions from huts to personal robes could not be sold, exchanged or given away without their joint consent.

According to Westermarck these privileges were not exclusively concentrated in certain North American tribes. Thousands of miles away in India, among the Kandha, women not merely commanded great respect but had remarkable rights. 'Constancy to her husband is not at all required in a wife, whereas infidelity on the part of a married man is held to be highly dishonourable and is often punished by deprivation of many social privileges. And a wife may quit her husband at any time, except within a year of her marriage . . . or within a year after the birth of a child, though, when she quits him, he has a right to reclaim immediately, from her father, the whole sum paid for her.'[20]

Polygamy was not so widespread among primitive peoples as popular legend would have us believe and even where it was practised many women did not resent but defended it. According to Winwood Reade, in certain parts of equatorial Africa he met with statements like the following: 'If a man marries, and his wife thinks that he can afford another spouse, she pesters him to marry again and calls him a "stingy" fellow if he declines to do so.' Livingstone recorded the comment of some Makalolo women when they learnt that a man was allowed only one wife in England: 'They would not like to live in such a country; they could not imagine how English ladies could relish our custom, for in their way of thinking, every man of respectability should have a number of wives as a proof of his wealth.'

Clearly, what European women today would regard as a very low if not—as in the case of polygamy—humiliating status, was looked upon quite differently by polygamous people themselves and the age-old truism repeats itself: upbringing accustoms people to accept and revere whatever they are taught. One tribe will convert into a high principle practices regarded by another as reprehensible. Hence the women involved in polygamous cultures had no sense of inferiority to the women of monogamous cultures, and the whole question of women's status becomes subtly relative. Among primitive peoples it was commonplace that husbands should purchase their wives and here, once more, the Moors thought that European girls, who commanded no price at all, must be very poor trash. In many cases the bride-price had a clear-cut economic connexion and was regarded as compensation for the loss of a girl-worker in the family.

All this inevitably poses the question—what scale of values determines the position of women in primitive societies? The answer is complicated. Westermarck examines the suggestion that rules of descent determine the status of women in many primitive tribes: 'As is well known among many of the "lower" races kinship is reckoned exclusively through the mother. This means that a person is considered a member of his mother's clan, not of his father's, and that property and rank succeed in the female line—for instance that a man's nearest heir is not his own but his sister's son.'[21] Westermarck does not find this very convincing. 'Among the West African Negroes the position of women is, in all appearance, no less honourable in tribes like the Eboes, among whom inheritance runs through males, than in tribes who admit inheritance through females only.'[21] Similarly the principle of economic determinism does not work out comprehensively. In the case of North American aborigines where the women help the tribe to 'acquire food' women are treated with more equality than in tribes where men alone provide the food, and it would follow that hunting nomadic tribes should devalue women, but in the nomadic Kara-Kirghis the 'female sex is treated with greater respect than among those Turks who lead a stationary life and practise agriculture'. In a word, each group or tradition has its own scale of values which, in the case of fifth-century Athens, put the emphasis on beauty, in the later Roman Empire on, in many cases, money, among North American aborigines on food production and in some early Anglo-Saxon groups on fertility.

*   *   *   *

When the Anglo-Saxons first settled in England the patriarchal spirit was already dominant, the father being absolute master in his family and his children so much property which he could sell or exchange as he chose. As with primitive tribes he could 'sell his daughters into wedlock' and even, if the necessity arose, his sons into slavery. In the days when St Augustine brought Christianity to the Anglo-Saxons a girl was regarded as the absolute property of her father and a wife of her husband. The laws of Ethelbert, the first Christian Anglo-Saxon King, contain careful provisions to meet the crime of stealing a daughter or wife. 'If a man carry off a maid by force, let him pay fifty shillings to her owner, and afterwards buy her from him.' 'If a man carry off a freeman's wife let him procure him another with his own money and deliver her to him.' The price of a young woman was sometimes so many head of cattle, sometimes a piece of land, sometimes a combination of both. In the course of time, the father sought to conceal the mercantile character of the transaction and the money became compensation for feeding and bringing up the girl with its own special description of 'foster-lean'. Over the generations this was refined again, until the father merely gave away his daughter, a custom which still prevails in the form today.

After the introduction of Christianity the father had it in his power to dedicate his daughter to a monastic life and 'in the middle of the seventh century, when Oswy, King of the Northumbrians, had defeated and slain Penda, the Pagan King of the Mercians, he gave his daughter to Christ, who thus . . . became her spiritual husband and she was consecrated to him in perpetual virginity'.[22]

Turning to feudal society Guizot[23] believed that life in the castle was favourable to the development of women and 'to that elevation of the condition of women which holds so great a place in the history of our civilization. This great and salutary revolution took place between the ninth and twelfth centuries. We cannot follow it step by step, we can only trace very imperfectly the particular facts which assisted its progress for want of documents. But that in the eleventh century it was about completed, that the condition of women had changed, that the spirit of family, domestic life and the ideas and sentiments which belonged to it had acquired a development . . . previously unknown, is a general fact which it is impossible to overlook.'

Nor is it possible to overlook the fact that Feudalism had a very powerful influence on the legal position of women. In the Chanson de Geste—*Le Charroi de Nîmes*—these lines occur: ' "One of these days," said the King to the knight William, "one of my peers will die; I will give you his land and his wife, if you wish to take them. . . . Take the land of the Marquis Berenges who has just died and take his wife with his fief." ' When Charlemagne returned from his wars in Spain he re-married *en masse* all the widows of the knights who had fallen there, since sentiment had little power to challenge the importance of title deeds and land tenure. Women, in these terms, as property holders, became pawns in the financial scheming of kings and knights.

According to Langdon-Davies it was not only the widow who married again and as fast as possible; nor was it the orphan alone who took what was given her in the way of a husband with hopeful thanks for her good fortune.

Davies is very disillusioned about the age of chivalry which he thought better described the attitude of feudal men to

97

horses, and barons to jousting, than society to women. There
were rituals in public when elegant knights fell on their knees
before gracious ladies and fluttering fragments of cambric were
treated with exaggerated reverence, but in private and in law
even the high-born lady suffered serious shortcomings. There
is a passage in the Chanson de Geste—*Mort de Gavin*—where
a lady named Blancheflor pleads with her husband, the
Emperor Pepin, to help the men and women of Lorraine. 'The
king hears her, he grows enraged, he strikes her nose with his
fist, four drops of blood fall from her and the lady says: "Thanks
be to thee; when thou wilt, give me another blow." ' It was
possible, it seems, for a lady of birth who went to counsel her
husband on matters outside her domain to be met with a blow
in the face but there were—as ever in medieval days—set rules
to the game, and it was carefully laid down that a husband
might strike his wife with his fist on the face or on the back for
contradicting him, and—here the divergence is ironic—for
adultery.

The high-born lady could recite stories and romances, she
could sing a little and accompany others on the viol; she could
sew, weave and embroider, she knew a little falconry and could
set a broken arm; but on social questions, or anything to do with
the great outside world, if she argued with her husband there
was, in some cases, a danger of violence.

The Christian dogma of the indissolubility of marriage may
have led to much unhappiness for some members of the upper
classes in feudal times but Christianity did try to lay down a
minimum age of twelve for marriage, which was intended to
break the habit of earlier child marriages. 'This formal de-
cision,' wrote Gautier, 'was not made to please noble families,
who scouted it. Feudalism had terrible needs indeed. That
the same baron could one day have two fiefs instead of one to
round off their manor and their property they did not stop at
any sacrifice, and they went so far as to marry scandalously
children of five. . . .'

According to Thomas Wright, many townswomen among
the upper class in medieval days were of very different mettle
from the ladies of the castle. Certainly the farces and popular
tales, the *fabliaux* and songs of the day, present the generality
of burgher women as 'ill-educated, coarse in language and
manners and violent in temper', and 'they tyrannize over their

husbands, and beat them and are often beaten in their turn'. Women of this class seemed to enjoy considerable freedom in choosing their husbands, but their education was scanty and once again they did not trouble their heads with politics or the wider world. According to Wright, they loved gadding about. This is easily understood when we remember that 'town life, as far as the male sex was concerned, was very much out of doors and women were left to themselves and therefore . . . sought some common place of meeting. This place was the tavern. . . .'

The tavern became as much a resort of women as men and since large families were the rule the wife could usually leave the older children to look after the younger while she 'set out for an occasional carousal'. Like the Romans, who used their palatial baths as social centres, many medieval communities had estuves where the women met and gossiped and these were said to be the centre of 'a considerable immorality'. The women of the towns and of the common class in the country 'were left much to themselves and were perhaps on this account more exposed to corruption'. Parish priests were said to be among the worst offenders, and in the popular stories of the time 'every woman almost has a priest, or a monk, for her lover', and no small part of the clergy lived with concubines 'who were acknowledged by the parishioners as wives and were commonly spoken of as "priestesses".'

To illustrate the determined individuality of some medieval peasant-wives the following story is constantly repeated by different authors. One day a peasant and his wife went walking and passing a meadow the peasant remarked that he had never seen a meadow so evenly mowed. 'No,' said the wife curtly. 'It is not mowed. It is sheared.' 'I tell you,' said the peasant, 'it was cut with the scythe.' When the wife persisted in contradicting him, the peasant threw her down and in a burst of ferocious anger took out his knife and cut her tongue out. 'Now,' said he, 'was it mowed or cut with the shears?' Whereupon the woman at once imitated with her fingers the movement of a pair of shears. Of course, the story illustrates not merely the independence of the wife but the possible brutalities of the times.

There were two other phenomena centred around women in the Middle Ages which need brief mention—courtly love in the twelfth and thirteenth centuries and, later, witchcraft. Cramped by her feudal life, the lady of the castle, looking out over the beautiful plains of Provence and elsewhere, sometimes sought to expand her emotional life by creating courts of love. 'Under a ruling judge, ladies gathered together and pronounced decrees upon the general theory of love, or gave judgments about specific points brought to their notice by individual lovers.'

At Les Baux in Provence, there remain today the ruins of an old chateau with its vast walls overlooking narrow streets, and it is easy, peering out from the turret of a wrecked tower, over the glimmering plain, at night, to hear the music of viols again, to pick up the words of the old chansons, to hear the elegant ladies talking softly at their courts of love. The refinement of feeling, the exaggerated rituals, the complex rules of conduct which gave high-born women such elaborate courtesy and respect, did not prevail for long, however; in any case they concerned a small minority of women. It would be absurd to deny that within the limits of rich living, of ritualized respect and prolonged leisure, many high-born ladies should have enjoyed their lives over long periods, and it is easy to understand the modern woman who craves to be carried back to the 'days of chivalry'.

There was, in any case, another way out for those women who found the interminable small talk about land, possessions, lovers, tourneys, and battles, the falconry and long stretches of empty idleness, intolerable—the Church. Maidens, widows or wives were all legally permitted to abandon their castle, home and responsibilities to become, by rigorous training, Brides of Christ. It was an inevitable part of the Church's attitude to sex.

Even at home with her husband the wife was exhorted to practise chastity; she was taught that Joseph and Mary lived celibate lives and though she and her husband might be granted the minor sin of getting a child or so, the sooner they achieved that ideal the better for both of them. Such married chastity was held to bring forth fruit thirty-fold, widowed chastity sixty-fold and virgin chastity one hundred-fold; but best of all was the lot of a consecrated nun. Widows might well desire to escape to the cloisters to avoid the trouble and dangers of feudal life; wives also were able to dissolve a marriage, however little the husband desired it, by taking religious vows; and many parents got rid of surplus daughters in the same way. Thus the Virgin became one of the feminine types of the Middle Ages along with the Feudal Lady . . . and the Witch. . . .[24]

A loathing for women marks much of early Christian teaching and Anselm of Canterbury wrote in *De Contemptu Mundi*: 'Woman has a clear face and a lovely form, she pleases you not a little, this milk white creature! But, ah! if her bowels were opened and all the other regions of her flesh, what foul tissues would this white skin be shown to contain.'

It was a complete belief in the horned devil, holding sway over thousands of evil and attendant spirits, which created an atmosphere where witches and their ruthless persecution became commonplace in the Middle Ages. The slow change in society's attitude towards witches is a novel means of measuring progress. In the seventeenth century 511 witches were tried in England and Scotland, and one continental judge put some 800 to the torture in sixteen years. In one year alone, the Bishop of Wurtemberg had roughly 900 burnt at the stake. A witch was executed in Scotland in 1722, and 1712 saw the last witch convicted in England.

Langdon-Davies is a highly prejudiced writer, but it was his conclusion in *A Short History of Women*, that 'the Middle Ages set up an ideal of womanly life that had no sort of connection with primeval facts; a despotic and misogynist religious institution and a militarist and uncouth civil institution conspired together to make women's life miserable'.[25] This is far too sweeping a generalization which sets out with the dangerous presupposition that one can measure the happiness of another individual in a long dead age, but it has some degree of truth.

When the fine free air of the Renaissance began blowing across Europe some of the superstition, subjection and nastiness surrounding the lives of many women was dispersed but, again, their lot in England under Elizabeth varied from class to class and group to group. There was a relaxation of the moral codes in some classes, religion no longer thundered quite so fiercely against sexual appetites, and the clergy gave up compounding erudite manuals of erotic disciplines, abandoned whatever concubines they had, admitted the weakness of their own flesh and began to marry.

The ideas of Death, the Christ Bride and the Devil ceased to hold men and women in quite such complete thrall, and an awareness of the joys of life here and now brought a new appreciation of women. In some classes, they became the partners of men in the revival of the arts of living and learning. Indeed, a small literature was especially created for women, if we are to believe Lyly's dedication of *Euphues*: 'It resteth, Ladies, that you take the pains to read it, but at such times as you spend in playing with your dogs, and yet will not pinch you of that pastime, for I am content that your dogs lie in your laps, so that *Euphues* may be in your hands, that when you shall be weary in reading of the one, you may be ready to sport with the other. . . . *Euphues* had rather lie shut in a lady's closet than open in a scholar's study.' There was a whole cult of lap-dogs at this period which makes Lyly's comment intelligible. Upper-class women carried them clasped to their bosoms, allowed them to sleep on their beds and dandled them with self-conscious charm on every possible occasion. Visiting foreigners were astonished at the freedom allowed certain classes of Englishwomen towards the end of the sixteenth century. They 'were not shut up as in Spain' but went to market when they pleased; they were allowed 'the free management of their houses', and they sometimes sat before their doors 'decked out in fine clothes in order to see and be seen by the passers-by'. Many women dressed boldly and wore 'doublets with pendent cod-pieces on the breast, full of jags and cuts'. Dutch visitors found that marriage conferred an astonishing degree of liberty and 'England [was] called the Paradise of married women'. W. S. Davis commented: 'In upper circles it is common enough for fine ladies to spend much of their time in the escort of fine gentlemen who are anything but their husbands. In lower circles plenty of dames foregather at taverns, tipple and gossip and presently glide home again telling their husbands the transparent fable—"I have been to church".'[26]

Education was slight for the majority of women and a high proportion of wives could not even sign their names, as was very evident from Shakespeare's second daughter Judith who could only 'make her mark'. Girls were 'given away in marriage' at thirteen, fourteen and fifteen, many marriages were 'arranged' and sometimes a joint family council would decide to betroth a girl as early as twelve.

Legally, women were still held very much in thrall. A married woman was almost completely in the power of her husband, 'her life only excepted'. She could be locked in the house at her husband's whim, she could be beaten 'with the lash or rods' and it was almost impossible to apply a legal remedy. Her property passed for all practical purposes into the possession of her husband on marriage and 'she [was] lawfully in a state of perpetual tutelage and minority'.[27] The question of divorce from a man who was a habitual drunkard, brutal or given to insane and dangerous rages, did not very often arise, because although, under the new Protestantism, divorce was granted by the bishop's court, it was more theoretical than practical and even when granted made second marriages very dubious.

Certainly women of the cultured classes were newly revered by some highly literate people. Thus England's Parnassus, an anthology of quotations published in 1660, contains these lines:

> Women be
> Framed with the same parts of the mind as we,
> Nay, nature triumphs in their beauties' birth,
> And women made the glory of the earth.
> What art so deep, what science so high
> Unto the which women have not attained,
> Who lest in stories old to look may trye
> And find my speech herein not false or fain'd. . . .

We must now discriminate between appreciating women as women and accepting them as co-equals with men, granted brains if not intellect capable of distinction in fields far removed from domestic life or maternity. Queen Elizabeth herself set the example and 'heightened the esteem in which her sex was held', but it was still a rare person who claimed that women could equal men in those spheres which had traditionally been regarded as male down the centuries.

The conflicting forces of Puritanism and profligacy presently broke into the spontaneity of Elizabethan life to stem and reverse the tide of emancipation. Puritanism came to regard women as capable of fulfilling one of two rôles. Either a woman must be a homely person, happy to play the background rôle of wife and mother, a modest, retiring and unquestionably faithful woman, or she ran the danger of becoming a courtesan. In the eyes of the Puritans any close attention to personal beauty was 'an invitation to licence', but some did not bar what they referred to as 'education for the fair sex'. The royal court took exactly the opposite view. Women should be beautiful creatures who spent their days either making themselves more delectable for male indulgence, or attending to a few delicate domestic duties. This attitude reached its climax in the circle of Charles II where 'women were not merely a temptation but a temptation to which one must incessantly and gleefully succumb. . . .' By the end of the seventeenth century the position of women had reached a very low mark and so far as one class of women was concerned, as Langdon-Davies colourfully overstated it: 'A religious prostitute in Phrygia in 1000 B.C. was in a higher state of development than a Christian mistress at the Court of Charles II.'[28]

Of course, Puritanism produced women like Lucy Hutchinson who achieved a thorough knowledge of French and Latin and some Greek and Hebrew, who translated Lucretius into English verse, outstripped her brothers at school, wrote her fascinating memoirs and did not believe in limiting her pleasures too much. 'I thought, when I had . . . every day performed my due tasks of reading and praying, that then I was free to anything that was not sin for I was not, at that time, convinced of the vanity of conversation which was not scandalously wicked; I thought it no sin to learn or hear witty songs and amorous sonnets or poems, and twenty things of that kind wherein I was so apt that I became the confidante in all the loves that were managed among my mother's young women and there was none of them but had many lovers and some particular friends beloved above the rest.'[29]

G. M. Trevelyan has described the position of upper-class women in the early seventeenth century very well:

The ladies of that day were forced to give a large part of their lives to household duties and had less to spare for society and culture. In the absence of country doctors it was the women of the house who practised the quaint lore of the art of healing—in part medicine, in part charm and white magic. Almost all the food, drink and delicacies of the land-lord's families came off the estate and in small manors the brewing of the beer, the salting of the Martinmas beef and the daily cooking were the province of the wife and daughters; even in fine houses it was their business to preserve the garden fruit, and to sew for household use or ornament during long hours that would now be either devoted to more intellectual or more athletic pursuits. . . . While the daughters of the well-to-do were not yet divorced from the business of life in the futile and languorous drawing-rooms to which Miss Austen's heroines were confined, on the other hand no professions or trades higher than manual were open to women, and scarcely any education was provided for them save that which each house could give. A very few clever women were classical scholars; a somewhat larger number were Puritan theologians or students of English. . . .'[30]

It was Daniel Defoe who protested eloquently against the lot of women in 1692 in his Essay on Projects: 'I cannot think that God Almighty made [women] so delicate, so glorious creatures, and furnished them with such charms, so agreeable and so delightful to mankind; with souls capable of the same accomplishments with men; and all to be only stewards of our Houses, Cooks and Slaves.

'Not that I am for exalting the female government in the least, but, in short, I would have men take women for companions and educate them to be fit for it.'

The position of women of the lower classes in the seventeenth century was sometimes appalling. From as early as Stuart times, large numbers of women were brought up to believe that work was degrading and thousands of other women were, in fact, degraded by long and exhausting hours of work, crude in character and impoverished in payment.

In the seventeenth century, once more, the relationship of one class to another, the rights, privileges, hours of work and payment of women varied widely, not only according to the nature of the work but according to the organization of the work. If production techniques are divided into three classes—Domestic, Family and Capitalist (as Alice Clark does in her very detailed study, *Working Life of Women in the Seventeenth Century*)—then much of the ordinary woman's 'production work' in the seventeenth century was domestic or family. Domestic production involved food, goods and service for the exclusive use of the family, such as growing vegetables, weaving clothes and looking after the family. Those who have not tried the long, arduous and very monotonous task of weaving enough clothes for a family of six or seven can have little idea of what it meant for one person, the wife, to face this task, possibly every year, but weaving was only one of many similar duties.

Family industry, as Alice Clark puts it, 'consisted of father, mother, children, household servants and apprentices; the apprentices and servants being children and young people of both sexes who earned their keep and in the latter case a nominal wage. . . .' The family became a unit based on the house, producing goods which were sold or exchanged in the outside world. Those women involved in family industry, provided trade was good, might do reasonably well because the profits 'belonged to the family and not to individual members'. During the father's lifetime he was expected to provide from the profits 'marriage portions for his children as they reached maturity' and when he died 'the mother succeeded to his position as head of the family'. Women of the tradesman class were generally well acquainted with their husband's business and secured 'possession of his stock, apprentices and goodwill' when he died. Frequently the widow carried on the business, quite efficiently, and women were especially active in the retail trade.

Some husbands found it worth while to free their wives from endless household tasks even at the cost of hiring servants to do the work because their wives had become too important a part of the business. Everything depended upon whether the business was conducted in or out of the home. Inside the home a woman could fulfil the same triple rôle as a modern professional woman, bearing children, helping to run the house and business and beyond the work of the modern woman, playing the part of nurse and doctor. In a society where sickness was rife, where every town and many villages were liable to outbreaks of smallpox and plague, this last rôle could be onerous. Add the work of teaching the young, occasional incursions into midwifery and some attempt at 'superintending the books' and it will be seen that the wife of a family business man had every minute of her time fully occupied.

As wealth increased and the iron hand of necessity relaxed some married women withdrew from active production to create the parvenu class so well described in Pepys's diary:

Nov. 13, 1662. Our discontent again and sorely angered my wife—who indeed do live very lonely, but I do perceive that

it is want of work that do make her and all other people think
of ways of spending their time worse.

Sept. 17, 1663. I see that she is confirmed on it that all I do
is by design and that my very keeping of the house in dirt,
and the doing of this and anything else in the house, is but to
find her employment to keep her within and from minding of
her pleasure, which though I am sorry to see she minds it, is
true enough in a great degree.

At the other extreme, life was very harsh for women involved
in agricultural work. A report made by the Justices of the Peace
concerning the agricultural poor of Hitchin said: 'When they
have worke the wages geven them is soe small that it hardlye
sufficeth to buy the poore man and his family breed, for they
pay 6s. for one bushell of mycelyn grayne and receive but 8d.
for their day's work. It is not possible to procure mayntenance
for all these poore people and their famylyes by almes, nor yet
by taxes.'[31]

It has to be understood that in the seventeenth century the
idea of a man supporting his wife was not widespread among
the working-classes. It was socially accepted that a woman
should help to support her children, and husband and wife were
mutually dependent. The father would probably provide rent,
shelter and protection and the mother food. If this gave the
woman considerable freedom of movement and many small
emancipations, it burdened her with responsibilities beyond
those accepted by the father.

Alice Clark gives it as her opinion that few children in the
wage-earning class were reared in the seventeenth century.
'Of those who reached maturity many were crippled in mind or
body, forming a large class of unemployables destined to be a
burthen instead of strength to the community.' This, she says,
was not so much the result of 'excessive work on the part of
married women' as of underfeeding and bad housing. 'In some
cases it even reached a point where the sacrifice of the wage-
earner's children was caused by the mother's starvation; vainly
she gave her own food to the children, for then she was
unable to suckle the baby, and grew too feeble for her former
work.'[32]

Her former work. Even when she succeeded in working in the
fields she could not hope to earn more than twopence a day

'with meate and drinke 6d. without'.[33] Her husband often worked on a farm at some distance from her 'home' and visited his wife and children on Sundays and holidays, bringing what money he could spare from his hopelessly inadequate wage. Hours of work for both sexes were appallingly long. There were occasions when 'the once lusty young woman who had formerly done a hard day's work with the men at harvesting was broken by this life . . .' and 'on the death or desertion of her husband the labouring woman became wholly dependent on the Parish for support'.[34]

In other trades things were better. As we have seen, many women entered the retail trade where tact, and general intelligence were more important than technical knowledge and manual dexterity. The woollen trade, on the other hand, repeated some of the hardships of agriculture in different form. The work was mainly done at home and made it possible to employ women and children indiscriminately, but the wages paid for 'spinning linen were insufficient, and those paid for spinning wool, barely sufficient, for their individual maintenance and yet out of them, women were expected to support or partly support their children'.

Long before the Industrial Revolution and factory work began, women and children were overworked and exploited, but as the eighteenth century swung into its stride the new British industrialists took ruthless advantage of the large and growing numbers of female workers, and the status of some women workers declined even more than in the seventeenth century. In 1800 a Home Office Report said: 'The people employed in the different manufactures are early introduced into them, many at five and six years old, both girls and boys, so that when the former become women they have not had any opportunity of acquiring any habits of Domestic economy or the management of a family. . . . The greater part of the working and lower class people have not wives that can dress a joint of meat if they were to have it given them. The consequence is that such articles become their food that are the most easily acquired, consequently their general food now consists of bread and cheese.'

In the Second Report of the Factory Commission, 1833, the point is repeated and the lack of domestic education deplored. The Report adds: 'Even if she had acquired the knowledge, she has still not time to practise it. In addition to the twelve hours' labour is an additional absence from home in the going and returning. Here is the young mother absent from her child about twelve hours daily. And who has the charge of her infant in her absence? Usually some little girl or aged woman, who is hired for a trifle and whose services are equivalent to the reward. Too often the dwelling of the factory family is no home; it is sometimes a cellar, which includes no cookery, no washing, no making, no mending, no decencies of life, no invitation to the fireside.'

As the British population leapt up spectacularly the social status of many ordinary women continued to decline. In addition to a number of enlightened spirits at the Home Office who put on record the terrible story of industrial exploitation, there were others who wrote from a higher sense of the destiny of women. It was typical of the early eighteenth century that when, in 1739, a pamphlet entitled 'Women not Inferior to Men' appeared it had to be labelled as by Sophia, a Person of Quality. Lady Mary Wortley Montagu was supposed to have been its author and the pamphlet is a powerful protest against restricting the rôle of women to sexual and domestic matters, vigorously attacking the prevailing system of education which left most women in a sad state of ignorance. 'Why is learning useless to us?' the pamphlet asked—'Because we have no share in public offices. And why have we no share in public offices? Because we have no learning.'

The beginnings of the feminist movement were now evident and in 1797 a lone voice was raised in the British House of Commons—apparently the first occasion on which the House discussed the matter—when Fox not merely asked, but himself answered the question: why shouldn't women have the right to vote? His answer was glib and immediate. Both the law of nature and the law of nations, he said, had made 'that sex dependent on ours'. 'Their voices,' he added, 'would be governed by the relations in which they stand to society.' He was tactfully expressing in parliamentary language part of the argument against female franchise, which all its opponents used in one form or another in the nineteenth century: that women would merely vote under the direction of father or husband, and become a female rubber-stamp to the traditional franchise. Fox referred to a number of absurd theorists on the subject and seemed to have in mind Mary Godwin—that 'hyena in petti-coats', as Horace Walpole called her—who, as 'a miserable spinster governess', had written a book called *A Vindication of the Rights of Women*. This book, derivative from Tom Paine's *The Rights of Man*, developed the theme that woman must acquire knowledge, broaden her mind, and educate herself until she could lift herself 'out of the terrestrial horrors of being man's plaything into the celestial glories of being his com-panion'.[35]

The stage was set for the first time in western history for women to reach out towards real equality with men, and presently the tensions mounted, the books and pamphlets multiplied and a holy preserve never before challenged in history, was at last invaded by women. A man now almost forgotten was one of the vital pioneers in the women's suffrage movement in England but his first attempt to present the cause in print carried a title not calculated to reach a wide audience: 'An appeal of one half the human race, Woman against the pretentions of the other half, Men, to retain them in political and thence in civil and domestic slavery: In reply to a para-graph of Mr Mill's celebrated article on Government.' This quotation followed:

> Tis all stern duty on the female side
> On man's, mere sensual lust and surly pride.

Some puritan streak in printer, type-setter or publisher translated the word 'lust' into 'gust', but the Appeal was power-fully written and marriage referred to as a mere superstition, 'called in aid by men when they wished to admit women to the high honour of becoming their "involuntary breeding machines and household slaves".'

Mr Roger Fulford has written a vivid and comprehensive account of the suffragette battle which followed, and anyone interested in its detailed history should turn to it. The typical middle-class outlook on any agitation for female franchise was ruthlessly represented in a letter which Queen Victoria wrote towards the end of 1870 to Theodore Martin:

'The Queen is most anxious to enlist everyone who can speak or write to join in checking this mad, wicked folly of Woman's Rights with all its attendant horrors on which her poor, feeble sex is bent, forgetting every sense of womanly feeling and propriety. Lady Amberley ought to get a *good whipping*.'

These were the days when respectable daughters never went anywhere without a chaperon, Father was an infallible and authoritarian figurehead, sex an unfortunate prerequisite to reproduction, men and women were carefully segregated in any activity which brought them into unmarried proximity, and professional careers unthinkable for 'persons wearing skirts'. Mrs Lynn Linton was busy writing severe commentaries on 'the decorum and morality of the young ladies who, under the lead of fashion, were just emerging from the restrictions of the crinoline'. To Mrs Lynn Linton, whose idea of the perfect woman seems to have been bounded by the lifeless, malleable doll beloved by Dickens, women who advocated the vote for their own sex were complete anathema; she called them, by turns, 'The Epicene Sex or the Shrieking Sisterhood'.[36]

In those days, middle-class women, who frequently reared enormous families of eight, nine or ten children, passed over whatever personal property they possessed to their husbands on marriage, did not qualify as ratepayers and therefore could not vote as the law then stood. This was the weakness of the early case for female suffrage. Despite the reforms advocated, all married women would have been excluded and the 'new outlook' seemed concerned with 'widows and affluent spinsters', and the like, a very suspect lot from the point of view of many middle-class gentlemen.

It is as well to repeat that the status of the ordinary working woman in the middle of the nineteenth century was still very low, her hours of work inordinately long and home life too often impoverished, anxious and down-trodden. Mr and Mrs Hammond's *Town Labourer* gives some evidence of the more extreme conditions:

When the Children's Employment Commission reported in 1842, women were working in the pits in the West Riding, in Cheshire, in some parts of Lancashire and in South Wales. . . . They were generally employed as 'drawers', i.e. in carrying or pushing the cars containing the coal 'won' by the hewers, for the men liked women in this capacity, finding them easy to manage and yet too spirited to let others pass them. . . . A witness told the Commission of 1842 that a married woman miner worked day and night, the day being spent on the mine and the night in washing, cooking and cleaning the house. . . . The working day varied; for men it was often twelve hours, for women and children longer. [37]

In one sense, middle-class women had once more been reduced to domestic appendages to their husbands, and in another, many working-class women were freed from domestic imprisonment only at the cost of becoming industrial drudges. Against this background the early agitation for female enfranchisement was doomed to ridicule, but as the century advanced, a period which produced such distinguished women as Florence Nightingale, George Eliot and Eleanor Acland could not so easily smother the growing determination of female militants.

It was not until the early nineteen hundreds that matters came to a head. On 9 February, 1907, the suffragettes organized a march from Hyde Park to Exeter Hall in the Strand which, despite heavy rain, found four thousand men and women (mainly women) trudging valiantly through the muddy streets. On 12 February Mrs Sylvia Pankhurst presided over what was called A Women's Parliament at Caxton Hall and on the words from their chairman 'Rise up, Women', the whole meeting filed out, formed a procession and marched towards the House of Commons. As Roger Fulford wrote: 'The afternoon was cold with gleaming sunshine and Mrs Despard [at the head preceded by an Inspector of Police] looked superb—picturesque but dignified. An observer once remarked that on these occasions she reminded him of the fighting Temeraire'.[38] Reaching Westminster Abbey, Mrs Despard saw deployed in front of her a strong police barrier, and the Police Inspector advised her to turn back, but she strode on, proud, silent, with nothing but her personality to urge the others forward.

'Suddenly a considerable force of mounted police rode into the procession and, with the help of the foot police, scattered the women, thumping them on the back. Mrs Despard and other leaders were arrested. Again and again the women tried to re-form and in the words of Mrs Pankhurst "the battle against the merciless hooves" lasted for some hours. Public opinion was unquestionably shocked; the *Daily Chronicle* published a cartoon the next mornings called "The London

Cossack", which showed a mounted policeman riding off in triumph from the field of battle with his victorious trophies—a collection of ladies' hats.'[39]

The remainder of the story is too familiar to need repetition. Everyone knows how women chained themselves to railings, how one threw herself beneath the hooves of a royal horse, others were imprisoned, some went on hunger strike, suffered the brutality of being forcibly fed and never hesitated to risk their jobs and reputations to drive home their claims.

It was bad enough in those days for women to speak in public and create mass public disorders, but to get themselves arrested and spend weeks in gaol was—in the eyes of conventional values—criminal behaviour. If they overdid their demonstrations and aroused retaliation that was sometimes brutal, few men living in those days expected the authorities to react otherwise. In itself, their prolonged and relentless campaign created steps in the emancipation of women which had no precedent down the ages. Women were thrusting through male restraints with spectacular courage and effect.

Between the years 1900 and 1914 a new movement among groups like the Fabians revealed women behaving in still more emancipated ways and there were even those prepared to have a child out of wedlock by a man they did not love, and if necessary 'go on the rates' to support it. Less spectacularly, women began to crowd the schools and colleges, took up games like hockey, appeared on male golf-courses and made their names as tennis champions. Careers were no longer completely barred to them and they put in an appearance in the City of London, and, most significant of all—as Roger Fulford says—they made their own friends. It was customary and correct to remain within the circle of friends which family introductions made possible in Victorian days, but now, young women dared to go out with men their parents had never even met. 'The contrast between the young lady of these pre-war years and little Miss Prunes and Prisms— the finished product of Victorian womanhood—is too obvious to need emphasis. Mrs Humphrey Ward gives an admirable portrait of the typical young lady of those times in her novel *Delia Blanchflower*. Delia has all the crispness and assurance of her contemporaries, and it is no shock to meet her, staying in a hotel in Switzerland alone and holding forth to a slightly frumpish collection of survivors from Victorian habits, with the confident assertion, "There is a new age coming and it will be the age of the free-woman".'[40]

On 28 March, 1917, Mr Asquith at last declared himself in favour of women having the vote. The Electoral Reform Bill became law in January, 1918. In 1920, the right of American women to vote, which was already possible in 28 states, became a provision of the Constitution. France did not follow until 1944.

It has to be emphasized that it was not the suffragettes alone who spectacularly liberated women. The steady increase in material wealth, the devices which simplified domestic work, the development of education, the rise in the status of the Common Man and the sheer enlightenment which came with greater knowledge of women's nature and physiology all contributed to break down traditional barriers, but much of the credit still goes to a handful of distinguished nineteenth- and twentieth-century women who were themselves the products of higher education. They worked, agitated, not for the vote but for the liberation of women. Simultaneously economic forces were creating a tremendous demand for women in offices and factories, and the old taboos were powerless against the needs of the new industrialists.

Today, in many parts of Western Europe and America, women are free in a wider sense than ever before. They move freely on equal terms with men and without chaperons, they wear clothes free from the smothering hypocrisies of the Victorian age, they live their married lives as companions and in many cases equals of their husbands, they have entered all the professions, invaded the House of Commons, become doctors and lawyers and regard the right to vote as an elementary right. As always down the ages, their social status varies from class to class but instead of using—exclusively—their bodies and beauty to achieve the highest distinction, like the *haetera* of fifth-century Athens, they can rely on professional distinction alone, on brains, talent or artistic ability. The classes are much more mobile than in the past. Education enables women of the humblest birth to stand a chance of reaching the highest places.

Once more it is the ordinary woman whose status has risen in the eyes of the community, who has at her disposal privileges once the exclusive right of the upper classes, who can afford to wear clothes which frequently make her quite indistinguishable from far wealthier and more exclusive ladies. It is doubtful whether any other period has produced such a revolutionary change in the status of the ordinary woman. It is even suggested by critics like Philip Wylie that the veneration shown to the Average American Woman, the privileges lavished on her, and the power she has to demand subservience from the male, has practically established a state of matriarchy in the United States of America.

Matriarchies have been known in primitive communities before, but nothing like the American situation seems to have arisen in Western civilization in the last two thousand years, and the trend seems to be towards even higher status for the ever more liberated young women.

In Europe generally, large pockets of resistance remain. The middle-class young woman of Roman Catholic Italy is still shrouded in protective rituals which hamper her freedom severely, but she is much more a free individual, taking a far wider part in the life of the community than her equivalent in ancient Rome. In Spain matters are worse. Far too many areas still regard and treat women in a manner not very different from medieval days. There remain at least a dozen countries where women have no political rights whatever, among them Colombia, Egypt, Ethiopia, Iraq, Jordan, Paraguay and Switzerland.

For the rest, the question has to be asked—does all this increase in status, freedom and variety of opportunity lead to greater happiness among those modern Western European women who are, in the widest sense, emancipated?

Certainly all the evidence indicates that the average woman *should* be happier. She is no longer a beast of burden, no longer a chattel, or a convenient body for sexual and domestic exploitation; her health is not ruined by bearing ten children in as many years; she does not go in continuous fear of pregnancy and when she works it is for limited hours under tolerable conditions. Her expectation of life is much greater, and pain, a far more constant and severe companion for women than for men, can be controlled in ways unknown to the past.

The age-old argument that in those days when women accepted their lot as the inevitable consequence of being alive they were relatively no more unhappy because they did not believe any other or better way of life existed, is not completely valid. Within the limited outlook of certain individuals this was true, but there remained a potential which, unrealized, left them, whatever they personally felt or thought, unfulfilled and impoverished as a sex. A stunted human-being may consider herself relatively happy but she is not necessarily a totally fulfilled human-being or as happy as she might be. Ignorance of an unrealized potential does not justify what may be limited forms of living or happiness.

Conflicts between the sexual and emotional elements in women's nature always existed and these were frequently reconciled by love. In turn, the sexual and emotional have often, in thinking women, been troubled by vague misgivings from the intellectual, and a repressed and stunted intellectual impulse was likely to be no less troublesome to peace of mind—and in some cases more so—than a realized one. Today, the rôles chosen for the fulfilment of the intellectual impulse certainly bring, *in some cases*, fresh tensions into a woman's life. Emancipation and fulfilment have been bought at the price of fresh nervous strains. A professional, intellectual or academic woman who raises a family of two or three children, finds herself hurrying back from work to a family run by a nanny, sees her children for hurried snatches in the early mornings and evenings and becomes a full-blooded mother only at the week-ends. A few organizations like the B.B.C. have recognized the difficulties of the newly divided or integrated woman, whichever way you look at it, and make provision for maternity leave, but the great majority still have no machinery for accommodating woman's new double rôle.

The woman who tries to combine the three rôles of mother, wife and professional woman, sometimes has a nerve-racking time in which she is overtaken periodically by a guilty sense of not fulfilling any one rôle satisfactorily, but these women are the exceptions. Today many women continue their jobs after they are married, but abandon outside work at varying stages of pregnancy. They may concentrate on motherhood for the next five years, rearing two children through their early years in that time, and return in their early thirties to professional life once more. In middle age, with their children gone out into the world and the home comparatively empty, they do not turn to small-scale gossip and back-biting about their neighbours for satisfaction, but continue an active and satisfying career. There are, at the moment, too many middled-aged wives untrained for any profession, who, when their children have grown up, are left in a terrible vacuum where their unused energies may be sucked into scandal-mongering, cinema-going, tea parties and dangerous tittle-tattle. In their case, emancipation has not gone far enough, but the great majority of younger women in the middle and lower classes appear to have benefited from it.

There are those who believe that the serried ranks of uniformly dressed girls who pour into offices and factories every morning and face the horrors of the rush hour in London and New York are no improvement on the circumscribed women of Athens who were kept in a state of happy subservience. This is a romantic view. It is true that emancipation carries certain penalties, but the advantages—especially for the average woman—seem to be overwhelming.

When we consider the free, educated, healthy young woman of today, who can earn her living and remain independent if she likes, or marry a husband of her own choosing, a woman who can come to childbirth voluntarily, three or four times in a lifetime with controlled pain, take an active part in the social and political life of the community and know that the social security services will buttress her in any disaster, and then remember the cloistered women of Greece, illiterate, married by arrangement at fourteen or fifteen, deprived of any political rights, untrained for any profession, entirely dependent on a husband, and liable to die from many minor illnesses—there seems only one answer to the question have women progressed?—whatever psychological subtleties would seem to confuse the issue.

Perhaps we might learn a lesson from Greece about sexual liberation which would reduce the number of young male and female neurotics today: perhaps we have increased the possibilities of neurosis in some women by releasing all their instincts and talents; perhaps there are those among us who look back nostalgically to the days when cow-eyed women remained happy concubines; but that women are now regarded on much the same level as men by most enlightened people in England, America and large areas of Western Europe is difficult to dispute. Whether they are any happier is a question which each individual woman must answer for herself.

CHAPTER SIX

Moral progress

'ALL progress, as distinguished from evolution or development, is in a sense moral progress, in other words, it is a movement towards a better state of affairs. We can, however, also speak of moral progress as meaning progress in morality. This seems to consist in the clarification of moral ideas, the removal of inconsistencies between moral rules, a clearer understanding of human needs and purposes, the enlargement of the area within which moral principles are applied and increasing approximation of behaviour to the demands of the moral code.'[1]

This very twentieth-century interpretation of the meaning of morals would not have been unacceptable to fifth-century Athens, but whatever slender thread connects the two outlooks, the Greek conception of morals was, of course, different from the Western European, the Roman, in turn, differed from the Greek and the Greek from the Egyptian. Every variety of conduct has, at some time, received social approval down the ages. It needs only the most superficial knowledge of primitive societies to realize that behaviour which we would consider brutal has often been elevated by the most solemn social sanctions into a lofty moral principle. At one time no more noble act could be performed than to sacrifice one's favourite daughter to a ritual death in the hope of arousing a wind for an idle fleet, and the sacrifice of a favourite son was an act of piety which no god worth his salt could ignore.

The climate of opinion in each civilization endorses certain social mores and the forces which bring this about may be economic, intellectual, sexual, the result of a dominant group imposing its will on the mass of people or a combination of all these. Between the irresistible power of a blood and iron dictator forcing his values on his fellows and the subtle permeation of personality by a sun-bathed climate like Greece, lies a whole forest of motives all contributing to an accepted code of conduct.

In Greece it was 'the full and perfect development of humanity in all its organs and functions . . . without any tinge of
asceticism, which held the highest appeal' and brought about one
form of conduct which still embarrasses modern moralists. In a
land of sun-bleached shores and rich vineyards where a steady,
tideless sea pressed against a beautiful coast-line it was not
unexpected that beauty should become the glowing core which
permeated the social mores. 'In no other period of the world's
history was the admiration of beauty in all its forms so passionate
or so universal. It coloured the whole moral teaching of the time
and led the chief moralists to regard virtue simply as the highest
kind of supersensual beauty.'[2]

Thus, a courtesan was often well placed in the social scale for
her beauty, and all Greeks admired the statues of Aphrodite
modelled upon her. Praxiteles carved, in gold, the form of
Phryne which stood in the temple of Apollo at Delphi, and
'when she was accused of corrupting the youth of Athens, her
advocate Hyperides procured her acquittal by suddenly un-
veiling her charms before the dazzled eyes of the assembled
judges'.[3] There remained, of course, large numbers of
courtesans who were little better than common prostitutes
living in what Lecky insists was abject degradation. None
the less, it became commonplace for the most venerable
philosophers, long past the indulgence of passions, to
make special pilgrimages to visit courtesans, and Simonides
and Pindar sang their praises in extravagantly beautiful
language.

The moral sanctions, as we have seen in my earlier volume,
relegated the ordinary Greek wife to a state of comparative
domestic 'drudgery' and it is not surprising, as Lecky says, that
'the more ambitious and accomplished women' from abroad
should find an outlet in the life of the courtesan. Women like
Aspasia attracted the poets and philosophers, the historians and
artists, and she gathered around her a distinguished circle of
men as ready to indulge her mind as her body until the great
Pericles fell under her spell and was presently passionately in
love with her.

In modern French history we have seen kings and politicians
deliberately indulging the great courtesans of their day, and
even English puritanism produced a worthy exponent of the
tradition in John Wilkes, but this was associated, in modern

eyes, with decadence. In Greece it corresponded to noble and virtuous behaviour.

There is no need to dwell on the free play of homosexuality and pederasty which the Greek code allowed. Apologists for greater sexual freedom commonly appeal to the classical detachment of fifth-century Athens where, as everyone knows, beautiful young boys were the lovers of adult men and family men frequently had male lovers. Family morals, as a whole, were very different from today. 'Irregular female connexions were looked upon as ordinary and not disgraceful incidents in the life of a good man.'

What were the philosophic theories which underlay a society where adultery and homosexuality were accepted as normal, where slavery was an automatic necessity of cultured living, women were frequently domestic serfs and unwanted children could be left to die in the open without violating any known moral law?

The early Greeks were driven by a superstitious belief in the magico-religious basis of law and morals. 'The Furies punished the parricide. The perjurer or the betrayer of his guest aroused the wrath of Zeus. The curse fell upon the offender and would work itself out in the fate of his children, if not in his own life.'[4] There was, in fact, a natural law established by the gods, which sanctioned moral behaviour and punished deviation. Gradually this changed, until the brilliant speculative minds in fifth-century Athens broke into these assumptions with the effect of a revolution and Zeno's dialectics shook 'the first principles of ordinary knowledge'. Heraclitus questioned the picture of reality presented by the senses, Protagoras came out with his bold doctrine that 'man is the measure of all things', and presently the Sophists applied those teachings to ethics. Travellers were finding, in foreign lands and customs, evidence which corresponded with the new intellectual theorizing. 'Herodotus told of tribes who were as scandalized at the Greek custom of burying the dead as the Greeks were at them for eating their dead.'[5]

It quickly became evident that the ancient idea of a moral law inherent in nature found no justification in observed fact. Natural authority for moral behaviour required an underlying identity in whatever land or situation one found oneself, and this was clearly lacking when clouds of superstition were subjected to rigorous examination. This new distinction between natural and man-made morals was crystallized in the Melian Dialogue ascribed by Thucydides to the Athenian delegates:

> As for the gods, we expect to have quite as much of their favour as you. . . . For of the gods we believe, and of men we know, that by a law of their nature wherever they can rule they will. . . . As to Lacedæmonians . . . of all men whom we know they are the most notorious for identifying what is pleasant with what is honourable, and what is expedient with what is just.[6]

The ferment of re-thinking which followed attempts to discriminate between 'what was natural in state law as opposed to what was merely a matter of human agreement', began with the assumption that 'every man aims at what is good for him, or at least at what appears good for him'. At first sight this seemed a selfishly romantic delusion which could be shot to pieces by the least ingenious analysis, but the implication that a debauchee relentlessly pursuing drink and sensuality was an ethically desirable person was explained away by saying that what *he* thought good for him was, in fact, bad. When cross-examined by the ubiquitous Socrates the young men of Athens were alleged to have answered that they held the pleasures of the senses, of avarice and alcohol, in less esteem than justice, wisdom, courage and temperance, which were the self-evident virtues of the good citizen. 'The abandonment of virtue is a proof, not, as has been urged of superior wisdom, but of ignorance of the real interests of human nature. . . .'[7] Intrinsically, this left the contradiction unresolved, because when enlightenment dawned on the morally illiterate and the fundamental precepts of good citizenship were driven home, they often pursued their vices rather more avidly, the very thought of wisdom, courage and restraint driving them to grasp immediate pleasures while opportunity remained.

It was characteristic of the woolliness of some Greek thinking and of the tortuous Platonic dialogues, that this discovery did not shake the belief of many philosophers in the moral value of sheer enlightenment. However, as Dr Hobhouse says in his very interesting book, 'To the Greek philosopher the question took the form: what is the character of that which is really good for a man, or in what does human well-being consist? The answer which they gave to it was essentially that it consists in the practice of justice as being that wherein human nature finds its best, happiest and most harmonious expression.'[8]

Aristotle carried this into loftier flights when he said that the ultimate aim must be to release man from earthly trammels to 'set the speculative wisdom free' and to soar into those divine places 'towards which all things move'. There were 'absolute spiritual' equivalents of beauty and goodness which were within reach of human apprehension. In ironic contrast, it was characteristic of the Athenian social mores that they should disregard the mass of slaves and women and legislate primarily for a privileged male class without violating their concept of social morality. Slaves might be beaten, sold or abused, women reduced to domestic drudgery and prisoners die of overwork or sickness in the mines, but the morality of ancient Athens remained untroubled. The sanctity and rights of every individual irrespective of class, profession or wealth was not an idea which bothered Greek thinking. Men were born immutably to their station; to treat them accordingly was not to abuse them.

Any quick sketch of Greek or Roman morals runs the danger of misrepresenting one period or another for lack of detail, and as I proceed to Rome I must make clear what is axiomatic to any scholar: morality underwent profound changes in the Homeric, Athenian and Hellenistic periods of Greece and the Roman code varied widely under the Republic and the Empire. This chapter can only give a brief and dangerously foreshortened sketch.

The sheer relativity of moral standards becomes sharply apparent when Lecky's view of Rome in his *History of European Morals*, is subjected to modern scrutiny. The Victorian outlook of the book recoils in greater distaste from Roman sexual morals than would the twentieth-century mind. Time and again Lecky allows his more liberal self to break surface, but the Victorian sexual code forces him to repeat the obligatory revulsions.

Certainly the morals of Rome varied widely from class to class as well as period to period and random examples show their immense diversity. There was a period when a husband could kill his wife if she was taken in adultery while he could commit the same crime and suffer no penalty.

In sharp contrast, Plutarch wrote of Cato: '[He] married a wife with more nobility than wealth. . . . He used to say that a man who struck his wife or son was laying violent hands on what was most sacred. In his eyes it was more creditable to be a good husband than a great statesman. . . . When his son was born he held no business (except the business of the state) so important as to watch his wife bathing and dressing the baby. She suckled it herself and she often put the slaves' children to her breast also, so that when they sucked the same milk they would have a natural affection for her son.'[9]

It was Cato of Utica on the other hand who divorced his wife and later, when she had acquired money, re-married her, such expediency passing with no more than a lifted eyebrow from his friends in his day. In Cicero's time divorce had become a straightforward arrangement either by the consent of both parties or at the desire of one party. Cicero had been married for thirty years and fathered several children when he abandoned his wife to marry a younger and much richer woman because he needed more money. As if the pendulum had swung too far the moral sense then recovered its impetus once more and Augustus passed a law which forbade adulterers to marry again and confiscated half their fortune.

In Trajan's day there were few women workers. Most women, if they were poor, spent the day at home going about their domestic work and if they were rich, idling around town, visiting friends, bathing and attending afternoon spectacles. The atmosphere was fertile for infidelity and matrimonial morals for many Roman wives varied in Juvenal's day from the expedient to the careless.

As for homosexuality, Otto Kiefer wrote in his *Sexual Life in Ancient Rome* which, of course, concerned an earlier period: 'We know from Catullus that it was perfectly common for a young Roman to have sexual relations with a handsome male slave.'

In the wider field of social morality we find ourselves at one with Lecky in his supreme distaste for the brutality of the gladiatorial shows and the whole military ethos. 'The career of the early republic of Rome, though much idealized and transfigured by later historians, was probably governed by these principles. The normal fate of the captive, which among barbarians had been death, was in civilized antiquity, slavery;

but many thousands were condemned to the gladiatorial shows, and the vanquished general was commonly slain in the Mamertine Prison, while his conqueror ascended in triumph to the Capitol.'[10] According to Lecky, the worst atrocities of Roman brutality in war-time were reserved for those cities where Roman ambassadors had been insulted or 'where some special act of ill-faith or cruelty had taken place'. He claims that the coming of Christianity revolutionized Roman military ethics by suppressing the gladiatorial shows, and 'steadily discouraging the practice of enslaving prisoners', but he has too romantic a belief in the chivalry of the Christian crusading knights who finally took the place of the Roman warrior.

At the military level Roman ethics under the Republic were full of contradictions. It was regarded as perfectly just that men who could, by any stretch of the imagination be called barbarian, should be treated as wild beasts and thrown to their equivalents in public arenas if they were not massacred in more straightforward fashion or simply sent *en masse* to swell the slave markets. Yet the declaration of war, even against the barbarians, was a matter of the nicest moral calculation. Crucifixion, too, which sometimes meant scores of men dying slowly in the utmost agony, was subject to elaborate justifications.

Under the Republic, the formulation of Roman moral codes was more dependent upon military and patriotic virtues than it was on religious. Roman education deified heroic patriotism. Roman religion performed a secondary rôle, deriving its driving force from the State or political inspiration. It was used not as a moral exemplar but as a means of reinforcing moral disciplines. Roman gods such as Jupiter did not spring from the dark forests of natural forces like those of Egypt or from the personification of superstitions like those of the Greeks; 'they were for the most part simple allegories, frigid personifications of different virtues. . . .' Religion was a means of reinforcing the sanctity of oaths, of patriotism, of civic virtue, a reaffirmation of the rights of the family, fostering in its worship of the dead 'a vague belief in the immortality of the soul'.[11]

The Romans envisaged a mysterious power called Providence which determined men's 'gifts of fortune' and the luck attending their enterprises, but 'man was master of his own feelings and was capable of attaining such excellence that he might even challenge comparison with the gods'. 'All mortals judge that fortune is to be received from the gods and wisdom from ourselves,' wrote Cicero.[12] 'It is a characteristic of a wise man,' wrote Epictetus, 'that he looks for all his good and evil from himself.'[13]

Upon these beliefs they developed their moral code which had periods of austerity under the Republic, and finally, under the Empire, dissolved into spectacular examples of the kind of depravity which occurs when great wealth and extreme poverty are no longer controllable in a disintegrating society.

As Lecky wrote: '. . . while the force of circumstances was . . . developing the ethical conceptions of antiquity in new directions, the mass of the Roman people were plunged in a condition of depravity which no mere ethical teaching could adequately correct. The moral condition of the Empire is, indeed, in some respects, one of the most appalling pictures on record. . . .'[14]

According to Lecky there were 'three great causes which impeded moral development—the Imperial system, the institution of slavery, and the gladiatorial shows'. It is very easy to assume with Lecky that what demoralizes us today would have demoralized the Romans yesterday. It has to be remembered that the gladiatorial shows were a brutally extravagant development of ancient sacrificial rituals when men were formally put to death to appease the dark gods, and the earlier moral sanctions were carried over into the gladiatorial arena. Many apparent immoralities had some sort of sanction down the whole history of Rome.

The man who lived parasitically on a rich patron, accepting largesse from him every morning and spending every afternoon in idleness watching the barbaric spectacles of the Colosseum, did not seem to suffer any qualms of conscience for the very simple reason that his way of life was not merely sanctioned by the social mores but actively encouraged. None the less, as Lecky wrote: 'In the first period of the Empire . . . the pages of Suetonius remain as an eternal witness of the abysses of depravity, the hideous intolerable cruelty . . . that were then manifested on the Palatine, and while they cast a fearful light upon the moral chaos into which pagan society had sunk, they furnish ample evidence of the demoralizing influences of the empire. The throne was, it is true, occupied by some of the best as well as by some of the worst men who have ever lived; but the evil though checked and mitigated was never abolished.'[15]

Lecky speaks continuously with the voice of Victorian morality. The notion that 'Ionian slaves of surpassing beauty and Alexandrian slaves famous for their subtle skill in stimulating the jaded senses of the . . . libertine . . .' should 'become the ornaments of every patrician house', profoundly shocks him, and he speaks of the slave population as a 'hotbed of vice' which contaminated all with whom 'it came in contact'.

Certainly the slaves tended to debase all labour of which they were capable, by accepting rates of payment far below those required by the citizen-worker and throwing him into the ranks of the subservient unemployed. Similarly there was no public attempt under certain emperors to check the growth of parasitic professions like spies, informers, hired gladiators, astrologers, religious charlatans, male prostitutes and boy perverts.

Social morality made clumsy attempts to accommodate these changes, but something more spectacular was required as one intoxicated Emperor after another began to assume attributes of divinity until it was related of Caligula that he had Jupiter's head removed from many statues and replaced by his own and once, during a thunderstorm, challenged, in a frenzy of vanity, the authority of the great god Jupiter himself. There were others who treated the apotheosis of human-beings with considerable levity as when the Emperor Vespasian, feeling death approaching, said in jest, 'I think I am becoming a god.'

Social morality under the late Empire tended to ignore poverty, brutality and licentious living to indict and punish the smallest disrespect to a possibly divine Emperor. 'It was made a capital offence to . . . undress near a statue of Augustus, or to enter a brothel with a piece of money on which his head was engraved.'[16] A woman who began taking off her clothes before the statue of Comitian was, in fact, executed.

Men were disinclined to marry in a society where sexual freedom offered every variety of experience without any very permanent ties and there was a whole class of men who did nothing but flatter their wealthy elders in the hope of securing an inheritance. 'Idleness, amusements, and a bare subsistence were alone desired, and the general practice of abortion among the rich and of infanticide . . . in all classes' checked the growth of the population.

What modern moralists would speak of as a sense of public spirit diminished and died under such conditions, and a disintegrated society endorsed the endeavours of each individual to achieve his own selfish aims with any degree of unscrupulousness. When Marius, under the Republic, proscribed certain opponents and threw open their houses to be plundered, none could be found who would carry through the act because a sense of public spirit would not permit violation of a distinguished man's property, but when the armies of Vitellius and Vespasian made a conquest under the Empire, 'the degenerate Romans gathered with delight to the spectacle . . . plundered the deserted houses . . . dragged out the fugitives to be slain and converted into a festival the calamity of their country'.

Imbued with twentieth-century European ethics we would regard Rome, under the Empire, as not exactly an exemplar of morality, and it is as well to repeat that so much of what seems to us appalling, in past ages, has found such remarkable justifications. The logic of events produced moral rulings in the past which are easily distorted when subjected to modern scrutiny.

*　　*　　*　　*

Morality takes many forms and has many origins. Sexual morality, social morality, private and public morality interpenetrate at different levels and the limits of this chapter permit only the slightest sketch of the general field. At first glance, it would seem that sexual morality has involved such complicated patterns of behaviour, and varied so widely from culture to culture, that any attempt to trace a line of progress would be mistaken. In Greece, as we have seen, marriage was taken seriously and monogamy remained the dominant pattern of human relationships but men were permitted every form of 'indulgence' from adultery to homosexuality and pederasty. In Rome of the Republic, monogamy was firmly established but men once again had wide freedoms before marriage, and pre-marital intercourse was accepted with no more than a deprecating smile. If any detailed evidence is needed of the variety of sexual behaviour we have only to turn to Westermarck's chapter on free-love and adultery in his massive two-volume work *The Origin and Development of the Moral Ideas* to see, among the so-called savage peoples, a bewildering panorama.

'The East African Barea . . . do not regard it as in the least disreputable for a girl to become pregnant, nor do they punish or censure the seducer.' Among the Wanyoro it constantly happens that young girls spend the night with their lovers, only returning to their father's house in the morning, and this is not considered scandalous. Over nearly the whole of British Central Africa, says Sir H. Johnston,[17] 'before a girl is become a woman (that is to say before she is able to conceive) it is a matter of absolute indifference what she does and scarcely any girl remains a virgin after about five years of age'. Among the Maoris of New Zealand 'girls were at perfect liberty to act as they pleased until married', and chastity in single women was held of little account. In the Solomon Islands 'female chastity is a virtue that would sound strangely in the ear of the native', and in St Christoval and the adjacent islands 'for two or three years after a girl has become eligible for marriage she distributes her favours amongst all the young men of the village. . . .'[18]

Westermarck being Westermarck and the product of late nineteenth-century English culture, it was once again obligatory that he should disapprove of such behaviour and it is some measure of the depth of indoctrination which can pass unnoticed in a highly intellectualized individual that he chose to explain away no small part of 'these divergencies' as the result of 'foreign influence'. The pioneers of a 'higher civilization', he wrote, 'are very frequently unmarried men who go out to make their living in uncivilized lands, and though unwilling to contract regular marriages with native women, they have no objection to corrupting their morals'.

Far more important, it is doubtful today whether modern anthropologists would accept the validity of his sources or the highly subjective and limited nature of his witnesses. That our own sexual code has been inverted, twisted and contorted into every contradictory shape down the ages, remains undisputed, and it is possible to find many examples where the sanctions applied to enforce chastity are as savage as other relaxations are 'loose'.

'Among the East African Takue, a seducer may have to pay the same sum as if he had killed the girl, although the fine is generally reduced to fifty cows. Among the Beni Amer and Marea he is killed, together with the girl and the child. . . . Among the Teda he is exposed to the revenge of her father. The

Baziba look upon illegitimate intercourse between the sexes as the most serious offence, though no action is taken until the birth of a child; then the man and woman are bound hand and foot and thrown into Lake Victoria.'[19]

The marriage system of modern civilized peoples emerged from the later days of the Roman Empire. Most relationships accepted as marriage then, would now be regarded as highly irregular and immoral. 'The Romans recognized,' wrote Havelock Ellis, 'that marriage was a fact and not a mere legal form; in marriage by *usus* there was no ceremony at all; it was constituted by the mere fact of living together for a whole year; yet such marriage was regarded as just as legal and complete as if it had been inaugurated by the sacred rite of *confarreatio*.'[20]

The wife retained full rights over her own property, the restitution of conjugal rights was unnecessary, divorce a private transaction as much open to the wife as the husband and there was 'no intervention of magistrate or court'. It was Christianity which gradually invaded this situation. A combined asceticism and hostility developed hand in hand with the Germanic conception of marriage in which the wife still remained a chattel.

'Among the Teutonic peoples generally,' wrote Havelock Ellis, 'as among the early English, marriage was indeed a private transaction but it took the form of a sale of the bride by the father or other legal guardian, to the bridegroom.' If the Christian Church insisted on hallowing such transactions with a benediction, it was no more or less than a similar ritual invoked to hallow the sale of goods under civil contract. There was no special religious marriage service either in the East or West earlier than the sixth century. It was simply customary to attend an ordinary church service after a private marriage. Not until the tenth century did the custom develop of celebrating 'the first part of the real nuptials' within range of the church, and presently the bridal mass was transferred 'inside the church'.

In the twelfth century the priest began to direct the ceremony, in the thirteenth he literally presided, and slowly what had once held private validity and possibly sacredness for two human-beings, was transferred to the church through *custom*, not law, and the rituals of ecclesiastical marriage achieved their dominance. Even so, Gratian's twelfth-century Canon

Law, on which modern marriage ritual came to be based—
confused as it was by the Peter Lombard school—accepted
marriage by mutual consent, without demanding a religious
ceremony, and as late as Milton, similar interpretations
persisted in some cultures.

So there it was. The practice of marriage, like the practice of
sex, had come through any number of convolutions before it
reached its modern state, and it is difficult to say whether a
Roman marriage of *usus*, which knew no religious sanction, was
morally any better than a modern marriage controlled by law,
convention and the church. Certainly the children had greater
security when the family unit was bound together by so many
inviolable bonds, but the unit might be a jungle of feuds, bitterness and frustration in which the very mind of a child turned
sour. We, of course, would say that the moral characteristics of
sexual relationship have progressed enormously since Roman
days, but the robust Roman spirit might easily find that laugh-
able. The modern woman has won for herself rights in marriage
which few Roman matrons ever knew, but in Italy the law
has now regressed again and created a situation where a wife
committing adultery can receive a two years' prison sentence,
while the man committing the same offence goes scot-free.[21]
Conceivably, some theologians would regard this as progress,
but any comparison in depth of sexual moralities leads into a
maze where one code simply has no meeting-place with another,
and any attempt to evaluate one against the other becomes very
difficult. As R. V. Sampson wrote in *Progress in the Age of
Reason*: 'It would, to cite an obvious example, be unreasonable
to expect a Muslim and Christian, however emancipated from
theological dogma, to agree upon the desirability of any *a priori*
code of matrimonial ethics. No system of rights and duties can
profitably be divorced from the historical social context in
which it is set.'[22]

As for the question—has sexual morality in general progressed?
—it is of course possible to say that not so many females of a
conquered country are brutally raped as in the past, sexual
violation seems to be far less frequent in Western Europe, and
women's new status has made their claim to sexual equality
more powerful. Whether the expression of sexuality is more
satisfying within the romantic modern European code which
demands love for one person as its correct concomitant, or

whether the classical indulgence of passion with several people did not yield wider and deeper satisfactions, remains in doubt. To modern Europeans it appears that love has transformed sexual morality and refinement of feeling has carried us into those high reaches of personality where two people meet in a more profound and satisfying way than promiscuity or its equivalents would ever permit; but we have no means of verifying such speculations.

Turning away from these highly subjective matters it is possible to move with greater certainty in the less mystical realm of social morality. We would regard a society where half the population was supported by charity in a state of 'semi-demoralized' idleness, where men were trained to concert pitch in order to mutilate each other to death, where women had little or no say in government, death by crucifixion was common-place and human-beings were sold in the market place like food or cattle, as morally inferior to our own.

Nor do early English communities with their savage penal codes and double morality permitting one class to commit crimes which meant death to another, seem to us very good examples of social morality. Feudal England took a step forward when each carefully divided class was conceded its own rights and could at least claim whatever protection those rights offered. There remained a primitive savagery, to the modern eye, in the power of the baron who so often took by force what he required, who could, if he chose, employ the most brutal torture to extract confessions, who had men hung, drawn and quartered for petty crimes and exercised despotic power over the lives of his subjects.

Fourteenth-century England had no moral qualms about the terrible gulf between the lavish way of life which centred around the gentry at the manor house and the often hard-pressed, over-worked and sometimes starving peasant who made that way of life possible. Sixteenth-century England became much more aware of the complex needs of the average individual, and the more extreme abuses relaxed, but the first stirring of public conscience on behalf of the less well-equipped members of the community did not have any very organized effect. Moral indignation at unnecessary hardship, attempts at widespread charity, plans to contain the unemployed, attempts to organize the crafts and trades, all revealed social morality awakening in piecemeal fashion. This persisted in the seventeenth and eighteenth centuries. Indeed, as Ginsberg has said, 'in the main the inspiration of the eighteenth-century theories of progress was ethical in character', but the monstrous tide of the Industrial Revolution presently overran good intentions, and the new cultural prescriptions of wealth and profit introduced fresh complications.

If a growth in the awareness of the needs and potentials of the Common Man represents a growth in social morality, then the long line which runs from Greece through Rome to Western Europe, England and America is encouraging. It is not, once again, a straightforward line. Different cultures had different moral traditions, some developing exclusively within themselves, some fertilized by outside influences. Each tradition tended to develop individually and some became distorted and died out entirely, but there were others marked by 'tendencies towards convergence'. Many reached a rough and ready agreement in condemning such habits as lying, cruelty, treachery, extreme selfishness and aggression. Similarly they converged in morally approving honesty, kindness, loyalty and industry. It was progress of a kind that men could universally accept moral precepts which, when they were practised, seemed to make the world a better place.

One such precept has become widely practised today. Social responsibility no longer emphasizes the needs of a rich, cultured or aristocratic élite, believing that in these classes alone lies the salvation of mankind. It is concerned to give every human-being equivalent rights, opportunities and protection, and in some eyes this revolutionizes social morality.

*   *   *   *

The time has come to give sharper definition to the word—morality. As Ginsberg has written: 'Like all social development moral progress does not necessarily involve changes in the genetic make-up of man. It consists rather in the building up of a tradition which makes it possible for each generation to re-acquire, perhaps more easily, what has been achieved by former generations and, in turn, to prepare the ground for coming generations. . . .'[23]

It does not seem that we possess an in-built thing called 'conscience' which can be said to be the centre of our moral sense, or that a divinely implanted will automatically distinguishes between right and wrong from the moment we are born. As Julian Huxley puts it: 'The ovum has no ethics, any more than it has a backbone. Ethics, like backbones, come out of non-existence, into existence *de novo* in each individual development. Somewhat as the physical stiffening of the backbone is later built around an embryological forerunner in the shape of the notochord, so the normal infant develops a forerunner for the moral stiffening of adult ethics. The Freudians call it the primitive super-ego. I will venture to coin a more non-committal term—the proto-ethical mechanism.'[24]

The human infant is genetically equipped with what Waddington calls an 'authority-acceptor'.[25] This leads him to take what he is told by his parents as authoritative, 'in the same sort of way as baby birds are equipped with an imprinting mechanism which makes them accept any moving object within certain limits of size as a parent'.[26] The authority-accepting mechanism receives and sets up as a seat of judgment the values and codes of behaviour first laid down by the parents. In effect this creates what is known as conscience. The authoritarian parent is internalized—and to some extent hated—because impulse so often wants to flaunt the rules made instinctual by the parent. Thus arises the 'instinctive feeling of what is right' and—because of the desire to act in quite a different way—'a sense of sin'.

Putting it in simpler terms it seems that there is no known biological gene which gives us the power to determine right from wrong. In whatever, precisely, instincts consist, there is no 'moral instinct' in the old-fashioned sense of both those words. The long process of adjustment to a hostile environment which early man underwent, slowly revealed to him that mutual aid was a necessary prerequisite to survival, and mutual aid meant taking into account the needs of others in the family, group or community. Presently, the disorganized impulse to work together led to its codification in social taboos, customs and moral laws. These, in early days, served the double purpose of placating the gods and protecting the community. Deeply ingrained fragments of such ancient laws remain with us partly because they correspond to our own requirements for survival, possibly because, as one anthropologist suggests, a certain modification of brain structure may have taken place over millions of years to accommodate repeated indoctrinations.

Ginsburg believes that there is a continuity in the underlying categories by which the 'moral impulse' has been codified down the centuries. 'It would be perfectly possible to classify the morals of the most primitive peoples by the aid of categories which have universal significance,' he writes. He then discusses the various headings given by Sir David Ross.[27] 'Fidelity, reparation, gratitude, justice, beneficence, non-injury and self-improvement' all describe principles which the majority of men might agree should be beneficial to their fellows. Most of these, it will be seen, are either direct expressions of mutual aid, or derivatives from it. Ginsberg goes on to say that Westermarck found truth-telling and fidelity to promises widely recognized in primitive societies: 'The Egyptians barely distinguished truth from right. The Babylonian Incantation Tablets condemn dishonesty not only in deed but in intention.'[28]

Another class of morals which provides compensation for wrongful acts and gratitude for services rendered is also universally recognized. Down the ages when one man damaged another man's property it was generally agreed that he should pay some compensation, and when he helped an injured friend, that friend should feel gratitude towards him.

However, in practice the compensation and gratitude vary so greatly as sometimes to modify the principle out of all recognition. Indeed, this qualification runs through all the categories laid down by Sir David Ross. It is particularly true of the principle that every man must be given his due, a principle which has had wide acceptance, but in totally different forms down the ages.

As Ginsberg writes, 'In a society where caste exists it is just to treat a pariah as a pariah: in feudal societies to give a man his due meant to give him what belongs to his status.' In short, giving a man his due in some societies meant working him fourteen hours a day for a pittance, insisting that he could not marry without the baron's permission and sending him to the scaffold if he stole a sheep. This is so far removed from what we today mean by giving a man his due as to belong to a different principle. The modern equivalent would be—giving a man his rights—and rights are not something arbitrarily apportioned by one class to another, but something distilled by reason from the nature of man.

Under another class of 'duties', according to Sir David Ross, come concern for life, integrity and freedom. Again, the interpretation of these 'duties' down the centuries, and the punishment which went with them, made it possible to burn a young woman for counterfeiting the coinage of the realm in the eighteenth century and sent a man to the gallows for homosexuality in the early seventeenth century.

As we have seen, the wildest variations always have justifications satisfactory to their day and age. Religious belief had a profound effect on all moral codes and the age which believed that a man guilty of heresy not only endangered his own salvation, but could, by his example, condemn others to eternal damnation, would consider it morally right to put that man to death. A change in religious outlook has now made it morally wrong to do any such thing.

If there has been one major change in the wellsprings of morality over the last two thousand years it is the change from a belief that morals should exclusively concern personal salvation and individual goodness—a principle characteristic of the old religions—to the belief that they should take account of social relations. In the past, providing the individual preserved his personal moral integrity intact, he was promised rewards of dubious certainty but splendid proportions in the hereafter. Today, religion is much more in touch with life and a new interpenetration between sexual, private, public, religious and social morals has qualified each. As Ginsberg wrote of personal goodness in a second brilliant little book: 'Though they single out elements essential to all morality, they are clearly inadequate when applied to the conditions prevailing in large-scale complex societies. Personal benevolence may have to be checked in the interests of the social order. Love and goodwill cannot in themselves suffice to remove the sources of conflict or help us in defining the limits of compulsion.'[29]

Another obvious factor which has influenced the development of moral codes since the early Christian Fathers is the growth of knowledge. As it became clear that heretical contagion did not necessarily pass by touch, or word of mouth, from one person to another, the moral law condemning heretics lost its force. As increasing knowledge showed that there was no strict correlation between a decrease in the population and widespread masturbation, the Jewish moral laws against it lost their stringency. As it became clear that a sickly child might turn out to be a worthwhile if not brilliant citizen, the moral sanctions which allowed a parent to expose that child until it died were qualified and finally, in our day, reversed.

The process called the rationalization of morals crystallizes the history of their development. What was, at first, dominated by obscure custom and usage, under conditions where no one questioned the validity of moral codes gave place to the mockery of the satirical writers, the reflections of the story-tellers, the vision of the poets and later to the critical analysis of the philosophers. In the first stage, moral laws were blindly carried out without the individual knowing what justification lay behind them. Sometimes the justifications were good, sometimes bad, but very few bothered to challenge their authority. There are many societies today where a similar unquestioning accept-ance of moral laws which modern knowledge has rendered ridiculous, persists.

In the second stage, critical analysis took two forms. Either it became an intellectual exercise in a vacuum, or a process of empirical enlightenment which led to modifications in the moral codes. There were many secular moralists among the Egyptians who learnt to modify moral behaviour as circum-stances demanded, and simply set down a series of maxims distilled from long experience. These were intended for every-day use by friends and relations. As moralists they did not rise above the level of motto-makers. There were others who tried to discover the underlying moral laws and even attempted to reduce them to a system. 'Perhaps the main contribution of this complex phase,' writes Ginsberg, 'is the gradual differentation of ethical norms from other norms such as the religious and legal, with the result that the problem of what constitutes the distinctively ethical element in social experiences emerges more clearly.'[30]

The last phase introduces semi-scientific elements. What were once considered unquestioned ethical ideals are now seen in relation to their effect on the community. If heavy sexual repressions result in an increased number of hysterics then it may be as well to liberalize the sexual moral code. If this appears to suggest a widespread substitution of empirical for intuitive ethics that, unfortunately, is not yet so, but certainly moral ideals are now frequently seen 'in relation to the con-ditions under which they can be realized'. Thus the moral stigma which attached to an illegitimate child in the nineteenth century was known to punish the child for a crime which it had not committed, and society did proceed to try to protect the child from the consequences of its parents' 'fecklessness'.

There remains what Ginsberg describes as 'the internalization and individualization of the conscience'. In the distant past moral sanctions were reinforced by fear of vengeance from the gods, and superstition was the origin and driving force of many moral precepts. In short, they were *external* sanctions based on fear of what might happen if the code was broken. Later societies recognized that certain moral acts had 'inherent ethical qualities' and external sanctions were converted into internal integrity. A man should not only behave well in the hope of winning the proper reward; he should do so because behaving well was desirable in itself.

As the moral conscience became internalized it emphasized individual responsibility. 'In primitive societies responsibility [was] collective and punishment vicarious.' In modern societies men came to be held *individually* responsible for their acts in criminal law, and were tried or punished as individuals.

In other words, morals in Western Europe have developed through the magical-superstitious to the mystical-religious, from the aristocratic to the rational and are now, according to the scientific humanists, entering the semi-scientific.

* * * *

Moving away from the theoretical to the practical le el for a moment, there remain a number of comparatively new influences in sexual morality today which have to be taken into account. Sexual morality in England and America has undergone dramatic changes in the past fifty years. Many theorists, like Professor Morris Carstairs, have pointed out that charity came before chastity in Christ's teachings and it was due to St Paul and St Augustine, one a 'reformed libertine', that chastity gained exaggerated reverence, and sex became a regrettable indulgence in many periods. Professor Carstairs showed, in the Reith Lectures of 1962, that there were many stable societies where chastity did not rank very high. 'The interesting thing is that pre-marital licence has been found to be quite compatible with stable married life.'

The onset of menstruation is said to occur much earlier in

girls today and commonly begins at twelve years of age, where before it was fourteen or fifteen. Earlier puberty in both sexes has brought about precocious sexual experiment and it would seem, from the evidence available, that pre-marital sexual experience is becoming accepted as a preliminary—sensible or otherwise—to marriage. In 1961, no less than thirty-one per cent of girls who married in their teens in England and Wales were pregnant before marriage, but a high proportion of these cases were not shot-gun or forced marriages because many of these young people were intending to marry anyway. On the other hand, it is clear that sexual patterns still vary according to class. Middle-class boys and girls delay sexual experience longer than their working-class equivalents.

Professor Morris Carstairs believes that today 'both the popular and the church-going types of morality have slipped into disuse. Popular morality is now a waste-land littered with the debris of broken convictions. Concepts such as honour or even honesty have an old-fashioned sound, but nothing has taken their place . . . the confusion is perhaps greatest over sexual morality. Here the former theological canons of behaviour are seldom taken seriously.'

Is it wiser to discover the precise sexual nature of a person who is to share the rest of your life before marriage? Many people think so today. Is it wiser to convert sex into a pleasurable, enriching experience, instead of a guilt-ridden indulgence? Again many answer—yes. Is it wise for the young to fulfil earlier physiological urges which bring sexual experience into the lives of boys and girls between the ages of sixteen and eighteen? Once more a qualified yes comes from some quarters and horrified condemnation from others. Patterns of sexual behaviour are not so sensitive to edicts issued by the Establishment today, and earlier sex and pre-marital intercourse tend to ignore periodic outbursts of indignation and condemnation. Compared with fifty years ago, sexual morality has undergone a revolution.

Whether it has progressed is a question which people answer according to taste, religious persuasion or upbringing. Looked at in the cool light of rational reflection, considered empirically, the effect of earlier and more open sexuality does not seem as disastrous as many puritanically indoctrinated Englishmen would have us believe. Indeed it may be beneficial. The conspiracy of silence about sex in the middle and late nineteenth century was broken only by men like Havelock Ellis and Sigmund Freud, and the misery and frustration which an austere code appeared to impose on large numbers of human beings, have given place to a better adjustment of sexual morality. The ideal would seek to harmonize the sexual urges of the individual with the needs of society and we are still—consciously and unconsciously—'experimenting' with new adjustments if we are not deliberately seeking the best balance. In some cases experiment has gone too far. In others not far enough.

The answers to many vital questions about sexual morality are still not clearly known. Is it wise for young people, liberated by the new sexual codes, to marry in their teens, when they may, later in life, develop into quite different people who, in maturity, would have made a quite different choice? Is it wise to allow the realization of the sexual impulse to anticipate emotional maturity? Generally, a great deal of ill-informed, highly speculative and very dangerous nonsense is talked about these questions by persons who speak in a ferment of moral indignation inherited from an age which could not face up to the facts of infantile sexuality revealed by Freud. Sometimes, when the facts are investigated by taking random samples, they turn out to be less iniquitous than is expected. In the case of teen-age marriages, for instance, it was found that in one representative sample they seemed to last as long as marriages which took place at a later age. The introduction of social-science techniques into the field of sexual morality may revolutionize our ideas of what is good and bad, and until the results of more detailed enquiries are available, most views carry little more weight than the highly prejudiced edicts of our Victorian forbears.

Social morality offers some equally interesting changes today. First, the concern which we now consciously have for something called posterity, a concern to play our part in maintaining and developing the highest standards to pass on a worthy heritage to those who will come after us. Second, the re-distribution of national wealth which has taken place not merely in America, Great Britain and the Scandinavian countries, but over a large part of Europe and Russia. Far into the nineteenth century, wealth lived alongside appalling squalor without too much distress and a fine culture in England flowered within reach of terrible poverty. Social conscience has created a social morality which redistributed national wealth so that extreme poverty and economic hardship no longer affects the working millions of England, France, Germany and America.

The third contemporary factor is a new concern for humanity as a whole. In nineteenth-century England, the condition of the backward people was the business of a handful of legislators who occasionally carried out piecemeal adjustments on a very limited scale, or relied upon the intervention of commonplace charity. Today, a new ferment of social morality has made the condition of the backward peoples a preoccupation of the great powers, and no one with any pretence to political morality can consider the world situation without taking it into account.

Once more a certain universality in the roots of moral impulse becomes apparent. Nothing could be more different than the political ideologies of the Eastern and Western blocs in Europe today and if there is something ironically disturbing in the spectacle of two gigantic powers both claiming to lead the peoples of the world to a new Jerusalem by utterly conflicting paths, there is something reassuring in the fact that both aim to release colonial peoples from malnutrition and extreme poverty. It would be naïve to assume that lofty moral motives alone have brought the great powers into consort on this point, since political strategy would demand a similar course in any case. Anyone involved in the current struggle cannot ignore the malnourished millions of the earth, since one nation or group may so easily upset the balance of power, weaken a defence system or cause loss of face in a world which is fast becoming one world. Sheer speed of communication and publicity now throws instantaneous light on incidents and issues which might in the past have remained comfortably obscure, or even have passed unnoticed. Many searching eyes now rove over the surface of the globe and it is hard to conceal anything of great consequence. Under the glare of modern publicity the pressures towards moral behaviour are greater, but the pressures are frequently ignored and the instruments of mass communication debased in the interests of propaganda.

The whole centrifugal movement towards one world must one day produce world government and a new code of world morals, but such statements have a completely romantic ring under present condtiions. It is reassuring to talk about world governments and world morals. It is quite another matter to know how to break down the vastly entrenched patriotisms of national sovereignty or the barriers of custom, language and morals which for all their underlying identities wear such different and intransigent masks. As the moral philosophers spend their days enquiring into the precise meaning of moral terminology and sometimes disappear in a jungle of subtlety, so the thought of laying down a moral code satisfactory to the peoples of the world leads into a smothering forest of difficulties.

Can we still risk asking and even dare to answer the general question—have we progressed morally? Well, Ginsberg thought that the development of moral behaviour had many hopeful elements and if it did not justify optimism there was little in the available evidence to warrant pessimism. Westermarck, in a detailed two-volume survey of the development of moral ideas, came to the conclusion that morality was 'more enlightened and reflective' today than in the past. Certainly the western world has progressed in the *theory* of moral values and we now understand far more about moral mechanisms than ever we did before.

Dealing in such a slippery currency as moral progress the only real law is that there is no law. Progress is not immanent in nature. Nor is there any discernible moral absolute, darkly working its will against the black hosts of evil in some cloud of spiritual subtlety. Indeed, T. H. Huxley believed exactly the opposite. 'The ethical progress of society,' he said in his Romanes lecture, 'consists not in imitating the cosmic process, still less in running away from it, but in combating it.'

If, by the cosmic process he meant non-human nature then he was right, but if he included human beings, he was wrong, because implicit in Homo sapiens is the potential which led to mutual aid, to moral codes and the refinements of modern morality. If we are part of the cosmic process then it is by combating *one side* of our natures that we shall emerge as moral —in the idealistic sense—human beings. In Western Europe much has been done which is encouraging. Indeed, dangerously freed from academic caution I hope I may be understood when I say that I think Western Europe has progressed in terms of social morality, if that progression is constantly in danger from reactionary forces.

Crane Brinton wrote a very interesting history of Western

morals and asked the difficult question—was the ordinary Englishman in 1901 a morally superior being to an ordinary Athenian in 416 B.C? 'The history-conscious observer,' he wrote, 'will perhaps have noted that these dates are those of Kitchener's organization of concentration camps in South Africa to cope with Boer guerilla warfare and of the Athenian attack on the little island of Melos; in the first some 20,000 Boer women and children died of disease, starvation, neglect and despair; in the second all Melian males were killed and the women and children enslaved.' Brinton, who is far too cautious to commit himself to any general belief in moral progress, does at least add: 'This was progress perhaps, for in 1901 formal institutional slavery had in fact ceased to exist in the West; but not quite the progress Condorcet dreamed of.'[31]

The word 'institutional' points the difference. Sporadic outbreaks of brutality are still common today and Nazi Germany witnessed a wholesale amorality among the S.S. and the German rulers which carried us back to the worst periods of Rome. The perfection of modern methods of persuasion and destruction made it possible to convert large numbers of simple Germans into Nazi fanatics and to wipe out millions of Jews, but the rest of the civilized world did not accept or endorse such behaviour as it so frequently did in the past. Civilized morality is still violated, terrible crimes are committed, but the great majority of modern European codes are now opposed to what, in Roman days, would have been 'institutionally accepted'.

Julian Huxley has outlined one of the biggest remaining problems. 'The most obvious is the prevention of the warping of the whole structure of personality, with accompanying primary ethical distortion in infancy and early childhood.' In short—education continues to indoctrinate the young with many values which are out of keeping with the modern outlook. Huxley remarks that if we could see the shape and nature of minds as we see the shape and nature of bodies we would, in the present state of their development, 'be horror-struck at their deformations and their dwarfish failures to develop'.

It is part of the machinery of consciousness that it resists for many and complex reasons 'the forces that are making for a higher and fuller consciousness'. Summoning every device to the service of this overwhelming impulse 'stunted spiritual growth masquerades as humility or acceptance of the decrees of Providence, sadistic projection as a crusade against evil, the excessive asceticism or moral rigour which springs from an unrealistic sense of sin and from failure to face one's own nature, as a badge of special righteousness'.

Failure to face one's own nature. We are growing much more realistic about what exactly we are and presently it may become more immoral to practise self-deception than to indulge in what was once considered sin.

Full moral maturity will depend upon admitting the consequences of our new knowledge, of rejecting non-realistic thinking, of refusing to 'put off the burdens of our conflicts and the responsibility of our choices on to the shoulders of some external authority'. Too much choking guilt and unnecessary conflict are created by distorted educational ideals. There remains the inspiring possibility that 'man can impose moral principles upon ever widening areas of the cosmic process, in whose further slow unfolding he is now the protagonist'. Perhaps he may even, as Sir Julian Huxley suggests, 'inject his ethics into the heart of evolution' and what was once a man-made intervention become part of natural forces.

CHAPTER SEVEN

Progress and religion

I T is characteristic of the Christian apologist that he rejects the humanist interpretation of the origins of religion while his humanist counterpart pours scorn on the divine inspiration of the Gospels. It is difficult, of course, for Christian scholars like Professor Baillie or humanist exponents like Julian Huxley to escape the presuppositions which belong to their different creeds, but it is ironic to find a scholar of the calibre of Baillie straining to assimilate the idea of progress into Christian dogma while Huxley colours his humanism with his own special brand of revelation. If the modern scientific humanist would have no truck with the religious tinge in Huxley's creed he equally rejects any divine inspiration in Buddhism, Christianity or any other form of religious experience. Man is to him a mysterious encasement of flesh and blood but earth bound, subject to severe pressures from the universe and capable of inventing any number of desirable gods to explain away his painful predicament.

How, in fact, did early religious practices arise? One explanation flatly contradicts another, but some nineteenth-century anthropologists put it all down to a series of events as inevitable as evolution. When the thunder spoke out of the sky before a ceaseless torrent of rain washed away the crops of primitive man, he assumed that the great rolling sound, which had similarities with the voice of wild beasts, belonged to a bigger and better beast, but this beast could not be seen, was much more mysterious and had to be granted intangible characteristics. When the great burning disc of the sun relentlessly poured its power over the earth, sucked up the dew and ravaged his crops, he could only understand it if he saw it in his own likeness. Continuously there were intangible forces hovering around him which struck into his life. One of these was a force which came to dominate all others and was known to later generations as death.

When, for countless mornings and afternoons he had worked, eaten and talked with his father, and suddenly, one day, the living, breathing reality collapsed and ceased to move, he was bewildered. What evil power could have brought about such a savage and altogether inexplicable transformation? What, who, where were the mysterious forces which could so easily strike his father down? Inevitably, after his father died, vivid memories lived on and sometimes, perhaps, the son heard his words, his sayings, echoing on the air . . . from where? From memory or reality? Was he still alive in fact? Or was some intangible part of him persisting on the unseen air? His spirit—still speaking—from—the beyond?

Any speculation about the thought processes of primitive man must invite ridicule and phrases like 'intangible part of him' presuppose a vernacular which he did not possess, but if such language did not clothe his thoughts, it seems imaginatively convincing that such thoughts would have occurred to him as first one and then another natural disaster threatened or overtook him.

Put into Freud's own words: 'What primitive man regarded as the natural thing was the indefinite prolongation of life—immortality. . . . It has been regarded as perfectly natural and not in the least puzzling that primitive man should have reacted to the phenomena [of death] by forming the idea of the soul and then of extending it to objects in the external world.'[1] It also seems likely, as Freud believed, that in the mind of primitive man the souls of those who had lately died were sometimes transformed into demons and the surviving members of the group were driven to protect themselves by taboos against their hostility.

Writing of primitive tribes still extant, whose habits could, in fact, be observed, he added: 'They people the world with innumerable spiritual beings both benevolent and malignant: and these spirits and demons they regard as the causes of natural phenomena and they believe that not only animals and plants but all the inanimate objects in the world are animated by them. . . . These souls which live in human beings can leave their habitations and migrate into other human beings.'[2]

Further justification for attributing life to inanimate objects occurred in Hume's *Natural History of Religion* (Section III). 'There is an universal tendency among mankind to conceive all beings like themselves and to transfer to every object those qualities with which they are familiarly acquainted, and of which they are intimately conscious.' Thus there was a voice in the babbling brook, stones spoke, the growl of thunder came from some hidden monster and the 'voice' of the dead father, detached from his decayed body, hovered on the air. Whenever the lightning struck, death came, or the earth split volcanically, it was the work of one or other of these hidden spirits and clearly it was as well to keep in with them. In the event, there were many occasions when makeshift rituals and piecemeal attempts at propitiation did not seem to work very well, and the evil spirits continued to bring disaster down on different tribes. In consequence there arose a number of magic-men and voodoo doctors, who codified magical rites which the tribe then performed with varying degrees of success and failure. Sometimes the magicians were successful enough to be given high rank and power and became the equivalent of the early Christian Fathers of magic. Sometimes the Thunder, Rain and Sun Gods conspired against them and they were first publicly humiliated and then subjected to savage mutilations which might lead to a more painful death than would have been their lot at the hands of their accepted divinities.

Some modern anthropologists severely qualify much of this. Not direct animism, but a magical-emotional approach pleases them more; not the intellectual deduction of a concealed spirit but a vague emotional awareness of a power hidden away in things.

These explanations of the origins of religion are most powerfully resisted by Christian apologists like Christopher Dawson. He writes: 'The dynamic element in primitive culture is to be found rather in the sphere of direct religious experience than that of conscious rational enquiry.' The more passionate advocates of Christian revelation tend to fall back on phrases which require an act of mystical insight before their meaning becomes clear—the intuition of pure being—while the down-to-earth apologists for animism are crudely clear in most of what they say.

Durkheim believed that religion was nothing else than 'the divinization of the social consciousness', but Dawson will have none of it. On the contrary, 'the sphere of religion is that which lies outside social control, and the primary religious instinct is that of dependence on superhuman powers. . . . Hence primitive religion is characterized by its universality and vagueness and it is impossible to isolate a single definite type of religious belief and practice as the source and starting point of the whole development.'[3]

Starting point? Well, it would be easy to claim that the universal idea of spirits possessing inanimate objects was the starting point of religious practice. Vagueness? Dawson himself gives some interesting examples where broad religious beliefs have been formulated in a very clear-cut way. When a missionary pointed out to a Maori 'that his religion was false since it taught that everything had a soul', Dawson records the Maori's answer: ' "Were a thing not possessed by the wairus of an atua —the shadow of a god—that thing could not have form. What enables us to know a material object is not its physical nature but the spirit that possesses it. Moreover, every being possesses an eternal element the toiora of the enduring world—and the toiora of the universe is nothing else but the soul of the supreme god—Io, the Self-Determined".' High-class mumbo-jumbo of this kind is not sympathetic to modern rational ears but the thirty-nine articles of Maori belief were obviously not so very vague to the Maori.

Christopher Dawson believes, in company with Andrew Lang, that 'mythology and religion, in the strict sense of the word, are two different things which have become inextricably entangled with one another but are quite distinct in origin'. Was the mythology of Jesus Christ quite distinct in origin from the Christian religion? Christopher Dawson goes on to ask— what could be more profoundly religious than the song of the Pawnee warrior?

> Oh you who possess the skies.
> I am living. I in you entrust my fate
> Again alone upon the warpath.

Mr Dawson claims that he can find nothing in mythology to justify the Pawnee warrior's song, and it follows, once again, that religion and mythology are clearly divorced. In fact, the Pawnee warrior can be seen as the living justification of the theory of animism. According to this, he has placed a spirit behind the thunder, the clouds, the storms, the vast and intimidating expanse of empty sky, which dominated his existence. Seen from the viewpoint of modern psychology it was fear and superstition which drove him to personify the One who possessed the skies, not a pre-existing religious impulse. By personifying an unnamed terror he made it explicable in terms which he understood. Unpersonified, he could not come to terms with it, because it could not understand him.

Sir James Frazer gives endless accounts of the links between human and divine characteristics in primitive religious practice, some of them reaching right up to the present day: 'Every night when the sun-god Ra sank down to his home in the glowing west he was assailed by hosts of demons under the leadership of the arch-fiend Apepi. . . . To aid the sun-god in this daily struggle, a ceremony was daily performed in his temple at Thebes. A figure of his foe Apepi, represented as a crocodile with a hideous face . . . was made of wax, and on it the demon's name was written in green ink. Wrapt in a papyrus case . . . the figure was then tied up with black hair, spat upon, hacked with a stone knife and cast on the ground.'[4] There are still people today who stick pins into wax images of their enemies in the hope of destroying them.

I repeat Mr Dawson's conclusion in order to reframe it: 'The dynamic element in primitive culture is to be found rather in the sphere of direct religious experience than in that of conscious rational enquiry.' The opposing school would answer: 'The religious element in primitive culture is to be found in the sphere of direct rationalization of experience rather than in some pre-existing pool of religious consciousness.'

It is possible to range through centuries of anthropological literature from Andrew Lang and Sir James Frazer to Freud and Christopher Dawson watching this battle develop, and most fascinating among it all is the rearguard action of the Christian apologists as they seek, first to fend off and then to assimilate new scientific knowledge. Whichever school the reader finally accepts, the facts of religious history which follow are less in dispute.

It is an easy step from the great mythological Sun and Rain Gods to the magico-religious basis of the Greek divinities. Polytheism—believing in several gods—was a natural fore-runner of monotheism—belief in one god—and the Greeks indulged the instinct generously. As we have seen, the tempestu-ous behaviour of the Greek gods was clearly derivative from the less enlightened habits of some of their savage forerunners.

Not unexpectedly there was fierce rivalry in the Greek Valhalla and many Homeric battles were fought among the gods in a manner surprisingly reminiscent of the worst impulses of wanton adventurers on earth. Christopher Dawson, a very learned man, has some penetrating things to say about the origins of Greek, Indian and Persian religion, and he points out that 'the new [Greek] mythology of the Olympian deities was of far less importance to the religious man than the due performance of the sacred rites whose origins were deeply rooted in the archaic past'. The precise nature of the gods 'was open to many interpretations and men were free to follow temperamental inclination, providing they maintained an exact and scrupulous performance of the Rites, for that alone could ensure the safety of the city and the fertility of the soil. . . .'

The Greek belief in a higher reality of absolutes which transcended common experience and remained perfectly poised and unchanged in some Empyrean had something in common with the oriental renunciation of everyday reality. Plato believed in a world of eternal forms 'where abides the very Being with which true knowledge is concerned, the colourless, formless, intangible essence visible only to the mind, the pilot of the soul'.[5] If only a man 'had eyes to see the Divine Beauty, pure and clear and unalloyed, not clogged with the pollutions of mortality and all the colours and vanities of human life'[6] he would rather enter that world than remain on this so much duller earth. Platonic mysticism differs from its oriental counterpart in seeking to penetrate the Absolute not by renunciation and asceticism but by knowledge, thinking and scientific discipline.

According to Dawson it was in 'the first millenium B.C.' that 'a cultural change of the most profound significance passed over the world, a change that was not confined to any one people or culture but which made itself felt almost simultaneously from India to the Mediterranean and from China to Persia'. When we enquire into the precise nature of this change we are told that it was 'due to the first appearance of new spiritual forces', but in what way these forces were 'new' is never clearly defined. Mr Dawson tends to dismiss the religious literature of Egypt and Babylonia as 'half-comprehended relics of a vanished world' but the authors of Hebrew literature and the Upanishads, the teachings of the Hebrew prophets, of

Confucius and Lao Tzu, are 'of perennial significance and value'.

In place of the 'new spiritual forces' it is simpler to say that men reorganized their relationship to the universe in new and different kinds of religion which stemmed from the old, took account of more reflective attitudes and a growing body of knowledge. All had the common purpose of trying to reconcile their harsh lot on this earth. Religion was, in part, a way of organizing and containing suffering. It was in the very nature of the sufferings which the majority of people seemed to undergo in their everyday lives that they should dream of a golden age placed in the past or future when life was, or would be, less arduous. The Athenians systematized this in their cyclic interpretation of life with a slow decadence at last giving place to another golden age, and the Christians came to see the golden age both as a time of divine innocence in the past and a heavenly hereafter. Even today it is commonplace in contemporary civilizations for older men to speak of 'the good old days' and at least one explanation of the origin of the idea of the Fall of Man is at once evident.

Consider next the religion of Rome. Under the Republic, as we have seen, Roman religion played a secondary rôle in Roman education and Roman gods—Jupiter, for instance—did not spring from the dark forests of natural forces like those of Egypt or from the personification of superstitions like the Greek.

Clearly Roman religion was a very makeshift affair from the Christian point of view and when the early Christian martyrs first began to trouble certain Roman consciences they were quite prepared to save them from the slaughter if they simply extended their hands and swore the oath—By Jupiter—a piece of expediency unacceptable to more profoundly religious peoples. It puzzled many a worldly Roman that a man would rather be torn to pieces by wild beasts in the arena than conform to this simple rite.

The history of the rise of Christianity is too well known to need any very detailed exploration here and I will not dwell on the early struggles with Roman authority, the appalling slaughter of Christians in the Colosseum, and the slow but persistent spread of the teachings of Jesus. Professor Toynbee has summed up its very early history in his book *Civilization on Trial*: 'After two hundred and fifty years of comparative tranquillity, the Empire suffered, in the third century of the Christian era, a collapse from which it never fully recovered, and at the next crisis, in the fifth and sixth centuries, it went to pieces irretrievably. The true beneficiary of the temporary Roman Peace was the Christian Church. The Church seized this opportunity to strike root and spread; it was stimulated by persecution until the Empire, having failed to crush it, decided instead, to take it into partnership.'[7]

Suffice it to add that the main characteristics of Christian mythology, the Messiah with magical powers, the death by crucifixion and the resurrection from the dead were already interwoven into many myths preceding the birth of Christ. Indeed, as Robert Graves points out in his unpopular but brilliant book, *The Nazarene Gospel Restored*, there are 'striking literary resemblances between the canonical Gospels and Flavius Philostratus's Life of Apollonius'. Robert Graves writes: 'Jesus's symbolic acts became misrepresented as miracles, at a time when Gentile Christianity had met with a strong rival in the "gymnosophism" of Apollonius of Tyana, an ascetic philosopher who flourished under Nero.' Graves does not give us Nero's dates but they are perilously close to those of Jesus— A.D. 37-68. 'Apollonius,' Graves says, 'was believed to have cast out devils, raised the dead, accurately prophesied several public disasters, appeared in two far distant towns on the same day, vanished into thin air from the Imperial Judgement Hall at Rome, and at last ascended into Heaven—whence he occasionally revealed himself to those who disbelieved in his apotheosis. The Gentile Christians were anxious to prove that Jesus had done equally wonderful things, forgetting his stern refusal to gratify the multitude by idle display or to let his disciples use magical incantations. . . . He had even declined all credit for his feats of healing. . . .'[8]

Much more interesting perhaps is this passage in Graves's book: 'A hundred years after the publication of Philostratus's *Life* [of Apollonius] Eusebius felt obliged to attack it in a treatise "occasioned by the parallel drawn between Apollonius and Christ by Hierocles". Hierocles, one of Diocletian's provincial governors, had remarked that "whereas the tales of Jesus have been concocted by Peter and Paul and a few others like them (liars, uneducated, and wizards) the history of Apollonius was written by Maximus of Ægæ, and his constant companion Damis the philosopher, and Philostratus the Athenian, all men of the highest education, lovers of truth and of mankind. . . ." '⁹

It is no part of my thesis to pursue the tortured textual quarrels between biblical scholars about the precise nature of the Gospels, or the evidence for the divinity of Christ. Later, we shall have to ask the question—can we, with all our new historical and scientific knowledge, accept Christ as divine, or was he a very distinguished and unusual messiah in a long line of messiahs?—but for the moment I am concerned with the early history of Christianity and its impact on progress in religion.

Certainly Christianity introduced a new historical perspective which did not see life as fatalistically predetermined in a series of drearily recurring cycles but envisaged a 'divine drama whose successive acts were the Creation and Fall of Man, his Redemption and his glorious restoration'. Origen among the early Christian Fathers analysed the illogicality of the cyclic theory of history and wrote: 'If we accept the theory, then Adam and Eve will do in a second world exactly as they have done in this: the same deluge will be repeated; the same Moses will bring the same people out of Egypt, Judas will a second time betray his Lord, and again Paul will keep the garments of those who will stone Stephen.'[10]

In place of this 'confused nonsense', Christianity claimed 'a new principle of divine life had entered the human race and the natural world' which would raise mankind to a higher order. The Fall of Man had brought Christ to earth as the first born of the new creation which would lead to the Redemption and the 'glorious restoration'. This world on earth and the infinite world beyond were no longer mutually exclusive but inter-penetrated one another 'and even the lower world of matter and sense was capable of becoming the vehicle and channel of the divine life'.

It is perhaps partly upon this assumption that Christopher Dawson claims for Christianity a considerable rôle in the history of progress but the idea of a Fall, Redemption and Restoration does not meet the requirements of the modern idea of progress and can indeed be seen as simply imposing another and no less fixed cycle on history.

According to St Irenæus, as quoted by Dawson: 'God

arranged everything from the first with a view to the perfection of man, in order to deify him and reveal His own aspirations, so that goodness may be made manifest, justice made perfect, and the Church fashioned after the image of His Son. Thus man may eventually reach maturity, and, being ripened by such privileges, may see and comprehend God.'[11]

Progress, in short, is progress towards God. Christopher Dawson speaks of the new civilization which began to emerge in the early middle ages as in a very special sense a religious and not a political creation. Dating the period commonly referred to as the Middle Ages is no longer a simple matter and one historian will place its beginning as far back as 300 and another close it as late as 1453, but if we take the period from the fifth to the fifteenth centuries the canvas is enormous. Somewhere in the early days of this period, Dawson points out, religion gave men a common spiritual link which transcended political feuds and warring factions. 'In the East the imperial unity was still all inclusive and the Church was essentially the Church of the Empire, in the West it was the Church that was the universal society and the state was weak, barbarous and divided. The only true citizenship remaining to the common man was his membership of the Church, and it involved a far deeper and wider loyalty than his allegiance to the secular state.'[12]

It is impossible to overlook the fact that after the first inspired spring of Christianity and the days of Jesus it underwent a fall no less devastating than that which the Christians refer to as the Fall of Man. Indeed, the history of the Christian religion fits far more convincingly into the pattern of a time of divine innocence, a fall, a redemption and a glorious recovery than all attempts to mould our modern anthropological knowledge in the likeness of Christian mythology. From the time when Constantine the Great adopted Christianity the Christian outlook underwent a dramatic change. Where before it had claimed that religious belief was a personal matter over which no one should exercise coercion, it quickly reversed this view and presently set out to persuade every man, woman and child that the one true God was the Christian God.

As we have seen, under Pope Innocent III, during the twelfth century, the fanatical desire to sweep away all heretics and establish 'pure' Christianity resulted in the terrible crusade

against Count Toulouse when appalling scenes of bloody warfare led to the pitiless execution of heretics by hanging and
burning, even down to women and children.

Can this be considered part of 'the common spiritual link
which transcended the unpleasant political feuds and factions
of the barbarous states'? Was 'the only true citizenship—which
remained to the common man'—worth having on these terms?
Quite clearly there occurred a prolonged period in the Middle
Ages when one Pope after another exploited religious principles
for what we would consider debased ends.

If it is possible to excuse the conduct of a long line of Popes
on the grounds that primitive superstitition drove them to
ruthless suppression, it can only be said that progress of
religious thought suffered a severe setback from that fine free
air of fifth-century Athens when a multiplicity of gods seemed
preferable to the authoritarian brutality of the One True God.
Where, now, was the wonderful upsurge of new spiritual life
which Christopher Dawson so much admired?

The question becomes more urgent because Christianity
can stand up to and outface the horrors characteristic of certain
stages in its development. It is not entirely true, as Christopher
Dawson says, that 'in so far as civilization survived it was
directly dependent on the Church, whether in the Great
Carolingian monasteries . . . or in the cities which came to
depend on the bishops . . .'; but Christianity certainly played a
part in that survival. It was unfortunate that until the eleventh
century most monks remained incarcerated in their monasteries
and their contribution to civilization was very much cut off
from the real world outside. In the eleventh century, however,
they were impelled by the force of their own ideals to leave the
peace of the cloister and to throw themselves into a semi-
political struggle.

As Dawson says, this bold reunion with everyday life found
its most courageous expression in the mendicant orders like
the Dominicans and Franciscans, who were free to rove the
countryside concerning themselves as much with social services
as with religious matters. It is also true that this inevitably
brought such spheres as education, social welfare, the care of
the sick and relief of the poor under the influence of the
Church, but that influence did not seem to have much effect if
widespread illiteracy, hopelessly inadequate social services, the

spread of disease and abysmal depths of poverty were any measure.

Dawson seems proud of the fact that the Church even exercised 'a direct influence on war and politics' and 'could launch the armies of Christendom' into crusades, without mentioning the brutal suppression which was characteristic of far too many spiritual crusaders.

There was what Dawson regards as a danger in the twelfth century that as the Church became inextricably interlocked with the state it might 'itself be secularized by the growth of wealth and political power', but the 'dynamic moral energy of the Augustinian tradition' counteracted this. The Church had retreated so far from everyday life in the tradition of the monasteries that it needed a very large swing in the opposite direction to over-emphasize its secularization. However, as Dawson writes: 'In place of the severe figures of the Byzantine Christ, throned in awful majesty as ruler and judge of men . . . appears the figure of the Saviour in His human weakness and possibility.'[13]

There follows the interesting assertion that 'the great intellectual synthesis of the thirteenth century' was not merely a 'triumph of theological dogmatism' but 'the foundation of European science'. Dawson supports this conclusion with a quotation from Harnack that 'Scholasticism is nothing else but scientific thought'.

Of course, in modern terms, there is a wide distinction between the logical cheeseparing of scholasticism which tended to be overwhelmed by the luxuriance of its own evolution, and the rigorous induction of hypotheses from observed phenomena characteristic of science. The deductions of scholasticism would be regarded today as about as unscientific as Plato's speculations on the nature of the shadows thrown by the fire on the wall of his caves. The mad proliferation of deductive detail which should have given birth to the phrase 'reductio ad absurdum' was remote from the rigorously disciplined inductions characteristic of modern science. Perhaps it is possible to show that by observing and recording certain natural facts some schoolmen could be described as the forerunners of natural scientists, but such observations were not exclusively the work of schoolmen.

From the repressions, the brutalities and sheer ignorance of the Middle Ages came the Reformation to change the character of religious belief. The Latin world and certain German provinces remained faithful to Rome, Luther dominated Scandinavia and Northern Germany, England became Protestant—'but above all Anglican'—and France Catholic and Gallican. Strong nationalist characteristics were now apparent in every creed.

As for Luther, the religious leader of the movement, he presented the paradox of a man with ideas derived from Wycliffe and Ockham, essentially medieval thinkers, creating a revolt which changed the face of Christendom. He represented the spirit of German nationalism fighting against the invasion of foreign ideas, against the Italian Cardinals, against intellectualism, and all forms of spiritual repression. As we have seen, in no time at all, he himself assumed something of the authoritarian rôle which he had undermined.

Before the outbreak of the German peasants' revolt the Twelve Articles were drawn up under the influence of evangelical preachers like Schappeler and Hubmaier and called for the abolition of serfdom and the preaching of the pure Gospel. Luther sympathized with these Twelve Articles but rejected the peasants' appeal to violence. When the peasantry ignored his advice and resorted to arms, he not merely joined their opponents, the lords and princes, but passionately called for a war of extermination against them. In part, it was his powerful appeal *Against the Murderous and Thieving Peasant Bands, May 1525* which gave religious sanction to the quite ruthless suppression of the rising, and the savage retribution of the princes embittered relations between the classes to such an extent that all hope of reconciling religious and social reform vanished, and Luther was denounced as a traitor who had become the pawn of the peasants' oppressors. As with the earlier Crusades, once again it became clear that the Christian Church was quite prepared to endorse brutal suppression to get its way, and now it was converted into an instrument to reaffirm and reinforce the privileges of a ruling aristocracy. The peasants, it seemed, must still rest content with a promised hereafter and must not expect to realize even the most elementary characteristics of Christian Socialism on this earth.

A new interpretation of divinity presently appeared as Luther simplified the Catholic tradition and stripped away its intellectualization. Dawson puts it admirably: 'The divine was no longer conceived as pure intelligence—"luce intelletual piena d'amore"—the principle of the intelligibility of the created universe. It was regarded as a despotic power whose decrees predestined man to eternal misery or eternal bliss by the mere fiat of arbitrary will.'[14] To offset this the new Protestant outlook rejected the ascetic withdrawal of monasticism and 'substituted the standard of practical moral duty'.[15]

There was much in Luther and the Reformation which might qualify, in modern terms, for the word progress, but Dawson believes that the idea of progress only appears in early Protestantism in the old apocalyptic form.

The development of scientific thought in the sixteenth century, the conception of the world as 'a closed mechanical order governed by mathematical laws', brought about further adjustments in religious outlook and produced the Cartesian system which interpreted mind and spirit as disparate worlds only to be reconciled by a Cartesian deity. The late sixteenth and early seventeenth centuries saw the rise of the Puritans and the Jansenists. Religious interests continued to permeate every side of life but they were without the unity of their counterparts in the Middle Ages, and presently many factions were warring against each other as it became freshly apparent that the Gospels were open to multiple interpretation. 'In the course of less than fifty years (1640-1690) the Government [in England] had been successively Presbyterian, Independent, Anglican and Catholic and none of these had proved strong enough to suppress or eliminate rivals.'[16]

The revolution of 1688 was the beginning of the secularization of the English State with John Locke as one of its most distinguished pioneers. This secularization went hand in hand with a new unifying factor throughout many parts of Europe. In the Middle Ages, one inviolable interpretation of Christianity had given the appearance of spiritual unity to many different countries, and now the development of scientific knowledge brought together men as diverse as the Catholics Copernicus, Descartes and Galileo and Protestants like Newton, Kepler and Leibnitz. A new force had entered European life, almost unnoticed, but those who wish to see a revival of European spiritual unity never mention the long history of scientific unity. Beginning with the scientists of the seventeenth century, it has gradually extended its hold, building a ritual of methodology, a liturgy of jargon and a deification of truth which give it all the unifying possibilities of religious life, with none of its super-natural obligations.

The tendency to turn away from minute examination of theological dogma and to settle for more rational interpretations of Christianity, reached its height in the speculative world of the French philosophers of the eighteenth century and their English counterparts the Deists. Dawson claims that 'when the philosophers of the eighteenth century attempted to substitute their new rationalist doctrines for the ancient faith of Christen-dom, they were, in reality, simply abstracting from it those elements which had entered so deeply into their own thought that they no longer recognized [their] origin'.[17]

It is true that some aspects of Christianity belonged to certain deistic systems, but most deistic thinkers did not so much forget the origins of these ideas as deliberately reject the supernatural consequences surrounding them. Indeed, as Dawson himself later says: 'All these were desupernaturalized and fitted into the utilitarian rational scheme of contemporary philosophy.'

We come now, very briefly, to the Abbé de Saint-Pierre and the Encyclopaedists. As J. B. Bury wrote: 'Between 1690 and 1740 the conception of an indefinite progress of enlightenment had been making its way in French intellectual circles, and must often have been a topic of discussion in the salons, for instance, of Madame de Lambert, Madame de Tencin and Madame Cupin, where Fontenelle was one of the most conspicuous guests. To the same circle belonged his friend the Abbé de Saint-Pierre, and it is in his writings that we first find the theory widened to embrace progress towards social perfection.'[18]

It is also, in the strict sense of the word, the point at which the modern idea of progress begins, despite the claims of Christian apologists to pre-date it centuries back in the heart of Christian history.

The French school quickly reacted on the English, but it is instructive to remember that 'the prevailing tendency in Britain at that time was to regard the belief in earthly progress, not as an alternative to the traditional Christian outlook, but as a supplement to it'.[19] The French school had developed its ideas in deliberate opposition to the Church, and some in England followed suit, but the great majority remained within the religious milieu. The influence of French ideas upon English and German thought was considerable, and time and again 'these ideas were . . . worked into as much as could be retained of the existing religious setting'.[20] It was from the French school, none the less, from men like Fontenelle, St Pierre, Comte, Fourier and Condorcet, as we have seen, that the modern British belief in progress sprang, a belief not so very much concerned with the possibilities of the hereafter.

The most famous piece of progressive religious writing was Lessing's *The Education of the Human Race* (1780) which represented the 'Old and New Testament revelation as a progressive process of divine education by which God had led the human mind from a state of tutelage towards a final state of independent thought. . . .'[21] Herder's *Ideas Towards a Philosophy of the History of Mankind* was published soon afterwards, and saw 'the progress of humanity . . . as a natural process in which God leaves man to work out his own salvation by the exercise of his own reason'. These two men were the fertile breeding ground from which sprang the idea of 'world religion as a progressive development of human discovery, culminating in the teaching of Jesus of Nazareth'.[22]

Almost simultaneously with the publication of Herder's *Ideas Towards a Philosophy of the History of Mankind* Kant published his *Idea Towards a Universal History in a Cosmopolitan Interest*. This was followed by his famous *The Critique of Practical Reason* (1788). Kant saw development not in terms of increased human happiness or material progress but in mankind's apprehension and fulfilment of the moral laws immanent in nature. Happiness he thought could only 'be added by the transcendent action of God'. Since it seemed to Kant that the chances of humanity achieving moral perfection on this earth were remote, then there must be some other means of satisfying the ineluctable demands of nature and bringing 'our wills into perfect conformity with the moral law'. This led him into his famous proof of the immortality of the soul. If we were destined to fulfil the moral laws immanent in nature, and life on this earth offered us no such possibility, there must be a life beyond the grave where we could satisfy the unconditional demand for endless moral progress. He added a striking new characteristic to the conception of the hereafter and nineteenth-century religious thinkers were not slow to exploit it. In the past, heaven had appeared as a massively static construction, undisturbed by change of any kind, where perfect serenity accompanied perfect bliss and time, in the temporal sense of the word, created neither boredom nor aged a single soul. Now, suddenly, Kant saw it as a 'prolongation of the earthly quest and task, so that after death men will resume their development from the point at which death had interrupted it'.[23] As Baillie remarks, it was a signal triumph for the general idea of progress that 'it should thus have found its way through the gates of pearl into the City of God'.

Seen in these terms, the idea of progress was carried to an even more remote conclusion by that maddeningly imprecise philosopher Hegel. Belonging to the German school of Fichte and Schelling, he believed that 'the structure of all experience is given *a priori* in the nature of Absolute Spirit, and the clue to the nature of the whole is implicit in each separate part'.[24] This substituted for the term 'progress', the term 'development', the first concerning itself with the history of mankind from the Renaissance into a yet unrealized future, and the second concerned only to interpret past history.

It was characteristic of the German idealists that they saw history as a series of successive stages each one logically unfolding from the last and all contained in the underlying matrix of life. They were, it seems, more concerned with demonstrating the process of interlocking development than with development 'in the direction of a greater good'.

As Baillie points out, 'the absence from Hegel's pages of any particular outlook on the future is certainly remarkable'. The French and English philosophers had seen progress in history as something extending into the present and future, but 'Hegel gives the impression of being content with what has already been achieved'. As we saw, spiritual progress with Kant finally burst through the gates of heaven 'into the everlasting life of the saints'; and now, with Hegel it enters 'into the very life of God'.

*　　*　　*　　*

There is a point in this very brief analysis of such a wide and complex period of religious readjustment, where the recurrence of terms like—Absolute Spirit and the Very Life of God begin to demand sharper definition if they are not to become so many emotionally charged and hopelessly obscure labels. There is another point where fresh exegesis of Christian mythology threatens to become boring.

Christianity has undoubtedly progressed enormously since those primitive days of the Old Testament when an aboriginal mythology was advanced as a satisfactory explanation of the creation of the world and the breath-taking appearance of Man. As we have seen, the continuous development of knowledge forced the theologians to revise their reading of the Gospels. Sometimes they fought a rearguard action against every new truth and refused to budge from a fundamentalist position. Sometimes the alacrity with which they assimilated scientific discoveries and refused to abandon the supernatural element in their creed, shocked secular thinkers, but there were others prepared to admit the validity of a long line of adjustments.

Certainly it made things very difficult for theologians when the earth was shown to be no longer the centre of the universe but a mass of cooled gas revolving, like many other bodies, round the sun. Certainly, belief in the uniqueness and immortality of the human soul suffered a serious setback when Darwin showed that we derived from the animals, and further confusion arose when Freud saw man not as a rational, free-thinking human being forging his own destiny, but as an organism continuously the victim of unconscious drives so deeply hidden that we did not know their precise origin. Each of these new discoveries has been assimilated into Christian doctrine, some think successfully, without the surrender of intellectual integrity, some at the cost of such contortions that the whole rationale of Christianity has been invalidated.

When it came to be realized that the earth and its inhabitants were not likely to 'cease upon the midnight' within a few hundred or even a few thousand years, and that Judgement Day would have to be relegated to a time theoretically so distant that no date could any longer be given, the idea of a Kingdom to come needed radical re-examination. It was one thing to promise a paradisal hereafter within an easily discernible time; it was quite another to say that Heaven had unaccountably disappeared over the horizon and might not be encountered for a hundred thousand years. However, there were two interpretations open to nineteenth-century scholars.

As Baillie says: 'It was generally concluded that Jesus sometimes spoke of the [Kingdom of God] as an order of things to be introduced by God at the end of earthly history, but sometimes also as an immanent reality already present in the hearts of believers and through their agency gradually permeating the society of men; but it was confidently felt that the former represented the Judaistic cabinet in which Jesus' teaching was set, and the latter His own real view.'[25]

When we read of Jesus having 'a view', as if a view were no more than an opinion and an opinion horribly open to human contradictions, it all sounds very odd, but this 'view' is necessary to Baillie's idea of Christian progress. He reads the New Testament as revealing a conjunction between that 'sense of present fulfilment' with the 'expectation of that final glory in which history will one day culminate'. The 'sense of present fulfilment' is concerned with the new kind of life opened on earth by the descent of Christ, a life with considerable possibilities, and the 'final glory' with the realization that human ills and sufferings will only yield in the long run 'to the perfect blessedness of the heavenly Kingdom'.

In a passage of the utmost solemnity which must be read in context to get its full flavour, Baillie manipulates simple images with a naïveté which should leave a sardonic amusement in the mind of the least intellectual Christian: '. . . the New Testament regards the earthly scene as a platform *across* which men must pass obliquely one by one into an unseen world which is "always there alongside". . . .' Baillie proceeds to question this interpretation with the following paragraph italicizing the subtle difference between the words *across* and *along*: '. . . the dominating picture throughout the New Testament is rather of the earth as a platform *along* which men walk, and on which one generation succeeds another, enjoying even now the blessings of a life hid with Christ in God, and waiting in hope for a fullness of glory which will supervene upon the close, not of each individual biography, but of earthly history itself, when the platform will finally be swept away to make room for a new heaven and a new earth.'[26]

It is astonishing that a modern Professor of Divinity has lived through a scientific age fraught with profoundly revolutionary knowledge only to achieve this childish interplay between crossing and traversing an earthly platform as his interpretation of progressive Christianity. It seems closely related to the imaginative world of a child playing with trains, rather than a highly educated member of the human race trying to come to terms with divinity.

However, so much of Christian teaching today is difficult to reconcile with modern knowledge. Even fine scholars like Dr Dodd find themselves driven to re-interpret some of the basic tenets of the New Testament in such a way that they virtually disappear for the common lay reader. The New Testament places 'the historical process between a Creation at the beginning and a Last Judgement and second Advent at the end',[27] but Dr Dodd no longer reads this literally at its face value. 'The myth of a Last Judgement is a symbolical statement of the final resolution of the great conflict. Serious difficulties are raised if we attempt to treat it as a literal and quasi-historical statement that the succession of events in time will one day cease.'[28] 'Doomsday simply takes a cut across the time-stream at any point and reveals the triumph of the divine purpose in it. But this triumph is something actually attained, not in some coming Day of the Lord near or distant, but in the concrete historical event of the death and resurrection of Jesus Christ.'[29]

Once again the rational mind boggles at language of this kind and the deceptiveness of the imagery used. At one point in his book, Baillie says that the Christian faith 'does offer . . . a very confident hope for the future course of terrestrial history' but when we enquire what this is, we are told that—'it is a hope for the success of an evangelistic campaign and above all, it would seem, for the progressive success of foreign missions'. In its more elaborate equivalent, he falls back on sentences like: 'We must recover that sense of standing on the threshold of a new historical economy (or dispensation), that sense of a noble prospect opening out before us, that sense of the power of the Spirit and of the inexhaustible resources now available to us,' 'that adventurous zeal for the renewal of humanity and that confidence in ultimate victory of which the New Testament is so full . . .'[30] etc. etc. Professor Baillie, in such passages, has compensated for what he describes as an 'apparent defeatism that characterized so much of traditional Christian thought'.

Accepting Weber's argument that 'history reveals a number of essentially disparate spiritual traditions, each with its own characteristic and untransplantable religious outlook, moral code and taste and style in art', Baillie cannot admit Weber's further conclusion that when a religion, regarded as universal, is transplanted, it loses its original identity. Thus the Hinayana Buddhism of Ceylon is something very different from the Mahayana of the Far East, and 'the various Christian sects of later times' are 'religions as separate from one another as they all are from primitive Christianity'.[31] This would, of course, place Christianity on equal terms with Buddhism and throw fresh doubt on its exclusively divine inspiration.

Not unexpectedly, Baillie is much happier with Toynbee's conclusion that the religious impulse carries over from one civilization to another, that the birth, growth, maturity and decay of secular civilization is subsidiary to the growth of religion. As Toynbee himself puts it: 'If . . . so far from its being the historical function of higher religions to minister, as chrysalises, to the cyclic process of the reproduction of civilizations, it is the historical function of civilizations to serve, by their downfalls, as stepping-stones to a progressive process of the revelation of always deeper religious insight, and the gift of ever more grace to act on this insight, then the societies of the species called civilizations will have fulfilled their function when once they have brought a mature higher religion to birth.'[32]

In the end, for Baillie, progress comes back once more to this, 'the . . . embodiment in the life of humanity of the mind that was in Christ and a growing up in all things unto Him who is the Head'.

Now it may be easy to convince Christians of such a manifest destiny because it rests on the belief that Christianity 'approximates more closely to final religious truth than any other religion'.[33] Christianity is their yardstick of measurement and other religions merely the 'forerunners of Christianity, partially foreshadowing its truths', but what of the millions who substitute Buddhism for Christianity and believe in an entirely different destiny? How do we finally know that we were not born to perfect as far as possible our life on this earth, rather than prepare ourselves for another and unknown hereafter? Professor Toynbee believes that 'the Christian soul can attain, while still on earth, a greater measure of man's greatest good than can be attained by any pagan soul',[34] but this is merely an assertion. Millions of profoundly religious people, alive today, would be shocked at any such idea. It is the weakness of many religious propagandists that they assume their own religion to be the only acceptable criterion of religious progress.

As Professor Ginsberg has written: 'The religions of the world may in future learn more from each other than they have in the past but I cannot see any ground for believing that any one of them, however modified by its contact with others, is likely to provide a basis acceptable to all for the spiritual unification of mankind.'[35]

*　　　*　　　*　　　*

Such is the tenacity of Christian spiritual life that the ruthless attempts made, in the Soviet Union, to stamp it out have not met with the success which the Communists expected. At different times the party has tried direct suppression and persecution, penalties for speculations dangerous to the State, penetration by deliberately faked rival churches and propaganda designed to show that the scientific truths on which Marxism is based can have no meeting-place with supernatural divinities. Evidence on the results is conflicting.

The younger intelligentsia among the Russians argue that it is only the older generations who cling to these 'outworn myths', and yet Stalin found himself forced to try a policy of compromise, granting religious organizations a certain toleration in exchange for their support. Today, many religious sects survive with varying degrees of life, from the Orthodox Church to the Protestants, from the Catholics and Jews to the Buddhists and Moslems, and although statistical evidence is hazier than in England or America, according to Leonard Schapiro, 'more than half the adult population described themselves as believers in 1937'. As Schapiro commented, numbers are not nearly so remarkable as 'the tenacity with which a religious body can survive in the face of all efforts directed against it as compared say with a political party. The mensheviks and socialist revolutionaries, for example, have long disappeared, virtually without trace.'[36] The Communist Party has certainly succeeded in penetrating but does not fully control the Church in Russia, and that is a remarkable enough phenomenon when we remember the ruthless powers at the disposal of an authoritarian state.

Unlike England or America, the government in Russia regards religion as regressive rather than progressive, but as we have seen, the relationship between religion and progress has undergone drastic changes down the ages. In England, the number of churchgoers has dwindled. In America statistics tend to be confusing.

Certainly Christian *doctrine* has progressed. Many of the absurdities of the Old Testament are no longer taught, no one today would think of torturing a heretic, physical force has disappeared as a form of religious coercion, a much more liberal attitude to controversy has developed and different creeds are less intolerant of one another. In many parts of Western Europe today, men and women are free to choose their own religion. In others, far more subtle means of persuasion have arisen and in countries like Spain the 'heretic' is still at a disadvantage.

Christian doctrine apart, can Christianity claim to have been interested in the idea of progress from its first beginnings? Professor Ginsberg has written: 'Christian theologians seem to have become deeply interested in the idea of progress only after it became a dominant element in Western thought. The Catholic Church has on occasion explicitly repudiated it, and Protestant writers find great difficulty in coming to terms with it.'[37] Dean Inge believed that Christianity was incompatible with a general theory of progress,[38] and Edwyn Bevan said: 'We should beware of supposing that it is possible for us to trace any approximation in the course of history to the Kingdom of God.'[39]

Has the record of the Christian religion contributed to human progress in any large degree? It is easy to remember the brutality of the Crusades, to recall the fate of heretics under the Inquisition, the repression of freedom of opinion, and the dark forest of sexual misery created by men like St Paul whose only way of expressing one of the most profound, complex and richly satisfying of our instincts was to say—it is better to marry than to burn. Countless generations of people have been driven by Christian doctrine to associate sex with sin in such a way that a mountain of artificial guilt has crushed its free, happy expression and what was once spontaneously innocent became self-consciously sordid.

There is much to set against this. The preservation of culture in some of the darkest periods of history, the gradual enlightenment which struck away intolerance and some of the worst absurdities of Christian doctrine, the gradual growth of a spirit which was humane, tolerant and in some respects wise, and the unifying power of Christianity with its valuable anticipation of an international world. Above all, there is the simple fact that, delusory or not, the Christian God has sustained countless millions of people in their suffering on this earth and made it possible for millions more to survive, to face up to living and find a certain spiritual exhilaration from sharing a divine purpose. No one will ever know how to measure these things against one another. At the most one can say—if the Christian religion did a great deal of harm in the past it has made life a better and more tolerable thing for many generations since the Renaissance, except perhaps in its sexual philosophy.

Does the Christian mythology survive the growth of scientific knowledge, and does it still represent a satisfactory explanation of man's relationship to the universe in terms which meet the far more exacting needs of his new spiritual awareness? For many scientists today, Christianity can never rise above the status of a man-made mythology which was the inevitable product of grappling with a harsh and hostile nature down a thousand generations. They cannot grant divinity to Christ or see anything other than a reassuring fairy-tale in the story of His Birth, Death and Resurrection. Certainly, the growth of scientific knowledge has forced the theologians to chip away at the original ideas of the Old Testament until they are no longer recognizable. When something said to be divinely inspired has to undergo so many human modifications before it ceases to trouble the intelligence, can it possibly satisfy our new and much more informed awareness of man's place in the universe? There is a sad correlation between the gradual conquest of hostile nature, the slow growth of knowledge, of material security and earthly satisfactions, with a steady diminution in the Common Man's belief in Christian doctrines. It would seem that his readiness to believe is in proportion to the material conditions under which he lives.

According to one view there have been three great philosophic interpretations of tragedy down the ages. The straightforwardly tragic which belonged to the classical age, the anti-tragic to the Christian age, and now the non-tragic which belongs to the scientific age. It is possible at last to avert premature death, to cure many forms of disease and to anticipate and prevent natural disasters until what was inescapable in the past can now be contained, and the breath of the Furies blown scornfully back in their faces. No longer subject to his old inescapable fate, Man is now busy trying to shape that fate to his own liking. Where before he believed in a manifest destiny, now he is trying to create his own destiny. Once it was accepted that men had to suffer and this acceptance was organized into religions, but now the sting has been taken from a great deal of suffering and the question has to be asked—is it possible to think any longer in such spiritually picturesque terms as a Fall, a Redemption and a Kingdom of Heaven? The beautiful images wilt under intellectual acids. The mind is uneasy trying to assimilate the Christian mythology.

Freud believed that religion was an illusion, one of those splendidly elaborate sops to widespread neurosis by which men preserved themselves in a permanently infantile state. For him religious ideas arose, like 'all the other achievements of civilization, from the necessity of defending oneself against the crushingly superior force of nature'.[40] God, for him, became simply the transfiguration of an earthly father into a heavenly Father, a deification made necessary because the child was appalled to lose the strong, warm, guiding hand which had watched over his years of growing up. 'God was the exalted father and the longing for the father was the root of the need for religion.'[41]

Like Havelock Ellis, Freud saw what Ellis described as the 'ghouls of the church rushing in to take possession of the plastic, unformed mind of the child' before the child was capable of thinking for itself, and implanting irrevocably the seed of the divine ordinance. It was a habit of which the Christian Church complained in Communism. The Communists indoctrinated unformed children with political beliefs, the Christians with Christian beliefs. Indeed each clearly saw something of a rival in the other, one deifying secular gods, the other a Divine God.

The results of both, according to Freud, were unfortunate: 'Think of the depressing contrast between the radiant intelligence of a healthy child and the feeble intellectual powers of the average adult. Can we be quite certain that it is not precisely religious education which bears a large share of the blame for this relative atrophy? . . . Is it not true that the two main points in the programme for the education of children today are a retardation of sexual development and premature religious influence? Thus, by the time the child's intellect awakens, the

doctrines of religion have already become unassailable. . . .
When a man has once brought himself to accept uncritically all
the absurdities that religious doctrines put before him and
even to overlook the contradictions between them, we need
not be greatly surprised at the weakness of his intellect.'[42]

It is a serious challenge. It remains to discriminate clearly
between the religious impulse in man and Christian education.
Any deeply conscious human being must, at some time, find
himself aware of his relation to the universe whether it be in the
depths of the night, when hidden fears come up to take possession of him, whether some malignant illness threatens him with
prolonged pain and premature death and he knows that the
black curtain may at any moment descend, or whether, standing
alone in an echoing street late at night, the 'otherness' in life
suddenly presses in on him. Religion, in these terms, need not
have anything to do with dogma or doctrine but is simply a
man's awareness that he is, in some mysterious way, related to
the fixed stars, interstellar space and the whole fantastic spectacle
revealed by the night sky. Christianity is one codification of
this awareness. It is one of many. There are others yet un-
explored. Religion, in short, need have nothing to do with the
acknowledged creeds of the day. It is capable of manifold
expression and perhaps we shall yet find a creed which does not
require the suspension of intelligence, or the careful indoctrination of children.

A man may be spiritually conscious when he listens to great
music in a sense no less profound than when he takes Com-
munion in an incense-laden church. The transcendence of
poetic expression may carry him through material barriers into
another dimension. Profound thought, prolonged absorption in
creative work, inspired love, all lead into spiritual awareness
which is quite divorced from Christian dogma.

One of the leading exponents of Religion without Revelation,
Professor Julian Huxley, has put forward a biologist's religion
in terms which resemble the Christian framework closely
enough to annoy some of his would-be disciples. He believes
that the world is advancing in a spiritual direction, but not on
the Christian principle. The process of evolution has no God
directing its forces. Spiritual values are an implicit part of
the blind movement of material forces. 'Consquently,' as
Christopher Dawson puts it, 'the religious impulse must find

its satisfaction in a conscious co-operation with this cosmic trend. . . .'[43]

In his book, *Religion without Revelation*, Huxley will have nothing to do with a personal God, be it Jehovah, Allah, Apollo or Amen-Ra. Some theologians represent Huxley as agnostic, but he specifically states 'I am not merely agnostic on the subject. It seems to me quite clear that the idea of personality in God or in any supernatural being or beings has been put there by man . . . I disbelieve in a personal god in any sense in which that phrase is ordinarily used.'[44] He may be agnostic so far as the existence of another life is concerned and he does not deny the phenomena of telepathy and clairvoyance, but spiritual life is, to him, a refinement of material life and finds it final expression in the recent work of Pierre Teilhard de Chardin.

I have read this book, to which Professor Huxley contributes a preface, and I must admit I find both book and preface confusing. In an attempt to explain the nature of the book, Huxley himself is sometimes driven back on phrases like— 'If I understand him aright'—and—'Here his thought is not fully clear to me'. Chardin's invention of a new jargon does not help matters very much, and I feel it is wiser to quote Huxley's analysis of Chardin, which sharpens the focus of many a rambling chapter. When 'man's thought and his resultant psychosocial activity', writes Huxley, 'is confined to spreading out over the surface of [the earth] idea will encounter idea, and the result will be an organized web of thought, a noetic system operating under high tension, a piece of evolutionary machinery capable of generating high psychosocial energy . . . I visualized this selective web of living thought as the bounding structure of evolving man, marking him off from the rest of the universe and yet facilitating exchange with it. . . .'[45] In other words, 'the intensification of mental subjective activity—' would lead to 'the evolution of progressively more conscious mind'. Chardin infers 'the presence of potential mind in all material systems, by backward extrapolation from the human phase to the biological, and from the biological to the inorganic'. As a result 'we must envisage the intensification of mind, the raising of mental potential as being the necessary consequence of complexification, operating by the convergent integration of increasingly complex units of organization'.

It is easy to see why the Roman Catholics would not allow

Chardin to publish this book in his lifetime because it obviously involves complete acceptance of evolution. More relevant to my immediate purpose, it carries Huxley's belief that spiritual life is a refinement of material life to its logical conclusion. As Huxley says, sometimes Chardin seems to equate the future of all this 'hyperpersonal psychosocial organization with an emergent Divinity'. In fact, Chardin can be found fitting the evolutionary facts into the Christian doctrine in a very familiar manner and what we have, in the end, once again, is a new kind of God. Elsewhere something less supernatural but highly metaphysical appears: 'the incipient development of mankind into a single psychosocial unit with a single noosystem or common pool of thought is providing the evolutionary process with the rudiments of a head. It remains for our descendants to organize this global noosystem more adequately. . . .'[46]

Organisms first become individualized from inorganic matter, then personalized with insights into their own behaviour, and finally transcend 'their merely organic individuality in conscious participation' with one another. The cephalization (differentiation of a head as the dominant guiding region) in the individual, is now being universalized and the rudiments of—so to say—an internationalized consciousness, developed.

All this very inadequately represents some of the subtle reasoning in Chardin's interesting but grossly over-praised book. It is better to read the book itself. It has to be added that one of the most distinguished biologists alive today considers the book something of a fake and perhaps even worse. In a review of *The Phenomenon of Man*, Professor P. B. Medawar has accused Chardin of 'habitually and systematically cheating with words'. Using the full weight of his brilliant technical knowledge, Professor Medawar undermines the scientific validity of one statement after another in the book. 'People,' he writes, 'should not be taken in by such a bag of tricks as this. . . . If it were an innocent passive gullibility it would be excusable; but all too clearly, alas, it is an active willingness to be deceived.'[47] Re-reading the book in the light of the technical details of his review, it certainly becomes highly suspect.

* * * *

One enormous question remains unanswered—what is the future of religion? Is it possible that we shall one day, not so

very far away, see a new religion which will more nearly
satisfy modern intellectual, emotional and spiritual requirements?

Or will men simply outgrow and abandon the old religions
without replacing them? We have seen polytheism give place
to monotheism in Western Europe. Will this in turn be followed
by so to say—no-theism?

The English empirical temperament has created many fine
institutions but the Church of England, at the moment, is not
one of the most successful. Incorporating scientific knowledge
in the nineteenth century it partially admitted defeat and these
concessions may have been dangerous. Today, some intellectuals
have returned to the Christian fold in one form or another and
there has been an increase in church-going among upper middle-
class people anxious to find spiritual consolation for post-war
social reforms which benefit classes other than their own.
Otherwise, the Church of England gives every sign of being in
decline. Perhaps it was a mistake to try to incorporate the
monster Science into Christian theology. It weakened the
Church's claim to exclusive rights in spiritual sources and in
para-psychology had a dangerous rival.

Dr John Robinson, Bishop of Woolwich, caused a stir in 1963
with his book *Honest to God*. He expressed a belief that
Christians, in this generation, must detach themselves from
their mental image of God as a supernatural person; he looked
forward to 'radical reformulations for the Church in almost
every field, of doctrine, worship, ethics and evangelism'; only
then, he felt, could Christianity become relevant to modern
secular man. God was teaching us that we must live as men who
could get along very well without Him. Simultaneously,
Bonhoeffer propagated the idea that man had reached a stage in
evolution where he would grow out of his need for religion.
Dr Alexander Vidler was asking penetrating questions about
Christian belief, and the theme of yet another book was self-
evident in the title *Objections to Christian Belief*. Everywhere
voices were questioning the very fundamentals of the Christian
faith.

For the rest, Freud believed that we can dispense with
religion in the old sense of the word and this, in his view,
instead of crippling or impoverishing mankind, would release
us at last into full maturity. Without religion we would stand

austerely and daringly face to face with the rigours of reality, a toughened and newly inspired species ready, if necessary, to go down before the forces of evolution but full of hope of a quite different kind from the past. Freud believed that it is only those in whom 'you have instilled the sweet—or bitter-sweet—poison from childhood onwards' who need the prop of religion to face the troubles and cruelties of life.

As he wrote of those men who had—in his view—been sensibly brought up without religious training: 'Perhaps those who do not suffer from the neurosis will need no intoxicant to deaden it. They will, it is true, find themselves in a difficult situation. They will have to admit to themselves the full extent of their helplessness and their insignificance in the machinery of the universe; they can no longer be the centre of creation, no longer the object of tender care on the part of a beneficent Providence. They will be in the same position as a child who has left the parental house where he was so warm and comfortable. But surely infantilism is destined to be surmounted. Men cannot remain children for ever: they must in the end go out into "hostile life".'[48]

CHAPTER EIGHT

Political progress

I T is melancholy to think how much human suffering, frustration and despair have been caused by pious men who formulated beliefs based on false conceptions of the universe and translated these into forms of government which they imposed on their fellows with all the ruthlessness of religious fanatics.

As Sir Isaiah Berlin has written: 'In politics . . . men tried to conceive of their social existence by analogy with various models: Plato at one stage, perhaps following Pythagoras, tried to frame his system of human nature, its attributes and goals, following a geometrical pattern . . . there followed the biological pattern of Aristotle: the many Christian images with which the writings of the Fathers as well as the Old and New Testaments abound; the analogy of the family which casts light upon human relations not provided by a mechanical model (such as that of Hobbes); the notion of an army on the march with its emphasis on such virtues as loyalty, dedication, obedience. . . .'[1]

Sometimes these systems challenged and overwhelmed one another; sometimes one adopted the better or worse characteristics of another; sometimes one powerful element in government—absolute monarchy—repeated itself for centuries. It was a long time before the State came to be seen as a great co-ordinated endeavour in which people of diverse interests, class and talents could co-operate to fulfil the higher purposes of human existence as revealed by the steady growth of insight into the nature of the universe and the nature of Man: but let me begin at the beginning. No analysis of patterns of government—however brief and this chapter must necessarily be a very foreshortened affair—can overlook the writings of Aristotle. There is space only to glance at Aristotle's *Politics*.

It is characteristic of the more reactionary thinkers today that they play down the obvious shortcomings of this work and too easily embrace an ethos full of contradictions for the modern mind. It remains astonishing that a man without any technical knowledge of political economy in the modern sense, should have written such a book fourteen hundred years ago. If exaggerated reverence for Greek civilization still tends to generate too high an admiration for his work, Aristotle's *Politics* cannot be avoided in any discussion of political progress. In some respects its influence on modern thought and behaviour remains pernicious. In others it is rich in the most stimulating ideas and deeply explores problems which still trouble us today.

Aristotle conceived of the State as an organism and said that an individual could not fulfil his true purpose unless he was an intrinsic part of that organism. A State, in Aristotle's view, should embrace enough people, land and sources of sustenance to be more or less self-sufficient, but it should not be 'too large for constitutional government'. Its area should not extend beyond that which can be seen in its entirety from a hilltop or its citizens become so numerous that they do not know each other's characters. As for its purpose, a political society 'should exist for the sake of noble actions, not of mere companionship'. 'The State is the union of families and villages in a perfect and self-sufficing life, by which we mean a happy and honourable life.' The final aim of the State was the 'good life'.

Taken within the context of the Greek city state and Greek values all this had a validity which it completely lacks today. We still subscribe to the ideal of the good life but our definition of such a life has undergone severe qualification, opposing political philosophies give different interpretations of the word 'noble' and our cities no longer bear any resemblance to the Greek city states.

The division of the classes in a Greek city state established a limited number of citizens with the right to rule and vote and a much larger class of slaves who were kept permanently in thrall and disenfranchised. Working men, in our sense of the word, were not eligible for citizenship. 'Citizens,' wrote Aristotle, 'should not lead the life of mechanics or tradesmen for such a life is ignoble and inimical to virtue.' Husbandmen should be slaves from foreign lands and citizens should busy themselves with the duties of owning property, governing or acquiring culture. According to Aristotle, Nature herself distinguished which were slaves and which citizens, and any man *naturally* inferior should accept the rôle of the slave without question.

Precisely how the naturalness of inferiority was determined is never established and at many points throughout his *Politics* Aristotle's failure to develop his thesis in detail makes it unsatisfactory reading to the modern eye.

As Bertrand Russell wrote: 'War [according to Aristotle] . . . is just when waged against men who, though intended by nature to be governed, will not submit and in this case, it is implied, it would be right to make slaves of the conquered. This would seem enough to justify any conqueror who ever lived; for no nation will admit that it is intended by nature to be governed and the only evidence as to nature's intention must be derived from the outcome of war. In every war, therefore, the victors are in the right and the vanquished in the wrong. Very satisfactory!'[2]

When carried to its logical conclusion too much of Aristotle's thought leads to equal absurdities in modern eyes, but several great precepts in the book remain valid. A government is good when devoted to the interests of the whole community and bad when exclusively concerned with its own class. Aristotle develops this into more questionable fields. Three forms of government are bad, he says—tyranny, oligarchy and certain forms of democracy, and three are good—monarchy, aristocracy and constitutional government.

The Greek idea of democracy was in some ways less effective than ours when only a small proportion of the populace could vote, and more effective when it appointed magistrates and lawyers by lot and, in extreme cases, allowed an assembly of citizens to decide separate issues by vote above the law. In our day and age, with the complexities of modern law, it would be absurd to elect lawyers by popular vote, but General de Gaulle has recently overruled the Chamber of Deputies by going to the people with a referendum.

Education, in Aristotle's view, was for the children of citizens alone, but slaves could be taught comparatively menial activities like cooking and agriculture. Citizen-children would learn to read and write, to draw and play musical instruments, but these would not be carried to the point of vulgarization where they might earn money from such activities. The whole object of education was not to learn what would be useful but to learn what would increase virtue, and the kind of person idealized was a cultured gentleman, a man combining a deep interest in learning and the arts with something vaguely defined as the 'aristocratic mentality'.

The way in which these principles worked out in practice was very unsatisfactory to the modern mind. In the days of Pericles, the brilliant life of Athens, enriched by philosophy, poetry, drama, architecture, sculpture, the beginnings of science and medicine, threw up a comparative handful of men who fulfilled the image of the ideal man, but large numbers of ordinary men and women remained illiterate, unfulfilled and denied those basic rights which our conception of government demands for everyone. This scantiest of sketches does no more than touch a few of the precepts put forward by Aristotle and inadequately represents the subtlety and complexity of his thought, but other matters claim our attention.

It is necessary to determine what criteria we propose using to discriminate between the relative value of one form of government and another. In the widest possible sense of the word any definition of progress, especially in forms of government, can rapidly deteriorate into such highly subjective terms that it becomes, ultimately, a matter of taste. One group prefers the form of government which best suits the aims, privileges and possessions of its class, and another an exactly opposite form for similar reasons. Despite the lofty pretensions of their calling the views of many philosophers down the ages have coincided with the 'pecuniary interests' of their class and Aristotle was no exception. As Bertrand Russell has written: 'Greek philosophers belonged to, or were employed by, the land-owning class; they therefore disapproved of interest. Medieval philosophers were churchmen and the property of the Church was mainly in land; they therefore saw no reason to revise Aristotle's opinion. . . .'[3]

It was axiomatic to the Greek mind that the values of a group of 'high-born citizens' were superior to the values of the mass of the people, and they felt themselves under a moral compulsion to impose these values on society by a minority rule. Today, we realize that the potential of many slaves may have been very high and social organization has undergone dramatic changes to permit the expression of that potential in many more human-beings.

The question now asked in many parts of the world is the one implicit in many chapters of this book—does social organization operate in such a way as to give each individual, irrespective of class or creed, the chance of fulfilling his best potential?

Ask the question of history itself, and it is very difficult to get any precise answer. Certainly there were many generations of Greek slaves whose potential was severely limited by the operation of the principles contained in Aristotle's *Politics*.

Some forty thousand citizens in Athens—a small proportion of the total population—were expected, at one time or another, to attend the Assembly, form part of the Council and fulfil the obligations of minor civil servants from guardians of the arsenals to guardians of the Acropolis. Some citizens found their public work a full-time job and were paid compensation by the State. There were, in fact, ten groups of fifty Councillors who took it in turn to be available in the rôle of what we could call permanent civil servants and they were paid. Every so often the ordinary fisherman, shopkeeper or craftsman, providing he had citizen status, broke away from work for a day to attend the Greek House of Commons as a temporary member. Once more he received payment from the State for his day's work, and he could directly influence his own social destiny by speaking or voting for or against whatever measures were under discussion. Within the small limits of the Greek city state he could bring to bear far more influence on state measures than his counterpart in the twentieth century, but for every citizen there were seven or eight slaves and metics who were politically powerless.

Three forces combined in the end to bring down the Greek political system and way of life: the insistence of every city on absolute sovereignty, the growing strife between rich and poor within the cities and the arrival of the Roman legions.

Turning to Rome, the Senate, or Council of Elders, was the most permanent feature of Roman government and consisted at the outset of three hundred members, all patrician by birth. During the monarchical period the King was the sole arbiter who appointed the senators. The substitution of two elected consuls for the King, when the monarchy was abolished, did not radically change the Senate. Theoretically it remained secondary in power to the magistrates, as it had to the King, and was really an advisory council of consuls meeting only at their pleasure, but in practice the magistrates rarely disregarded the advice of the Senate.

Forces were at work during the age of war and conquest

which brought about changes in the old constitution. In the end it no longer recognized any order of nobility, the patricians were no longer an exclusive and privileged caste and all offices of state were, in theory, open to anyone.

In fact, this outward form of democracy was converted into an oligarchy. In defiance of the law, a privileged class still claimed the title of nobility. Under their rule the Senate, not the assembly, continued to govern Rome, and the magistracies and the Senate were in their power. The occasions when the assembly was called upon to decide big issues of policy became steadily more rare and in most cases decisions were taken by the Senate without any reference whatever to the people.

The majority of the new nobility in A.D. 146 were of plebeian, not patrician origin, the titles being appropriated by men who had achieved the consulship. In theory any citizen could aspire to these distinctions, but like many ruling classes the old and the new nobility presently joined forces to form a new and exclusive order. Towards the end of the period, once again a select minority had achieved a monopoly of political power and the attempts of outsiders to work their way into the Senate by popular approval or political manœuvre were usually frustrated.

As early as 150, the clash between the people and the Senate on the one hand and the magistrates and the Senate on the other, brought about certain modifications which were partly the result of the conquests of the third and second centuries B.C., and presently proved fatal to the republic.

In the past, Rome owed a great deal to its smaller land-owners and now as they sank deeper into what seemed to be ruin, the senatorial system of government was seriously attacked by Tiberius and Gaius Gracchus. The Senate glibly identified itself with the wealthy owners of big estates who were crowding out the small land-owners, and Gaius put forward a legislative programme to counter this. He began by challenging the dreaded *senatus consultum ultimum* and with his first plebiscite won back the old right of appeal. Step by step, he robbed the Senate of the power to dispense privileges and rights to its partisans and removed the means by which they cajoled or compelled obedience. Simultaneously came the first dole system of any consequence in history—the grain-dole to the poor.

The agrarian reforms of Gaius did not have any lasting effect but his political reforms continued to stir up conflicts right down to the time of Cæsar who once more revised the senatorial lists, increased the numbers to nine hundred and had such influence over the elections that he could more or less control the Senate. All the early Cæsars paid deference to the Senate in order to give their rule a respectable air, but they did not suffer too much at its hands.

The day of the omnipotent rule of the divine emperors was at hand. The real government of Rome passed out of the hands of republican institutions into the hands of imperial prefects and commissioners. Under the Empire, the senate was deprived of any real power and became a pawn in the hands of successive Emperors, some struggling ineffectually towards what they considered enlightened moral conduct, but many intoxicated with their dictatorial powers. The ranks of political informers and spies were swelled as these professions became profitable. Under the later days of the Republic they were 'encouraged to denounce plots against the State', but under Augustus, the promise of a share in confiscated property increased their activities and they were so busy denouncing enemies of the Emperor that no one was safe from their accusations. Politicians, nobles and wealthy men came under suspicion to the point where they must abandon public life, or suffer financial ruin. The poor were conciliated not by any increase of liberty or prosperity but by gratuitous distribution of corn and by public games.

The Roman Empire underwent widespread fluctuation during its long history but was, on the whole, stable and peaceful from the accession of Augustus (30 B.C.) until the third century. Augustus did in fact introduce a method of social organization which took some regard for the welfare of the people in the provinces, and all classes from poets to business men praised him and found universal peace a great convenience.

By the second century an extraordinary state of affairs had arisen in Rome itself. At least one-half of the population was living on public assistance and the class system governing all forms of behaviour was very carefully devised to represent the values of a society reconciling bloated wealth and terrible poverty. As Carcopino commented: 'The majority of what we should nowadays call the middle classes vegetated in semi-starvation within sight of the almost incredible opulence of a few thousand multi-millionaires.'[4] Simultaneously, free bread and circuses were provided to keep the plebs in their proper places and gladiatorial shows which reached a pitch of splendour and brutality unknown in the history of the world.

The third century brought disaster. The army began to abuse its position and raised one Emperor to power in return for money only to destroy him and substitute another for more money. In the end it lost its fighting effectiveness and when the barbarians from the north and east invaded Roman territory they could not check their plundering and marauding armies.

Once again it can be said that Roman social organization served the interests of a number of privileged classes and sometimes met the claims of the 'lower orders' in ways which varied from the satisfactory to the novel, from the expedient to the barbaric, but any conception that every individual born had a right to equal opportunities and equal treatment did not play an important part in its philosophy.

Politically, the Republic developed the principle of the Senate with elected senators and made some attempts at democratic programmes; legally the Empire revolutionized legal machinery and rose above national to international law. Where the Greeks failed to impose supra-national values on the highly individualized city states, Rome introduced international government for the first time and the power of unification to produce peace was revealed under Augustus.

At different stages of Roman history the extension of civic rights certainly formed part of the attempts at a democratic programme but as L. T. Hobhouse wrote: 'Politically [it] was not compatible with the structure of the city state and could only be carried out by the Empire under which its effect was civil, legal, social and financial—not political. Eventually, through military expenditure and financial ineptitude, the Imperial Society degenerated into a caste system which was a principal cause of its fall.'[5]

*   *   *   *

Seen in relation to the early beginnings of man, the achievements in social organization of the Greeks and Romans were considerable. It is a long way back, in one sense, to what Hobhouse called the primary group in early societies, but there are still primary groups in undeveloped parts of the world today. The primary group was 'often no more than a little group

numbering all told anything from a couple of dozen to four or
five score persons who live together or habitually meet, innocent
of differentiation except by age and sex, generally but not
always united by kinship and if not akin, intermarriageable.
Some such groups seem to live with little or no intercourse
with outsiders . . . but more often we find it in active relations
with neighbouring groups, visiting, exchanging gifts, meeting
for ceremonial purposes and in particular intermarrying on a
recognized system.'[6]

As social relations between primary groups develop they
become the concern of a wider community 'and eventually the
larger aggregate acquires a true government of its own and
reduces the primary group to a subordinate place'.[7] Each
primary group has its own rudimentary ideas of justice which
may resemble or coincide with those of other groups, but
these, by one means or another, are finally integrated with or
subjected to the ideals of government and justice of the wider
community.

As a tribe absorbs into itself a number of primary groups
it does not necessarily weaken the kinship tie. Either one
particular class dominates the rest, and its leader becomes
recognized as the hereditary chieftain, or the heads of each clan
may form a governing council. 'As a circle of intermarrying
clans forms a tribe, so a little group of tribes may allow intermarriage, cultivate peaceful intercourse and grow into a certain
unity without subordination of one to another. Acting together
in common dangers and aggression, they eventually need a king
but his power is held in check by the clans. The clan chiefs
form his council and all important decisions go before a meeting
of the clansmen.'[8]

The central defence point of these clans may grow into a
settled community which becomes a town and eventually a city,
and at last we approach the conditions which were a prerequisite of the Greek city state. There now arises a conception
of community more comprehensive than any clan or tribe,
'but resting not on common submission to a superior but on a
nexus of reciprocal rights and duties'. The civic idea of government has in fact emerged. In Greece and Italy it concerned a
'narrow strip of territory with a dominating urban centre', still
compact enough to allow 'a personal gathering of the adult
male citizens and direct government by the assembly in the last

resort'. The civic state is based upon the idea of mutual obligations between all the groups involved and 'is the first expression of the idea of the community as an organic harmony . . . or partnership', based in turn on 'the rational will of free men and satisfying the true demands of nature'.

Thus a certain evolution of political organization up to and beyond the Greek city state can be classified in L. T. Hobhouse's terms. First, the 'little communities of kinsfolk and neighbours of high solidarity [which allow] little scope for development'. Second, a coming together of kinship groups into bigger tribes and communities involving subordination to more general principles. Third, a community subject to a chieftain or king where subordination has been ritualized. Fourth, the first attempts at the civic state 'in which the common life begins to rely on moral force and the willing co-operation of free men'. Such communities arose in ancient Greece and in the Middle Ages but were limited to city states. Fifth, the development of this principle on the national scale to involve a whole country or nation in civic contracts and responsibilities. The Roman Empire carried the same principle over into international affairs and we today are attempting to realize a similar extension.

Within these broad divisions a whole network of duties, obligations and rights was modified or enlarged and societies radically changed by forces which are too complex to analyse here.

Class distinction or differentiation of status played a very big rôle in determining the rights and duties of different groups. The simplest primitive communities knew no difference of status apart from distinctions of age, sex and possibly kinship, but as we advance in the complexity of social organization, distinctions begin to multiply. 'The chief acquires definite power', and if 'his office is hereditary his family shares his rank. Prominent men become privileged nobles and perhaps landowners. Industrial classes arise by the side of tillers of the soil; serfs and slaves come into being through war, conquest and trade . . . and hereditary castes are formed. . . .'[9]

The community, in its more developed phases, makes a series of demands on the individual to subordinate himself to social order and there seems to be a correlation between an increasing differentiation of social rank and a growing complexity of economic life.

N   183

If the 'archaic structure of the village maintains much of the old equality' as Hobhouse says, the kings, nobles and organized priesthood have overall authority and political, military and economic development tend to increase distinction of rank and privilege.

Against what seem to be the blind forces of social development the Greek democrats did make a stand. They set out 'to establish an equality of civic and political rights for all males who were personally free', and the matter did not end there. The Stoic ethic presently evolved to supersede the principles of the city state and it asserted the natural equality of all men. When Christianity arose it, too, claimed that all men were 'alike as sons of God', and if, in practice, people like St Augustine made some very remarkable exceptions, the Church came at last to range itself on the side of a partnership in the common good. St Thomas Aquinas expressed the view that liberty was the right of the members of the community to be ruled in their own interest.

However, when the ruling person came to be acknowledged as the representative of God the limitation on political action was concentrated in one person whose spiritual guidance should have kept his behaviour within limits prescribed by the moral teaching of the church of his day. This proved hopelessly inadequate. The substitution of a contract, in medieval days, between the ruler and the ruled, worked reasonably well in the hands of men like Manegold of Lautenbach, but badly in the hands of others.

In the Middle Ages the *lex regia* of Roman law was interpreted to mean that when the people set up a ruler they should define the limits of his powers and here began the idea of constitutional government, which was to have profound repercussions.

Magna Carta was thought to have changed the relationship between the ruler and the ruled dramatically. Theoretically it established the principle that a man could not be held under arrest indefinitely without a charge being preferred against him, trial by jury and the right of parliament to control taxation. Some modern scholars have suggested that the charter was drawn up mainly in the interests of the barons and a number of carefully chosen clauses included to attract general support. Certainly those who drafted the charter were at great pains to include not only baronial demands, but administrative reforms, and if it is difficult to tell which of their mixed motives became dominant, they did not exclude dis-interested ones.

In this very brief survey there is no room to deal elaborately with the political organization of feudal times. Those who believe in a caste system would have found the sharp distinctions between baron and squire, peasant and serf very satisfactory, but the political philosophy which believed that only the élite should be educated and such an élite largely selected on the hereditary principle is difficult to reconcile with modern know-ledge. The serf had far more duties than he had rights. In exchange for a minimum security he was expected to render extravagant service to his lord; the social machinery for re-dressing grievances was heavily weighted against him; above all, without any democratic rights, without any vote or power of voicing his opinion in matters of government he was politically impotent, and when he did try to organize and express his grievances by small-scale revolts against isolated castles he was quickly and brutally overwhelmed. In short, the concept that all men were alike as sons of God did not have any equi-valent in his earthly treatment.

Theoretically, the Middle Ages, largely as the result of the rediscovery of Aristotle, presented three lofty principles of government which did not seem to work out in practice. Government must be for the common good, it must be repre-sentative of the community, and whatever authority was exercised must be derived from the community. Under the influence of Aristotle and driven by some mistaken passion for unity, the Middle Ages adopted monarchy as the best expression of these principles and despite Magna Carta, did not stop to ask whether each appointed King conformed to any concept of goodness. Presently, sharper distinctions were made between a political and regal régime. Gradually, in Europe, the King came to dominate one country after another as absolute monarch, and England at last succumbed to the same principle under the Tudors and the Stuarts.

Between 1450 and 1600 the biggest revolution in terms of social organization was the rise of the nation state, headed in many countries by an absolute monarch. The enclosed Medi-terranean community of the Middle Ages gradually extended to embrace America and Asia and the rise of the nation-states involved a modification, if not decline in the power of those two great international institutions of medieval Europe, the Holy Roman Empire and the Papacy. What some historians refer to as the medieval synthesis was shattered by the combined effect of the Reformation and the Renaissance.

By the sixteenth century the whole machinery of political organization and justice was undergoing refinement but the results in the seventeenth century were not very happy. The story of the rise of democracy is a long and tortuous one which ranges as far back as 1640 and does not reach its climax until 1918. Macaulay in his *Essay on Milton* wrote: 'He lived at one of the most memorable eras in the history of mankind, at the very crisis of the great conflict between liberty and despotism, reason and prejudice. The great battle was fought for no single generation, for no single land. The destinies of the human race were staked on the same case with the freedom of the English people. Then were first proclaimed those mighty principles which have since worked their way into the depths of the American forests, which have aroused Greece from the slavery and degradation of two thousand years and which have kindled an unquenchable fire in the hearts of the oppressed and loosed the knees of the oppressors with an unwonted fear.'

Macaulay, in rhetorical mood, overstates the case. It remains true that John Milton's writings epitomized the spirit of his age. The development of Magna Carta and the Common Law, fertilized by the Renaissance and the Reformation, inspired a number of sects, some deeply religious, to propagate the democratic faith in the seventeenth century. The revolutionary movement was enlivened by the spiritual devotion and fearless efforts of countless individuals and groups scattered over Western Europe who worked to spread and develop the ideas of liberty and equality. In his 'Defense of the People of England' Milton wrote: 'No man who knows aught can be so stupid to deny that all men naturally were born free, being the image and resemblance of God himself . . . it being thus manifest that the power of kings and magistrates is nothing else but what is only derivative, transferred and committed to them in trust from the people, to the common good of them all.'

Presently England developed the spirit of rationalism and liberalism and John Locke expounded these principles in his *Two Treatises of Government* and *Letters on Toleration*. Locke formulated the two great basic ideas: 'that the foundation of all social life consists in the liberty, dignity and happiness of individuals' and that 'government is a moral trust dependent upon the free consent of the governed'. In these comparatively early days, England was the only European country which broke the power of absolutism, and the affairs of the nation slowly passed not only into the hands of a parliament, but one in which the House of Commons came to dominate the scene as the electorate steadily widened. Presently, the power of judges was separated from the political sphere, a Bill of Rights protected the liberties of the individual and the broadening sense of tolerance at last broke into and overwhelmed a number of forms of censorship.

These movements in Britain had reverberations throughout the world. In the virgin soil of the American colonies where there were no classes or institutions surviving from a feudal past, the new ideas took quick root. Tom Paine's pamphlets 'Common Sense' and 'The Crisis', the writings of the French Encyclopædists and Jean-Jacques Rousseau all encouraged the spread of natural rights, the rule of reason and the freedom of the individual in America and France. Thomas Jefferson, deeply influenced by the Encyclopædists, drafted the Declaration of Independence and the American Revolution reacted on France, which saw in America a wonderful example of a people who had broken away from the yoke of an unjust monarch. There followed that bloody and gigantic upheaval in European affairs, the French Revolution, which carried its influence throughout the whole of Europe and expressed the essence of the new faith in three great principles: the right to liberty of every living person, the equality of all men and the common sense of brotherhood.

One after another a number of reactionary governments in Western Europe were overwhelmed or qualified by the new principles, the United States of America became a proudly democratic republic and the tide finally ran over into that tremendous convulsion of Slav peoples, the Russian Revolution of March 1917.

It was clearly seen only by a handful of people that the political institution of democracy carried profound economic implications. The early revolutions in England of the seventeenth century and of France and America in the eighteenth century, had their inspiration in the middle classes, and they served to challenge, among other things, the feudal basis of an economy which restricted the liberties of the individual in economic development. In the beginning little was done to extend political into economic democracy but the new cries of liberty and equality awakened people to material possibilities of which they had never before dreamt. It needed a number of intellectuals among the middle and upper classes to realize that democracy would remain a hollow sham for what they referred to as The Masses, unless the fine gestures of political freedom were translated into economic realities.

The origins of modern capitalism are widely disputed among historians. The code of economic conduct involved in capitalism conflicted seriously with the accepted social ethics of the seventeenth century. As Tawney asked: 'What influence nerved [the innovators] to defy tradition? From what source did they derive the principles to replace it?' The conventional answer to these questions involved the exportation of precious metals from America in the sixteenth century, the growth of population, technological invention and improvement and the reaction of expanding markets on industrial organization.

Weber later pointed out that these conditions had existed in the past without producing capitalism. He then gave his own explanation of its origins. The men who led the new economic orders were *parvenus* who forced their way to the front braced by the Protestant view of a calling or vocation, which sanctioned the application of all energy and talents to whatever a man thought was his calling in life. As Tawney later put it: 'This conception wielded into a disciplined force the still feeble *bourgeoisie*, heightened its energies and cast a halo of sanctification around its convenient vices. What is significant, in short, is not the strength of the motive of economic self-interest which is the commonplace of all ages and demands no explanation. It is the change of moral standards which converted a natural frailty into an ornament of the spirit. . . .'[10]

Tawney qualified this in *Religion and the Rise of Capitalism* where he said that the capitalist movement 'owed as much to changes in economic and political organization, as it did to developments in the sphere of religious thought'.[11]

Whatever its precise cause, capitalism came to dominate the economic organization of industrialized Europe and presently

188

to reveal a number of shortcomings. Various forces arose to challenge its unqualified authority. The Chartists formulated a programme which included universal suffrage, annual elections to Parliament, and indemnities for parliamentarians, but their hope of realizing a *complete* democracy was undermined by a lack of emphasis on economic reform.

The socialist movement in France in the 1840s finally codified its demands in the Communist Manifesto of 1848 which insisted that true democracy was a contradiction in terms while a bourgeois society enabled a handful of capitalists who owned the means of production, exchange and distribution to exploit the wage-earners.

The great modern conflict was now out in the open. A third factor, characteristic of the British spirit of compromise, produced democratic socialism, a form of government which has undergone, like Marxism and capitalism, a variety of modifications until its critics complain that in its modern exponent, Hugh Gaitskell, it became indistinguishable from conservatism.

Three questions must now be faced. Have forms of government progressed in creating the conditions best calculated to realize the highest potential of the whole population, irrespective of class or creed? How do the rival claims of capitalism, democratic socialism and Communism compare today? Is democracy the best form of government?

In the most general terms, social organization in the past emphasized the interests of either the ruling class or the wealthy, the privileged or the influential. Athens offered a form of democracy which we cannot challenge today, but as we have repeatedly seen, it served a limited minority. Rome served the interests of special classes under quite different conditions. There was a time, in Rome, when former slaves made up the greater part of the Roman Cabinet under Claudius, but power was merely shifted from one ruling class to another without widespread dispersal or general representation. In the days of absolute monarchs, the Kings themselves lived in the jungle of court feuds and merciless vendettas characteristic of royal politics and sometimes were no more secure than the veriest slave but, while they ruled, they generally put the interests of a limited minority before that of the mass of the people. There were of course exceptions, but not many.

Ancient philosophers saw in democracy the paradox that the governed were in some mysterious way also the governors and this caused Aristotle to consider it the lowest form of legitimate government. The evolution of modern democracy is interlocked with the struggle to find some means of limiting political authority when it fails to serve the common good. From the earliest days of western civilization this struggle has found several resolutions. Its development suffered a serious setback with the rise of absolute monarchies but a number of theorists at last devised a means of applying constitutional laws to self-government.

Closely linked with the idea of limiting authority was the idea of political and social equality in a democracy. Social equality did not mean that all men were socially equal in all ways. It meant that distinction of birth or money did not give special political powers or privileges before the law. It remained to devise a satisfactory method of electing representatives and to determine the period for which they were entitled to rule without consulting the electorate. Various forms of suffrage came into operation. At different times all manner of qualifications have conditioned who has the power to vote, from commonplace discrimination by age and sex to more complicated laws of property, wealth and social standing. Full democracy did not come into operation in Britain until 1930 when women were given the vote for the first time at the age of twenty-one. America followed suit, and one after another western European countries matured into full-scale suffrage. Meanwhile, the three great arms of government—legislative, executive and judicial, otherwise, in England, the House of Commons, Civil Service and the Law—which had once been vested in one body and as such were open to serious abuse, had now split irreparably and each functioned in relation to, but independently of, the other, or so it was believed. Bagehot demolished the classical theory of the separation of powers in the British Constitution. According to him, behind the façade of separatism real power was concentrated in the Cabinet in which the executive and legislative functions were once more merged. In turn R. H. S. Crossman has recently demolished Bagehot. Crossman argued, in his introduction to a new edition of Bagehot's *The English Constitution*, that the Cabinet, like the Houses of Lords and Commons, was just another part of the façade with the 'efficient secret' of power resting today in the rule of the Prime Minister.

Despite Bagehot and Crossman, it seemed that we had come a long way from the primitive attempts at government which marked man's early beginnings and we had half-realized the dream of government of the people for the people by the people, but democracy at work revealed certain shortcomings. It is the paradox of the search for the equitable distribution of power that it cunningly defeats our ends at the very point where we seem to have made it minutely available to every individual.

We have, today, in England, achieved complete franchise and every man and woman can wield a vote at the age of twenty-one, but the vast increase in population and the complexity of the social machine reduces the average individual to a pin-point whose effect on sudden crises where his life, family and profession are mercilessly at stake is less than the mote floating helplessly in the beam of light. There is, again, the lethargy and indifference of the majority of voters. This is not so marked in general as local elections but it still means that elected representatives are not backed by the electorate as a whole. In local elections, as few as fifty per cent may vote, which means that local councillors are the elected representatives of a half-breed democracy which does not do justice to its underlying principles.

Within the political parties the inevitable imperfections of the democratic process under modern conditions are self-evident. The views expressed by a delegate at the Annual Labour Party Conference may correspond to the views of only a minority of the actual members of the party in that area. Similarly, it is possible for the Annual Conference to give its massive vote in favour of one course of action only to find itself in head-on collision with the much smaller, much less representative caucus of the Parliamentary Labour Party, and it has been known for the views of the Parliamentary Party to prevail.

In the case of the Conservative Party, although different resolutions are debated and voted on at Annual Conferences, the items included in an election manifesto are not necessarily the result of a majority vote.

Similarly, the trade unions had their caucus troubles which allowed militant minorities to work patiently and persistently in such a way that the democratic principle was undermined and a tiny minority, forceful, articulate and highly trained, seized control of a specific union of which they could not remotely claim to be representative.

Precisely similar troubles in the American Senate and Congress, aggravated by the existence of lobbying tactics far more efficient, rich and powerful than anything in the British House of Commons, re-emphasize the primitive nature of modern democracy. It is indisputable that rich and privileged minorities sometimes succeed in turning the democratic machine to private purposes and there are occasions when the power of Committees like the Rules Committee in the American House of Representatives can delay and defeat enlightened legislation in a way all too familiar to President Kennedy. While Sam Rayburn was Speaker of the House of Representatives he held unparalleled sway over its activities and under his persuasion the Rules Committee was enlarged from twelve to fifteen members and liberalized to the point where it ceased to be an implacable stumbling-block in the face of progressive legislation. Until then it was possible for the Southern members of the Rules Committee, in combination with the Republican minority members, deliberately to direct progressive bills into the arms of conservative Committees who were bound to reject them. When Rayburn died it seemed to sound the knell of any further liberal measures. Inevitably the three new members of the Rules Committee would not be replaced when re-election occurred, and the Rules Committee must sink back into the conservative mould of its original eleven members. In practice this did not happen, but the whole process is fraught with tactical dangers and subtleties which sometimes threaten to distort the democratic machinery.

In terms of cultural progress it is argued by the opponents of democracy that it tends to exploit the sheer weight of numbers to very bad ends as when newspapers vie with one another to achieve bigger and bigger circulations by appealing to the lowest common denominator and the test of television programmes becomes not their quality, but the size of the audience. Culture subsidized by mass votes is, in their view, in danger of becoming debased.

All these carpings must be seen in the perspective of democracy's tremendous—if not overwhelming—achievements, which are too familiar to need restatement. The rights and liberties of the individual under democracy are legally protected;

he has freedom of movement, expression and religion; he has free education, and an approximation to equal opportunities; he does not go in fear of arbitrary arrest; he can try to introduce himself as a political candidate at the local or national level and no one will imprison him if he chooses to challenge and criticize the very principles which give him this enriched way of life. So much more can be said in democracy's favour, but it is all so familiar to the western mind that the case can be taken for granted. It is a case which makes democracy by far the most successful and acceptable form of government to the present writer.

There remain two fundamental questions which have troubled some political theorists of the day. Is a democracy which stops short at social and political equality enough, or should it develop to include economic equality before it can be said to be a true democracy? Is there not a danger that the attempt to achieve social equality can be frustrated by wide economic differences, social classes being replaced by monied classes? British and American economies, derived from nineteenth-century *laissez-faire* theories, allowed employers, owners and industrial entrepreneurs to pursue their private objectives without state interference. This resulted in very wide variations of possessions, wealth and earning power which critics of pure, unbridled capitalism regarded as far too extreme.

It was once the policy of the British Labour Party to nationalize basic industries and to introduce a test of public service into the large areas which would remain under private enterprise. The precise balance of this mixed economy underwent radical changes when Hugh Gaitskell led the party, but democratic socialism remains a compromise between the business-man's free enterprise as represented by American capitalism, and the state-planned and some believe cold-blooded methods of Communism.

Some of the underlying principles of British democratic socialism have now been absorbed by the Conservative Party but if they accept a nationalized coal industry, a welfare state and a national health service, at many levels they have been busy over the last ten years restoring what they regard as 'freedom' to fields like rent restriction and recent studies have shown a growing concentration of wealth in fewer hands.

Certainly the theories of Marx have not borne fruit in

England. There has been no violent clash between the classes leading to revolution, but it must be said that he thought England one of the few countries where revolution was unnecessary. The British workers' increased share of the national income over the past twenty years is also in flat contradiction to the prediction of Marx that wages would fall to a dangerously low point where violence became a possibility.

The whole question of how far the system now operating in the Soviet Union itself is genuinely Marxist becomes very interesting because both Marx and Engels detested injustice and were concerned to free the proletariat from certain classes of restriction which now seem characteristic of some sides of Soviet life.

Marxism, one culmination of the search for a political system which would lead to government of the people by the people for the people, has been converted in Russia into a system resembling, in some respects, the oligarchies of ancient days but with quite different intentions, and the principle of democratic equality seems to have overreached itself and become unrecognizable.

Marx, as we have seen, propounded three great doctrines: the materialist conception of history which said that events were economically determined in a series of synthesizing developments; the labour theory of value which did not see why the surplus value of any product should be redistributed in the form of profits, dividends or unearned income to people who took no part in production; and the class struggle which saw a permanent clash between the interests of the proletariat, the *bourgeoisie* and the working-class until such time as a 'truly socialist state' had been achieved. In theory, Marxism set out to carry the principle of economic equality into final effect, but in practice it seemed to work out very differently. As Leonard Schapiro, Reader in Russian Government and Politics at the University of London, has said—'the Russian system, with its present defects, seems to have nothing to do with Marx'.

There is no doubt that the present Russian Government has improved the economic lot of the average worker and the old spectres of hunger and unemployment no longer persist. Housing conditions are still crowded and the general standard of living below that of America or England, but people are fed, clothed and housed better than they were under the old corrupt régime of the Czars. At the materialist level, which so concerned Marx and Engels, the Soviet state is reasonably successful and it has to be remembered that the abrupt, revolutionary change from the hereditary to the communistic principle of government is still relatively recent.

By emphasizing the comparative youth of this gigantic experiment in human affairs, Russian apologists seek to justify the limitations and restrictions which undermine the Soviet way of life in western eyes. Any young revolutionary movement, they claim, must exercise austere control until full maturity enables the correct relaxations envisaged by Marx, and, in any case, since the death of Stalin, such relaxations have become widely operative under Khrushchev.

It was Friedrich Engels who made the classic statement that 'freedom is the consciousness of necessity'. This definition is part of the official propaganda in the Soviet Union and other Communist countries. The *Soviet Political Dictionary* defines freedom as consisting 'not in any supposed independence of man from natural and social laws but in the possibility of understanding and utilizing those laws. . . . In the conditions of an antagonistic society the elemental character of social development does not give man the chance to develop his activity freely, but makes him the slave of necessity. Only communist society implies the transition of man from the realm of necessity to the realm of freedom.'

As Dr John Keep has commented: 'This outlook leaves no room for individual freedom in the western sense of the term. Communists acknowledge that "bourgeois" democratic political and civil liberties played a positive rôle in the rise of capitalism. But they are not deemed to have an intrinsic value in themselves and the degree of their implementation depends on the current exigencies of the class struggle. At present, the argument runs, where such liberties exist in the "imperialist" world they merely serve as an instrument in the hands of the exploiting class to dupe the masses into accepting its rule. Only under socialism do the people enjoy real liberty, of a superior quality than bourgeois freedom, for the constitution of the socialist states assures the citizens basic liberties (of speech, press, assembly, conscience, etc.).'[12]

Unfortunately these freedoms can only be exercised within

the Marxist philosophy. It is possible to criticize the detail of Communist planning in the interests of greater efficiency but the Communist plan itself is sacred and must not be challenged. It is as if we, in Britain, said—you may challenge the details of the Conservative Party's programme, but if you challenge the philosophy of conservatism you are liable to go to gaol. Since the Communists believe that any other system than Marxism is a criminal device for exploiting the masses, it is easy to understand why they relegate criticism to an internal rôle and have what we would regard as heavy penalties for any infringement of party policy. Indeed, past history gives them certain justifications for regarding some governments in this light, but they are even more powerfully opposed to what they regard as half-breed concepts like democratic socialism as represented by the British Labour Party.

Freedom of the printed word is tolerated in the Soviet Union provided it falls within the prescribed Marxist framework. In the western sense of the word this is not freedom at all. 'Marxist-Leninists have always regarded the press as a mighty weapon in the struggle for men's minds,' and in his address to writers and artists published in May 1962, Mr Khrushchev said their task was 'to educate the people in the spirit of Communist ideals'. This would 'awaken in them a sense of admiration for all that is beautiful in our socialist reality and inspire men to devote all their strength, knowledge and aptitudes to selfless service to their people . . . and make them implacable foes of all anti-social and negative elements in life'.

In May 1961, the official organ of the Central Committee published an article by P. Romashkin which dealt with the crucial question of the 'withering away of the state'. 'The party is striving for . . . a growth of the Communist consciousness of all members of society to the level of the vanguard. . . .' It 'is a task which is not less difficult but more difficult than the task of creating the technical and material basis of Communism. . . . Moreover until the historic task of constructing Communism has been accomplished it must be said of the Soviet state as well that it must not be weakened. . . .'

As Leonard Schapiro comments: 'Romashkin does not explain how the state should both wither away as Communism approaches and not be allowed to weaken. I fear, moreover, that Marx and Engels might raise an eyebrow at the suggestion that for the working-class to attain Communist consciousness will require longer than for the material bases of Communism to be constructed.'[13]

Perhaps this is not to take enough regard of empirical Marxism which learns by experience and modifies the original philosophy where it fails to work, but such theories can so easily become a cloak for a deliberate attempt to sustain a caucus in power.

When we remember the complexity of human life and values, when we recall the long and painful attempt to break open the secrets of social organization which have promised so much and led to endless suffering and confusion down the ages, there is a kind of arrogance in the political absolutism of Russia which it is hard to swallow. In the heady rush of his sociological discoveries Marx, who professed to study society scientifically and simultaneously indulged a messianic vision of the liberation of the workers, was full of contradictions, but it is doubtful whether his spirit rests easily today if intimations of what his disciples have done penetrate to whatever place he now inhabits.

*   *   *   *

There has been progress in political organization and representative institutions in western Europe. There has been progress in understanding the way in which social organization works. It has enabled many average men to reach new stature as individuals, but the picture, as usual, is very uneven. Some countries are more advanced than others. There are signs of a throwback in certain societies and men like De Gaulle are really benevolent autocrats disguised as democrats. Above all, in eastern Europe, the passionate denunciation of capitalist evils has reached that quasi-religious pitch where the facts are not too clearly seen and a new caucus government with a blind belief in its own infallibility sometimes seems to behave like the religious oppressors of old. The search for the realization of the Common Man has reproduced the age-old paradox: some revolutionaries among us reveal the tyrannical possibilities of their past enemies.

The modest attempt of democratic socialism to assimilate the best characteristics of capitalism and socialism in a form of government which does not censor the press, or freedom of speech, which does not send men to gaol for holding beliefs contrary to state beliefs, but which expects public interest to come before private profit and places the common before private good, does not flourish. The strong colours of capitalism and Communism are more attractive than the neutral compromise of democratic socialism. And we are a long way yet from that political golden age of which so many philosophers have dreamt.

CHAPTER NINE

Have we progressed?

IT is intellectually unfashionable today to have a philosophy of history. As R. V. Sampson wrote in his *Progress in the Age of Reason*: 'In the Anglo-Saxon historical tradition the term philosophy in relation to history is suggestive of a dangerous predisposition to erect systems of ideas on inadequate empirical evidence.' Von Ranke believed that the work of the true historian should be confined to establishing the facts without interpretation of any kind. H. A. L. Fisher put forward his famous proposition that he could not associate himself with those fortunate scholars who had succeeded in finding a pattern in history. Linked with these ideas goes the particular one with which this book began: that any belief in progress must be a romantic delusion.

We lived in an age of disillusion. The exuberant optimism of the early H. G. Wells was suddenly converted at the end of his life into the gloomy pessimism of *Mind at the End of its Tether*. The excited promise of steadily developing progress at all levels in the late nineteenth century collapsed under the brutalities of World Wars I and II. Arthur Koestler wrote in his autobiography: 'Since the end of the eighteenth century the place of God has been vacant in our civilization. . . . Now, however, after the shattering catastrophes which have brought the Age of Reason and Progress to a close, the void has made itself felt.'[1]

Early in the twentieth century Nicolas Berdyaev had written: '. . . we still go on with our endless tedious discussions about progress and reaction, just as though everything in the world had not been turned upside down and as though our old criteria had not lost every shred of significance.'

Such wholesale pessimism not only seems a little premature; it does not give us an accurate answer to the general question: Who precisely is it that disbelieves in progress today? Views still vary widely according to class, education, profession and upbringing, and no general picture is possible without the help of a sociological survey.

Moreover, as R. V. Sampson points out, at least two of the current political philosophies are derivative from the very Age of Enlightenment which meets with such widespread ridicule: the Marxists and what he labels rather vaguely as the Liberal Progressivists. As Sampson puts it: 'If the latter school are the direct descendants of the *philosophes*, the Marxists are no less the children of the eighteenth century. Marx attempted to achieve for the nineteenth-century proletariat what the Voltaireans had accomplished for the eighteenth-century *bourgeoisie*.'[2]

The New Pessimists have an immediate answer: Marxists and Liberal Progressives are now no less outdated than the lofty protestations of Comte, Fourier and Condorcet. In short, against the history of the last fifty years, the conceptual categories known as progress and reaction have ceased, in this view, to have any validity, whether in Marxist or Liberal Progressive terms. They have become, in fact, meaningless. Such an outlook, 'enunciated in innumerable books and periodicals, is closely paralleled by a revival of emotional faith and mass evangelism at a more popular level'.[3]

The Age of Reason, according to this analysis, has failed to fulfil its promise and the old gods associated with the Age of Faith are once more in the ascendant. Not only progress has been washed away but with it the old ideas derived from Darwin. Professor Julian Huxley wrote in his book *Evolution*: 'The purpose manifested in evolution, whether in adaptation, specialization or biological progress, is only an apparent purpose. It is just as much a product of blind forces as is the falling of a stone to earth or the ebb and flow of the tides. It is we who have read purpose into evolution, as, earlier, men projected will and emotion into inorganic phenomena like storm or earthquake. If we wish to work towards a purpose for the future of man, we must formulate that purpose ourselves. Purposes in life are made and not found.'[4]

So evolutionism, too, is dead. Societies and civilizations are not necessarily evolving and historians had better acknowledge the shortcomings of their trade and stop trying to trace development in the manner of the Enlightenment.

The proper exercise of the historian's function and his rôle in intellectual life have been examined more recently in a series of polemics between men like Toynbee, Trevor-Roper, Taylor, Berlin, Carr, Geyl, and Namier, but even when the dust had subsided and the clash of one colourful personality on another ceased, no one satisfactory definition emerged. Carr carried his thorny determinism into the heart of the enemy's camp, only to have Trevor-Roper protest that accident played a much more important part than Carr would allow; Berlin, locked in eloquent grapple with Carr, did not know whether determinism was false but defended the proposition that the individual can be responsible for his actions, and the remote and highly respected Geyl continued to stand by the famous passage in his book, *Napoleon*, which concluded with the uplifting thought that 'History is indeed an argument without end'.

It is difficult to stand against the weight of the arguments which seem to crush progress into a corner reserved for intellectual follies of the past, and some of them must be accepted, but first, they do not overwhelm the case which has been made out in the preceding chapters of this book for a qualified form of progress in certain fields, and second, a new definition of Progress still leaves that term very much alive.

*   *   *   *

It is possible to give so many interpretations of history, some static, some anti-progressive, some progressive pure and simple and some full of qualified ideas of progress, but few, if any, survive close scrutiny.

Considering what we mean by civilizations in general terms, two broad but mutually exclusive interpretations are worth a quick glance. There was the theory that within each self-contained society certain trends in law, morals, and social organization could be traced, creating a tradition which proceeded independently of any other tradition and therefore could not lead to any general enrichment or degeneracy. There was, with this theory, no cross-fertilization except perhaps in the religious field. Thus civilizations rose and fell in splendid isolation and there could be no general progress.

Professor Gordon Childe's excursions into prehistory and archæology seem to contradict this and he has clearly shown not only that there was a continuity between the civilizations of the ancient East, but that 'the links between these centres of civilization and the European barbarisms of prehistory are also more or less definitely established'. It is commonplace that Greek thought deeply influenced Renaissance England and that we ourselves have basic laws derived in part from the Romans.

If there are different traditions following a highly individualized course in different civilizations and no one steadily progressing international stream, these separate traditions do not always run to seed without first cross-fertilizing one another. It may happen: it may not. The picture of one culture integrating elements from another, sometimes beneficially, sometimes injuriously, becomes very complex. It may lead to development or syncretism. It may accelerate decline or growth. In the modern world, the interconnexions have developed enormously and, as we shall see, there are now extraordinary underlying identities between cultures which seem, on the surface, savagely opposed. In the world today, where intellectual anarchy is much more evident than in the past because of the diversification of knowledge, we can yet find definitions of progress which correspond in opposing societies.

Professor Carr in his latest book *What Is History?* describes progress as 'the progressive development of human potentialities, moving towards the right goals'. When we ask what are the right goals the brilliantly lucid Professor becomes ambiguous and we read that such goals 'can be defined only as we advance towards them and [their] validity . . . verified only in the process of attaining them'.

Professor Ginsberg is much more precise and interesting in his definition of the theory of human progress and has more sharply penetrated the emotional haze which surrounds the word progress today than any living thinker I can recall. It is his belief that 'there has been development in the efforts of men to gain knowledge and to organize human relations: that with this development we can trace certain trends which are either themselves progressive or show the possibilities of progress, as judged by ethical criteria; and that to turn these possibilities into actualities is to follow in the line of progress'.[5]

Professor Ginsberg believes in the possibility of applying a rational ethic to human affairs and by rational ethic he means an ethic 'based on a knowledge of human needs and potentialities. . . .' It would involve 'principles of justice . . . designed to exclude arbitrary power and to secure an equitable distribution of the conditions of well-being'.[6]

What are the factors which have changed our approach to and definition of progress today? In the first place, man's power to interfere with natural processes has increased to the point where he is no longer the victim of overwhelming natural forces and the old conception of tragedy can be challenged in a manner which would have astounded Plato and left even the visionary Condorcet agape with admiration. We can stop plagues decimating our cities, we can anticipate the weather, we can control the number of our children, make mechanical forces take the place of once exhausting physical labour, interfere with economic processes to prevent slumps and booms and we have recently cracked the genetic code in such a way that the control of human characteristics may, within our lifetime, become a reality. More than ever before man has the power to take charge of his own destiny and the old ideas of progress have to be recast in that light.

What have we found in the more specific areas investigated in this book? In one sense unexpected conclusions have been reached. As we have seen, it is commonly assumed among many modern intellectuals that progress is still a romantic myth and yet at the material, penal, moral, medical and religious levels, at the level of female emancipation, and to some extent social organization and freedom of thought, it seems, from our brief analysis, as if progress has a qualified reality in Western Europe, although no one is deluded into believing that a single straightforward line can clearly be plotted. The line, if a line exists at all, is neurotically disturbed.

There is no discoverable law of progress, but there is something in man which makes him set out to attempt to better his lot. This may, on occasion, lead him hopelessly astray, and in his wildly contradictory attempts man has sometimes run into cul-de-sacs comparable with those which occurred in evolution when the giant mastodons could develop no more and were overwhelmed and died. Contrary to cynical belief, man has learned from some experiences in history, and now, for the first time, has the power to interfere with his apparent destiny in such a way that he may succeed in injecting a higher degree of progress than we have ever known before. That is the possibility; not yet by any means the reality; but what exactly do we mean by progress?

In terms of these last chapters I am using the word progress to mean the development of Western civilizations in the desirable direction of creating those conditions which will realize the best potential in mankind. Immediately the question arises—what is the best potential? The best potential may vary with the needs of the day, but the mass of ordinary people might agree that it would involve realizing to the full, all those talents and capacities which contribute to the well-being of self and society. This enormous concept must involve equality of opportunity for education and jobs, equality before the law, freedom of movement and opinion, common rights for all humanity in many different fields and the encouragement of those qualities of intelligence, feeling, generosity, imagination and sensitivity which extend the boundaries of self-interest to involve the interests of others.

Obviously no clear-cut arrow-head of progress is driving immutably towards any such idealistic goal. The trouble, in fact, with progress is simple and self-evident. As one current in a given civilization moves in a desirable direction, another may set out cunningly to thwart it. There are many conflicting currents. For instance the laws, customs, morals and religion of a given civilization may have reached different stages of development, as in Britain today, and produce different influences. The morally enlightened regard homosexuality in a quite different light from the law, and custom in sexual relationships is more relaxed than the law admits. On the other hand, the ideals of a community may derive from religious roots and resist the pressures of scientific enlightenment towards its kind of moral progress. Comte, in short, remains vividly contemporary. The advance in different fields of thought and behaviour in a given community is at different rates. Even the 'sciences' reach the positive stage—'the stage in which theoretical construction and empirical verification are duly balanced and correct each other'—at different times. The situation becomes even more complex when modes of thought based on outdated knowledge persist in a modern environment of enlightenment.

Today, the tendency is for many of these factors to compromise with and converge on one another, and as we better understand the way in which men arrive at their attitudes, as knowledge explains the basis of prejudice, belief and behaviour, the chances of coming to a common understanding of what is meant by progress should grow. Ginsberg has written: 'The case for progress rests on the fact that in the course of historical development some degree of progress has definitely been achieved, that various possibilities of synthesis have been opened out and on the hope that with the advance of social knowledge and moral insight, the causes making for discrepancies or one-sidedness in development may be discovered and brought increasingly under control.'[7]

What of the principle that every progressive step brings with it disadvantages which neutralize true progress? Today we build gigantic cities offering a wealth of artistic and intellectual life, full of diverse activities in which the most abstruse and popular interests can find satisfaction and presently those cities are choked with a monstrous mass of traffic and noise and unexpected hazards assail the unwary citizen. We tame and enslave nature in the form of great masses of machinery which removes the exhausting burden of physical labour only to find the burden of monotonously repetitive jobs introducing a different kind of psychic staleness. We brilliantly flash moving pictures into myriads of homes employing technical skills which would seem to our forefathers sheer magic, only to interlard every other image with nauseous advertising ditties. The extraordinary fusion of the world by means of communication undreamt of in the past has led to the 'debasement' of mass media until every instinctual appetite is fed with a semi-respectable, semi-cheesecake substitute for real satisfaction. The uniform mass culture of television sometimes replaces local cultures in which men and women played an active part—in amateur dramatics, operatic societies, recitals, play-readings—and reduces millions of people to ciphers who stare at westerns, horse operas and vaudeville with the passivity of sleepwalkers, where before they shared in the creative process. The debasement by ad men of the appeal to the commonplace need for entertainment has riddled the world with pulp books, cheap advertisements and superficial satisfactions which debase the simpler appetites into profit-making pawns. The uses of literacy have been sold to ever-increasing newspaper circulations and the staccato stimulus of news-headlines and comic strips. The development of myriad devices for comfort has, in some eyes, reduced the sheer physique of human beings to a flabby softness where our former powers of physical endurance are rapidly diminishing. The emphasis on brain and talent, on higher education and intellectual pursuits has seriously multiplied the number of neurotics and psychotics, and the sheer tempo of modern life with its wild rush-hour tensions and its appeals to multiple appetites has, for the pessimistic, created a whole new category of conflicts.

The picture is, of course, not merely grossly exaggerated; it is in many respects a fake. The hazards of city traffic are incomparably less than those of the ancient jungle, or of everyday life in many other centuries. The psychic staleness of some factory workers does not apply to thousands of semi-skilled and skilled workers, bears no comparison with the animal exhaustion of the peasant and takes no account of the equal monotony of the peasant's tasks. The mass media cater for millions of people who are no longer illiterate and offer them, in some instances, articles written by writers which their local papers can rarely afford and in B.B.C. television, drama which does include plays from Ibsen and Shaw to Tennessee Williams and Arthur Miller. If the mass of television seems frivolous and unsatisfactory, catering as much for its advertising sponsors as its audience, there are a number of serious programmes with much higher standards which have wide audiences. If the great driving forces of profits and increased audiences, the motives of money-lust and sheer size appear to vitiate many sides of television planning, there are voices raised in protest, oases where other gods are served and some concern on the part of the more morally conscious television executives. Even some among the masses of national newspaper readers are turning away from the extreme presentation of the snappy tabloids to more serious papers like the *Sunday Times* and *Observer*. As for physical flabbiness, it cannot be so widespread when thousands of human beings performed wonders of physical courage and endurance in the last war, and even war itself, the most brutal negation of progress, has also revealed in a thousand unexpected places, those very characteristics—disinterested service, self-sacrifice, the sharing of burdens, idealistic behaviour—which are prime elements in the whole philosophy of progress. The increase in neurosis? We simply do not know how much neurosis existed in the past but the chances are that anyone threatened with a short, dangerous life working thirteen hours a day, without a medical service worth the name, would have acquired a system of superstitious fears far more compulsive than the common neurotic knows today. As R. V. Sampson wrote in *Progress in the Age of Reason*: 'If the Freudians have succeeded in awakening us to the magnitude of the task of expanding the rôle of intelligence in human affairs they have also provided us with the instruments of diagnosis and therapy exceeding in efficiency those available to our predecessors. If the forces of war are more terrible than in the past, the revulsion against war is more widespread and more intense than ever before. If the forces of racial intolerance and persecution are still with us, this fact needs to be measured against a new sense of dignity and equality which characterizes the Asian and Negro mental revolutions of our time. If the class war has not been eliminated, there is some evidence to suggest that the institutions and policies of welfare conscious governments have gone some of the way in achieving a more equitable distribution of national income. If we have witnessed the nihilistic revolt of Nazism against every civilized value, we have also seen its overthrow by an unprecedented display of democratic solidarity.'[8]

It remains true that there are many conflicting and neutralizing currents, many self-perpetuating eddies in the dark and mysterious stream which we call progress, but there is no law which says that one current effectually counters another, and no law which says that any movement which we might detect in the right direction, is an illusion.

The great new factor in the possibility of human progress is the enormous power we have to break into what were called natural forces and re-shape and re-direct them, even to the point of breaking open the atom and creating an explosion which, in five apocalyptic minutes, would destroy urban civilization as we know it. And there, of course, is the rub. We have, it would seem, progressed materially, morally and medically, the penal code has been revolutionized, patient enquiry has wrested endless secrets from nature, evolution has produced man, knowledge has widened out of all recognition and the free-ranging intellect is, for the most part in Western Europe, splendidly uninhibited, but we have not learnt how to control the results of some of our knowledge. It remains a fair guess that the Common Man today, with his liberties, opportunities, privileges and equipment, modern man living in an age where we have found qualified progress in so many spheres, is more likely to know greater happiness than did his counterpart in many past ages.

Bernard Shaw believed that happiness was constitutional. Certain people by disposition would be relatively happy under the most depressing circumstances. This is not true of the general run of human beings. Only the saint can be happy in excrutiating martyrdom. Happiness for the majority of mankind is the result of interaction between internal and external forces, between inheritance and environment, between the nature of the beast and the pressures of his upbringing and experience. If the social pressures and sanctions take account of the inner needs of the organism and the fortuitous intervention of shattering experience is to some extent controlled, if the individual is fully trained to cope with life and given opportunities to realize his best potentials, the chances are that whatever his or her innate disposition, he or she will stand a better chance of happiness, and a better chance of overcoming those shocks and stresses which the gamble of being alive release unexpectedly on the most beautifully cushioned individual.

Opponents of this view immediately cite Sweden—a clean, well-lighted place as Kathleen Nott remarked—where the individual is catered for from the cradle to the grave and yet the alcoholic and suicide rates are very high and a certain ennui invests a number of the population. Of course, comfortable ennui is better than tormented misery, but Britain, when the social security services were comprehensive, did not suffer any emasculation or spectacular increase in suicides and alcoholics. There is no law which necessarily correlates social security with a form of bored degeneracy. On the contrary, it can release people from commonplace anxieties into daring adventures, intellectual, scientific and even physical, which would have been swamped with far more material preoccupations in the past.

What constitutes happiness must remain highly individualized. One man's happiness may be another's misery, but there are some common prerequisites which the general run of humanity share. Progress in the terms defined in this chapter would provide them.

*   *   *   *

The H-Bomb apart, two powerful forces remain at work against further development. First there is the increasing specialization in professional and technical knowledge which can isolate one group in the community from another in a most perilous way. As A. N. Whitehead put it in his book *Science and the Modern World*: 'The dangers arising from this aspect of professionalism are great, particularly in our democratic societies. The directive force of reason is weakened. The leading intellects lack balance. They see this set of circumstances, or that set, but not both sets together. The task of co-ordination is left to those who lack either the force or the character to succeed in some definite career. In short, the specialized functions of the community are performed better and more progressively but the generalized direction lacks vision. The progressiveness in detail only adds to the danger produced by the feebleness of co-ordination.'[9]

Comte foresaw this long ago. He thought that the introduction of his positive stage into the social sciences would reconcile these differences and give a *vue d'ensemble*, but this has not happened.

The second danger has an equally insidious power to eat into the happiness of the individual and to remain quite inviolable to all our attempts as yet to bring it under control—man's love and sexual relationships. Into the serenity of the planned and protected world of the Welfare State, there can still break the wildest emotional storms of love, hate, jealousy and bitterness to qualify the satisfactions which a scientifically directed world may have to offer mankind. The subjective explosion of extreme jealousy in the lives of two people can be as agonizing as serious physical hardship, but at least jealousy and the emotions may not wreck the physical reality of living in a manner comparable with the trail of devastation left by an H-bomb. One can recover from hate, jealousy and the agonies of psychic suffering, but not from the direct fall-out of an H-bomb. Among all the conflicting currents one and one only stands out as a major negation of the rest, as a power which could send the stream of progress pouring catastrophically back to its source—the H-bomb. If we could remove this major threat, there would still remain many dangers but most of these are more susceptible to rational solution, and once solved the way would be opened to accelerating a progressive world. Implicit in the problem of the H-bomb is an age-old difficulty. In each civilization which has fallen into decay and finally destroyed itself in the past there arose a current, or force, which the ruling classes of the day did not understand and could not contain. Professor Toynbee has drawn attention to a remarkable parallel which bears one resemblance to our own dilemma, since its solution might make possible the control of the H-bomb.

As Toynbee says: 'On the time scale now unfolded by geology and cosmogony, the five or six thousand years that had elapsed since the first emergence of representatives of the species of human society that we label "civilizations" were an infinitesimally brief span of time compared to the age, up to date, of the human race, of life on this planet, of the planet itself, of our own solar system, of the galaxy in which it is one grain of dust. . . . By comparison with these orders of temporal magnitude, civilizations that had emerged in second millenium B.C. (like the Græco-Roman), in the fourth millenium B.C. (like the Ancient Egyptian) and in the first millenium of the Christian era (like our own) were one another's contemporaries.'[10]

It is Toynbee's belief that of the score of civilizations known to us 'the majority appear to have broken down already'. As for the method of collapse he writes: 'Briefly stated the regular pattern of social disintegration is a schism of the disintegrating society into a recalcitrant proletariat and a less and less effectively dominant minority. The process of disintegration does not proceed evenly. . . . In the last rally but one, the dominant minority succeeds in temporarily arresting the society's self-laceration by imposing on it the peace of a *universal state*. . . .'[11] The italics are mine. If, to the lay mind, phrases like 'recalcitrant proletariat', seem born of the inherited prejudices of Toynbee's class, and 'society's lethal self-laceration' remains picturesquely obscure, there is no mistaking the meaning of the imposition of 'the peace of a universal state'.

It is in this last task that the Greek civilization failed. 'The Greeks' attempt at an international political order was the so-called Delian League, founded in 478 B.C. by Athens and her allies under Athenian leadership. . . . But the Delian League failed to achieve its purpose. And the old political anarchy in the relations between the sovereign independent Greek city-states broke out again under new economic conditions which made this anarchy not merely harmful but deadly.'[12]

Even the Romans, with their ruthless military efficiency, when confronted by the same problem failed to solve it. 'The Roman Empire—which was really an international league of Greek and other, culturally related, city states—may be regarded as a tardy solution of the problem which the Delian League had failed to solve. But the epitaph of the Roman Empire is "too late". . . . It was a peace and an order that came four centuries after its due time.'[13] In a word, the problem of establishing some form of *international* world order which confronts us today confronted the Greeks and Romans and it should be a solemn and terrible warning that their failure to solve it was one of the main causes of the disintegration and collapse of their civilization.

Bertrand Russell has told us that we must today find some method of achieving world government or die, and there are those who take him to task for resounding rhetorical appeals which do not come to grips with the detailed difficulties involved. John Strachey is one of a number of people who have done some detailed thinking into the problem of world government and what, at first sight, to anyone familiar with the old League of Nations, the passionate patriotism of sovereign states and the irrational fears which divide Russia and America, appears a hopeless task, is given a dash of hope in his analysis. It is the tragedy of the modern situation that the force which could conceivably unify the world almost overnight—Communism—is unacceptable to the West and America, who see the enslavement of the human mind as the price to be paid for a world government of automatons. Yet the Communist doctrine says that any unification between bourgeois capitalist states is, by their very nature, impossible, while spontaneous forces render unification of proletarian socialist states inevitable.

Strachey will have none of this. 'The fact is that the Nation-State as an institution has survived the revolution after all. No one cares even to speak of China becoming part of the U.S.S.R. Yugoslavia could be brought to do so only by conquest. . . . In a word, the revolution has come and gone and lo and behold, China is still China, Poland is still Poland, Hungary is still Hungary. . . . Finally the U.S.S.R. is still very much Russia.'[14]

Strachey inverts the Communist dogma. He sees signs of states in which the capitalist relations of production still predominate, being capable of some form of unification, while the automatic unification of socialist states is no longer certain.

'If Communist nations turn out to be genuine nation-states after all, with most of the intentions, ambitions, passions and prejudices but with also the caution, desire to survive and sense of reality of other nation-states, is it so inconceivable that some time before the end of the century it may be possible to set up some sort of limited world authority constituted by both Communist and non-Communist nation-states but constituted for the one, sole, narrow but indispensable purpose of preventing the outbreak of full-scale war . . . ?'[15]

Once again we are in the realm of somewhat more precise exhortation, but Mr Strachey does not leave it there. He sees that a complete *rapprochement* between Russia and America is most unlikely while two opposing ideologies religiously divide their outlook, but he believes that there is one single survival issue on which they might be brought to agreement: nuclear war. Mr Herman Kahn has already proposed that 'the Russian and American Governments should sign a one-clause treaty binding themselves never to use their nuclear weapons except for the coercion of any State which itself used such weapons'.

Working through the United Nations, when the Suez crisis arose, for the first time America and Russia saw eye-to-eye in trying to stop the Anglo-French–Israeli war on Egypt, and they were so quickly effective that their power in unison to 'impose' peace, given that the 'delinquents' surrendered to the authority of the United Nations and did not lose face to any one particular power, was self-evident and encouraging. As Strachey has said—if Russia and America not only agreed 'never to use their nuclear weapons except in the special circumstance outlined above, but set out to prevent any other State acquiring or using nuclear arms, the H-bomb might yet be contained'. This second clause becomes increasingly urgent every day as the costs of producing nuclear weapons are scaled down and brought within the range of nations who are young, ambitious, less balanced and maybe, in terms of temporary leaders, unscrupulous enough to let loose atomic destruction from sheer hatred of a threatening rival.

*   *   *   *

There are four main reasons why the blanketing cloud of gloom which has settled on mankind about the almost inevitable use of nuclear weapons and the creation of a vast radio-active poison desert capable of crippling and destroying life for thousands of years to come, may be mistaken.

In the first place—a point which Strachey does not make—we have learnt, in mutilated reality, just what a small atom bomb explosion meant at Hiroshima, and the readiness to use the bomb has diminished. We have had several crises of an intensity which, in the 1914 period, would almost certainly have led to *international* war on a large scale: Berlin, Korea, Indo-China, Suez, Hungary, the U2 incident and Cuba. Neither the atom bomb nor the H-bomb has been used and it is becoming clear that the rôle of aggressor among the big powers is seen to be more dangerous than it has ever been before in the whole of history for the simple and obvious reason that reciprocal and almost instantaneous annihilation is not the desired end of premeditated attack. At the strategical level the use of the H-bomb has become suicidal. This is encouraging, providing we do not find ourselves in a situation where the fanatical leader of a nation approaching defeat in a limited war, decides to indulge one mad, glorious gesture of ultimate defiance and blow himself and the world to smithereens rather than surrender in the traditional manner. Hitler, given possession of the H-bomb, would probably have done this. Certainly, the dread of the new H-bomb, a mysterious sense of not knowing its precise power to wipe out cities and leave its fearful slime of radioactivity over the face of the earth, is in itself a deterrent, but not one calculated to check the irresponsible fanatic.

The third force for peace outlined by Strachey is the remarkable tendency for the 'economic and social systems of the advanced, industrialized nation-States to approximate to one another, whether they are capitalist or Communist'. Quite clearly one characteristic which he does not specifically mention—the tendency towards large-scale organization and planning—is common to both and both systems now consider the Common Man in a manner quite alien to the past. In both societies almost identical technical skills are in great demand and the type of executive required to run different industries in Russia and America is almost interchangeable. As with scientists, a point may be reached where professional preoccupations override national characteristics and a certain similarity of technical skills and outlook give alien peoples a common ground on which they can meet. Equally important as Strachey says: 'The American economy is a long way from the freely competitive "model" of the classical economists and would immediately collapse if it attempted to approximate to that model. On the other hand the growing success of the Russian economy in the *production* of goods and services may be expected to force it increasingly towards the development of some kind of price mechanism and competitive process. (And the development will not really be contradicted if the Russians choose to distribute a particular service, say transportation, free—i.e. paid for out of taxation—just as we in Britain choose to do in the case of medical attention for instance.)'[16]

There remains one other factor where the two blocs tend to converge—the recognition of the necessity for an international organization—but here John Strachey seems to overestimate Russian sympathies. The Soviet Union insists on complete observance of national sovereignty during what they call the present historical period, at any rate so far as Socialist States are concerned. Russia accepts collaboration between national states on the basis of mutual respect and coexistence but rejects the idea of surrendering any important prerogative to an international body. However, she works within the United Nations, even if the use of the veto seems to cripple UNO on a number of crucial issues. More important, perhaps, than the immediate nature of the organization, the general climate of thinking which realizes the necessity of some sort of world authority is a considerable advance on the old game of bluff, cunning and deception known as power politics which dominated the late nineteenth and early twentieth centuries.

We are in the eighteenth year of the Nuclear Age—eighteen years since the bomb was dropped on Hiroshima—and we have survived a number of alarming crises without a major war or the use of nuclear weapons. Eighteen years is a hopeful period to look back on. Can we look forward to a similar period of uneasy adjustment in the next eighteen years?

As we have seen, the future will be influenced by many forces not apparent in the past. One of these is the increase in the number of nation-states becoming members of UNO. Years of anti-imperialist indoctrination have so conditioned the Afro-Asian bloc that any new member state tends to suspect the

West more than the East and the danger of increasing votes sympathetic to Russia is powerful. We are, in this sense, reaping a terrible reward for our treatment of certain colonial peoples in the past, but a far greater trouble arises more immediately with the organization of UNO.

It dealt with Korea and Suez effectively, but it was sadly confused in the Congo and it is possible that UNO may lose the international respect in which such an organization must be held if it does not increase its striking power. There is one possible solution to this problem which interlocks with the terrible delta of indecision where the whole disarmament cause threatens to founder. At the moment each nation contributes men, money and equipment to UNO. Supposing this were extended on the principle that every item of disarmament accepted by each member of UNO would be passed over to UNO's new Striking Force, beginning, for instance, with the three great powers possessing H-bombs each handing over one H-bomb to UNO, with the men and equipment, including jet-bombers, necessary for its effective functioning. The remaining nations would contribute their most advanced equivalent to the H-bomb and in the second year, two such items for every member nation would once more be placed in the hands of UNO, and so on by the simple multiple of doubling the last contribution. Simultaneously, there must be either international agreement to suspend the production of all nuclear weapons or a security-checked suspension of tests. The enlarged UNO Striking Force would presently be equipped with enormously increased traditional and nuclear power and would have the ability, with the Council's sanction, to threaten to bring its full weight to bear against any aggressor state, big or small.

Today, UNO has higher international standing than the old ramshackle League of Nations, and the United Nations has the advantage of living in the jet age. Distances have diminished. Trouble can be dealt with more rapidly and effectively. For the rest, an uneasy lull may be possible if the enlarged armament of UNO goes hand in glove with a new approach to disarmament, and it is just possible that the ideal which inspired Thomas Mann in his last years may even yet become a reality.

He foresaw a period of compromise between Russia and

America in which growing prosperity modified their intransi-
gence, each bloc reacting on the other to qualify representative
institutions in such a way that America's aggressive belief in free
enterprise diminished, and Russia's insistence on world-wide
Communism admitted the possibility of other forms of economic life. Attrition through understanding is a better process
than attrition through strength. This period of compromise
might last at least twenty-five years, an interval long enough
for far better relations to develop between the two blocs and
who knows—a prolonged peace?

The second possibility is a sudden war of annihilation in
which urban civilization as we know it collapses, and the world's
atmosphere is poisoned for years to come. There is a third
possibility—a limited H-bomb war in which not the big powers,
but smaller ones, newly equipped and cocky with nuclear
weapons, let loose, in a moment of hysteria, enough H-bombs
to destroy millions of people and pollute, say, the whole of the
Middle East. This might come as such a shock and reveal the
terrible consequences of nuclear war in such appalling reality
that the world would, at last, be brought to its senses and
driven to reconsider world government in quite different terms.
A less than total nuclear war would wipe out whole cities, throw
urban civilizations into confusion and leave a terrible drifting
trail of poison, but there would be survivors and it would not
necessarily mean the end of Man as a species.

Assuming Man survives, he may pick up the threads of
civilization again, but certain prerequisites are vital and within
our power to provide. We should, now, at this very moment,
be busy micro-filming and burying, at hundreds of strategic
points, two classes of modern knowledge. First, those practical
details for medical treatment, restoring food and water supplies,
housing and clothing which a totally disorganized community
thrown back to its primitive beginnings and suffering from the
effects of radiation will desperately need. Second, those basic
discoveries of science, medicine and the arts which are the
flower of our civilization. Clearly there must also be a system
of sign-posting, in many languages, which makes it impossible
for the whereabouts of this buried intellectual treasure not to be
discovered. These are the least efforts we can make to contribute
to the easier survival of whatever remnant struggles up from
the nuclear jungle to continue the amazingly resilient and

perhaps indestructible human story. But I am cautiously optimistic. I think there is every reason to hope that we shall not get an obliterative nuclear war. Instead, I see a slow and painful period of compromise dragging us through a series of crises and threats to a saner epoch where peace predominates.

CHAPTER TEN

A glimpse of the future

T URN away, for the moment, to this more hopeful view of the future. Consider what might lie before us if, for one motive or another—expediency, morality or hard common sense—the horde of H-bombs remained inert, became, in time, anachronisms, and a hundred years from now underwent a ceremonial burial in the Atlantic with the full ritual due to the outdated monsters of a dead age. The prospect then becomes remarkable.

Come down into the wide streets of the future, observe the tree-lined boulevards, the slender towers rising three hundred feet into the air with myriad inhabitants whose lives are no longer driven by the rush to work for eight hours a day, but literally reach their work within ten minutes' walk, and work for only four days a week. New towns of sixty thousand inhabitants centred in clusters of crystal skyscrapers are scattered through the countryside, each town with its own work area where all the equipment for the new forms of work is available and the old problems of rush-hour travel no longer exist. Each town has its factory area and each factory its electronic brain, a vast apparatus of mechanical cells capable of controlling the work of hundreds of machines for weeks at a time. One man only is required to watch the signals which indicate when something is wrong with a 'brain', and the only other human elements are the maintenance men, the highly skilled electronic engineers called in from time to time to check over the machinery. The factories are spotless, smokeless, gleaming metal honeycombs intersected by giant steel corridors and apart from the subtle smell of heated metal there is no other disturbance to ear, eye or nostril.

These electronically fed factories have provided one vital antidote to what were called, in the rhetorical past, the horrors of the machine age. Until the year 1980 too many men and women were still trapped at factory benches carrying out soul-destroying repetitive work whereby, in the course of a year, they

pulled similar levers and saw drop away an infinitude of bolts
or nuts. Now the machine works itself and the workers have
been released from drudgery into a hundred different activities
of a highly personal and more significant character. Across in the
big banks, what was once a thriving hive of young men and
women clerks has become a softly humming desert where
electronic machinery receives, records and carries out myriad
small and tedious calculations. Counter clerks have gone and in
their place stand mechanical-clerks who accept your cheque,
credit your account, cash your cheque and answer queries with
the unchanging good-humour which only a machine, untouched
by weather or temperament, can know.

Remarkable developments have overtaken the social and
political scene. In the far distant past, social birth was very often
the passport to privileged education, status and wealth. As
successive Education Acts equalized educational opportunities,
young men and women from the lower and middle classes
began to lay claim to jobs and incomes once thought beyond
their reach, but the principle of promotion by seniority still
clogged the Civil Service and many other fields. Gradually, as
Michael Young foresaw in his brilliant book *The Rise of the
Meritocracy*, class distinction by birth and money gave place to
class distinction by merit, selection for promotion ceased to be
a matter of years of service and became a question of ability.
Those with I.Q.s in the 140-160 range quickly rose to the top
as methods of selection were made more scientific and the
principle of re-testing I.Q.s every five years, far into life,
enabled late developers to find their proper level. The New
Meritocracy was a society where income and status no longer
had anything to do with birth or social class but depended
entirely upon merit—and there was the rub. The capacity to
solve any number of problems with brilliant logical insight
might be accompanied by a deeply neurotic temperament
which made the top I.Q.s intolerable husbands or wives not
gifted with co-operative ways. Far worse, the great mass of
people whose I.Q. did not rise above 110 found themselves
progressively less and less employable as the electronic machines
took over the simple routine jobs they were accustomed to fill,
and the work of technicians and higher executives proved beyond their powers.

What in the past were known as morons now included the

simpler people whose I.Q.s fell below 100 and they were subjected to the kind of scientific scrutiny which left no doubt about their inferiority. In the past, the simple-minded person had always been buoyed up by the belief that he might seem simple-minded according to the limited means of assessment available, and there was no guarantee that such assessments were true. Now, the science of intelligence measurement had been brought to such a pitch of perfection that there could be very little doubt about who was moronic and who was not.

Meanwhile, the effect of the New Meritocracy on organizations like the Labour Party and trade unions was catastrophic. The Labour Party had served a vital purpose in slowly undermining the old hereditary distinctions of class and privilege which produced self-contained castes. It had broken into and cross-fertilized the classes. When the new talent-classes replaced the old social classes a savagely ironic fact became apparent. There could be little class mobility when scientific assessment fixed your class I.Q. and the inexorable accuracy with which the selection now skimmed off the best talent from the 'lower classes' and crowded it into the top echelons was devastating to the trade unions.

As Michael Young wrote: 'By 1990 or thereabouts all adults with I.Q.s of more than 125 belonged to the [new] meritocracy [or higher classes]. A large proportion of children with I.Q.s of over 125 were the children of those same adults. The [top intelligences] of today are breeding the top of tomorrow to a greater extent than at any time in the past. The [I.Q.] élite is on the way to becoming hereditary.'[1] Class discrimination had come full circle. The clamour for freedom from the caste system of the past had led for a time to intensive mobility between the classes but now the talent-class system had automatically created new and even more watertight divisions, and with them new class snobberies.

The Labour Party, as such, ceased to exist. As the rough, manual jobs were steadily taken over by the machines the old idea of labour changed and the growth of white-coated technicians suggested to the brilliant men still leading the outdated Labour Party that it should change its name and its ideals. The Labour Party became the Technicians Party concerned to further the belief in technical progress, in research and higher standards of work and leisure.

It was a preoccupation with the growing problem of leisure interests which caused severe political troubles in the year 2000 when the Populists, representing the mass of low I.Q. people, rebelled against the idea that the Technicians, representing the high I.Q.s, should legislate for compulsory education for leisure which would save the hundreds of thousands now working less than thirty hours a week from frittering their leisure time away gaping at television screens.

Engineers, artists, teachers, scientists, administrators and even salesmen were still in great demand, but their hours of work had diminished and they did not include the large numbers of low I.Q. people virtually unemployable in a complex modern world. These were the biggest problems of the day—the tremendous increase in the number of people no longer employable in electronified industry and the widespread increase in leisure.

Three attempts were made to solve them. A small minority of low I.Q. men and women had become 'assistants' of a special kind to higher I.Q. households, helping with the cleaning, children and the background chores. At first glance it bore some resemblance to the slave-aristocracy of ancient Athens but these men were not in any sense slaves, and their employers were not absolute masters. Indeed, even the label 'servants' was carefully avoided and they were known professionally as— assistants. Many more thousands were taught the rudiments of research and encouraged to join the huge teams of research workers now amassing new knowledge in every field and solving problems at a rate out of all proportion to the past because of the vast numbers of research workers available.

Education for leisure was encouraged to concentrate on research and the arts. A sustained propaganda campaign over many years was designed to persuade men and women to find an interest in painting as well as sport, in literature as well as crime novels, in music as well as dancing, in amateur theatricals as well as television; and it became commonplace to continue trying any number of new interests until something absorbing came up. Works of craftsmanship which made one home different from another were in greater demand than ever before, and a whole new resurgence of craftsmen was partly employed by this increasing market which allowed the individual to reassert himself in his work and his leisure.

It was the problem of leisure which drove the Technicians Party to introduce their Bill into the reconstituted House of Commons, a Bill intended to make leisure education compulsory. They felt that too many idle people spent their days in the new Television Pleasure Domes, too many people simply drifted away their time, and potential criminals were the result of having a surfeit of undirected leisure. The home life of many people encouraged whole families to sit hypnotized in their television rooms where one whole wall was a stereoscopic television screen. Middle-aged couples sat for hours watching the television newspapers which were piped directly from visual newsrooms, and the many events which were literally photographed and broadcast as they took place held hundreds of thousands more in prolonged states of arm-chair passivity.

Fully aware as they were of all these dangers, the Populist Party, representing the lower I.Q.s, remained fiercely opposed to certain clauses of the Leisure Education Bill and they headed off its first reading in the House of Commons by persuading the Union of Maintenance Men to call a strike. It is now possible for the twenty thousand members of the Maintenance Union to paralyse the whole of industry because if they strike, industrial electronic machinery begins to overheat, to seize up, to fail to programme itself, and in a very short time industry simply comes to a standstill. A new and modified Bill will come before the House next year making it compulsory for anyone under thirty—not the nation as a whole—to take Leisure Education, and it is expected that if this becomes law it will, over the next ten years, remove the worst strains of drifting aimlessness from the mass of younger and lower I.Q.s in the Populists' ranks.

The whole basis of education is undergoing radical changes. It was Bertrand Russell who anticipated one major change many years ago in his book *Has Man A Future?* which is still read today with ironic interest. 'The young should no longer be taught to over-emphasize,' he wrote, 'the merits of their own countries, to feel a pride in those of their compatriots who had shown most skill in killing foreigners, or to adopt Mr Podsnap's maxim "Foreign nations, I am sorry to say, do as they do do". History should be taught from an international point of view with little emphasis on wars and much emphasis upon peaceful achievements whether in knowledge or art, or in exploration or adventure. The education authorities of a single country should not be permitted by the International Government to stir up chauvinist feeling or to advocate armed rebellion against the International Government. . . .'[2] Certainly education now plays down extreme competition and sets out to 'make young people aware of the possibilities of world-wide co-operation and to generate the habit of thinking about the interests of mankind as a whole'.

We are much more scientifically minded than in the past and the whole trend of education is to remove subjects like mathematics from the cold world of cyphers into the realm of philosophy. As Dr Bronowski wrote of those now distant days: 'We teach mathematics not as a way of thinking about nature, but as a vocational technique for adding up bills; and then, alarmed at the mental desert that we have created, we make our pupils read Julius Cæsar so that they may know that there are higher things to do with one's leisure. Is it any wonder that, after this destructive schooling, many adults can think of nothing to do with their leisure except to watch synthetic dramas in historical or cowboy costumes?'[3]

It has become commonplace now, to teach the scientific method as it once was the scriptures, and every intelligent pupil absorbs the first and second laws of thermodynamics as he once memorized the Ten Commandments. A new and far less ambiguous set not of Commandments—heaven preserve us against the dictatorial terms of past teachers—but of Principles is taught and repeated in schools. Books are not nearly so important in education as they were and television has deeply invaded the classrooms.

In 1961 only one-half the boys with intelligence enough to win a degree in America and only a third of those with I.Q.s as high as 145, went to university. Today, the change is revolutionary. Very few pupils equipped to qualify miss a university training, but the emphasis now, of course, is on technical training. Where before, university education was intended to teach people to manipulate words and numbers, now as much emphasis is put on mastering natural laws and the behaviour of circuits.

The wider emphasis is on the whole man. Everyone is encouraged to practise at least one art. Students have far more leisure to absorb literature, painting and music, and in adult life the enormous increase in leisure has created a tremendous demand for better novels and plays. By far the greatest artistic development is now beginning to take place in television where competing stations and programmes backed by state subsidies are able to experiment with new television art forms, which will make it far less time-wasting to sit in front of a television set.

The ideal man is no longer seen as an 'extroverted good mixer who combines back-slapping geniality with aggressive drive'.[4] Such men have their place but the ideal is a more thoughtful less aggressive, more sensitive less simple, more kindly less selfish person, who not merely achieves a high standard of living and multiple material comforts, but tries to contribute something to the general well-being, and has a different kind of virility from extrovert drive.

As Huxley wrote years ago: 'The important ends of man's life include the creation and enjoyment of beauty, both natural and man-made; increased comprehension and a more assured sense of significance; the preservation of all sources of pure wonder and delight, like fine scenery . . . the attainment of inner peace and harmony, the feeling of active participation in embracing and enduring projects. . . .'[5]

Not merely education, but the basic economy has been changed to try to meet these needs. We know now that civilizations will be remembered not only for their great wealth or contributions to sheer comfort, but for their philosophic attitudes, for their achievements in art, science and the laws of government, for 'their success in liberating human life from the shackles of fear and ignorance'. In the past the western economic systems were based on 'expanding production for profit; and production for profit . . . in expanding consumption'. People were persuaded by enormously expensive mass advertising campaigns that they must buy a new model car, refrigerator or house at any cost, and this led to a 'gross over-exploitation of resources that ought to be conserved, to excessive advertising, to the dissipation of talent and energy into unproductive channels and to a diversion of the economy as a whole away from its true function'.

All this is changed. Profit as such is limited by law, and salary scales range from £500 to £5,000, no one earning more, no one less. The artificial expansion of a market for goods has given place to an attempt to satisfy real human needs, to evaluate the product not only for its utility but for its quality. Sociological surveys have taken the place of the old market surveys. The object is not merely to find out what the consumer wants, but what serves him best in the light of full knowledge of any given situation and commodity. We knew years ago that a random sample of a few thousand citizens can be selected in such a way that it represents the entire population from which it is drawn. By interviewing the few thousand it was possible to formulate their needs more precisely and to avoid the loaded questions which men bent on making large profits sometimes used in sampling techniques.

*   *   *   *

The prophecies which Bertrand Russell made about the future of education have all come to pass; his prophecies about international government have not. Many years ago we saw the old League of Nations die of inanition. Later we witnessed the humiliation of UNO, the second world organization, because the narrow patriotism of national sovereignty would not surrender to an international Striking Force capable of quelling trouble wherever it arose. The H-bomb came into the hands of a number of lesser powers; two, in the Middle East, went to war, and in the desperation of a stalemate between their opposing forces, they used H-bombs against each other. The results were so catastrophic, the drifting clouds of radiation so deadly, the millions of mutilated bodies so appalling, the eye-witness accounts of survivors so horrifying that the world was shocked into forming a third, new and far more powerful international organization—the United World Organization. It now has an H-bomb Striking Force which for the past twenty years has enforced peace throughout the world. But World Government, no; we are still remote from that ideal.

Bertrand Russell also spoke of the dangers of world population. It was expected, in the old days of 1950-60, that within fifty years the population of the world would double itself, but this estimate did not take sufficient account of the distribution of oral contraceptives which, by 1970, began to take serious effect, with the result that the reproduction rate slowed down considerably. A vast increase has occurred in world population but the expected increase in malnutrition and starvation, as world food supplies were stretched to their limit, has been avoided by new methods of production. In the distant nineteen fifties not more than nine per cent of the land surface of the earth was actually cultivated and another sixteen per cent was 'pasture producing some human food but much less per acre than arable land'. These figures are now radically different. Twenty per cent is deliberately cultivated, and areas once complete deserts have been reclaimed to increase pasture-land to twenty-five per cent. Simultaneously a development of the old organic chemical Krilium has revolutionized the very nature of the soil. Describing the action of the early forms of Krilium Sir George Thomson wrote: 'It acts by surface processes and since a monomolecular layer absorbed on to a surface alters its properties and molecules are small, a handful of material can alter a surprisingly large surface.'[6]

Today, the yield from chemically treated soil is roughly twice what it was in the past, but doubling the world's food supplies was not enough. In the 1960s a very high proportion of the world's population was either underfed, malnourished or continually threatened with starvation, and it was not enough merely to keep millions of people on a similarly restricted diet. As the world population doubled, the available food had to be trebled to raise the standards of nutrition to a reasonable level. Two new methods have worked very successfully. The first was developed from the Chlorella species of algæ, which grows as a green mush in bright sunshine. It was found that dried Chlorella gave a yield of $17\frac{1}{2}$ tons per acre against the 1 ton per acre of wheat in Britain and the protein content was fifty per cent against only twelve per cent in wheat. We now have vast areas of Chlorella water crops under cultivation. Similarly, in some specially controlled areas, a new kind of sea-animal has been bred which short-circuits the long, clumsy and inefficient processes of nature. These processes fed the algæ to very tiny organisms which in turn fed larger organisms and proceeded, through an elaborately wasteful chain, to nourish even larger animals. Now, the new Sea-Scavenger lives directly on the algæ and produces large quantities of animal protein to vary the vastly increased vegetarian diet which we can offer the once under-nourished peoples of the world.

*   *   *   *

Working hours as we have seen are now down to seven hours a day for four days a week, holidays sometimes extend to six weeks a year, even the humblest person has had prolonged excursions to the far places of the earth and the new supersonic jet aircraft can reach America in $1\frac{1}{2}$ hours, without strain. As the giant airliners—nearly a mile long they seem, lying silent on the aerodromes—increased in size and speed, carrying five hundred passengers at a thousand miles per hour, it became necessary to stop the torrent of small private planes from choking the air lanes, and presently all private planes were abolished and public transport only is now available. At the great Central London Air Table, once a week, one of the ten space-ships takes off for the moon and the sight of its glistening black hull, less in size than an airliner, but so much more complicated in design, slowly rising vertically into the air under pressure from enormously powerful jets which suddenly, at a height of a thousand feet, cut out and leave the craft hovering there, silent, in the sky, unsupported it seems by anything, is still one of the spectacles which set thousands craning skywards and fill with a hushed awe the watching crowds. Space-ship Aventura is the most modern, most remarkable feat known to modern engineering not because of its nuclear-powered engines, but because it is made of the new and still very rare alloy which is unaffected by the pull of gravity. Once this ship has been driven into position it will stay there, quite impervious to the ancient law which drags every escaping body crashing back to earth.

The voyages of these space-ships have made new knowledge available. We had long ago established that there were many other galaxies of greater consequence than ours scattered like gigantic dust through the universe, but now we also know that we may not, after all, be the highest point of the evolutionary process because men's minds have been darkened lately by a disturbing discovery. Our scientists have established that there is life on Venus and that it is a kind of life with which we cannot communicate because, although it uses a form of intelligence, it has nothing to do with consciousness as we understand the word. Scientists are now desperately trying to crack the code of what are referred to as 'electrical murmurs' which appear on delicate screens specially sensitized to the atmosphere of Venus.

Crack the code. On earth another code has recently been cracked with results far less dramatic than were expected by the new scientific romancers whose novels still sell in their hundred thousands. This is the genetic code. As Sir George Thomson wrote many years ago: 'Present-day methods of breeding depend more on shuffling about existing genes . . . than on assisting the naturally occurring mutations. It seems likely that in the future more use will be made of mutations deliberately induced. In this connexion I can't help feeling that the highly developed methods of what are called electron optics may be of great service.'[7]

They were. Geneticists have now successfully unravelled some of the fantastic multiplication of conflicting possibilities which arise in the cock-shy of the genes, and some attempt at controlling two characteristics has been made, but religious scruples have stopped the full-scale experiment whereby a conditioned fœtus was to have been nurtured under artificial conditions to full maturity. The clash between the churches and the sciences still persists because the geneticists feel that they may be able to check and frustrate the growth of those characteristics which produce criminals and maladjusted people, and the churches argue that the neurotic wellsprings of criminals may equally well produce artists or writers. Responsible politicians are also alarmed at the possibility of placing in the hands of any group of scientists the power of conditioning the character and therefore the behaviour of thousands of people.

The words 'churches', 'writers' and 'politicians' are rapidly becoming old-fashioned. Religion is no longer centred around the ancient churches which have become museum pieces cherished for their beauty as shrines of the old ways of religious life. The Christian mythology has ceased to have supernatural significance and is seen now as a poetic interpretation of the martyrdom of man in his long struggle from pain, obscurity and victimization into the far more serene, satisfying air of the present. The whole Christian doctrine, with its emphasis on an immortal soul exclusive to homo sapiens, found itself in difficulties when mysterious new forms of life on other planets were discovered to possess intelligence in high degree of a different kind from what we knew on earth, but were quite without any sign of Christian inspiration. Could—'they'—whatever precisely they were—be possessed of immortal souls?

Would the Church need to send its missionaries soaring through interstellar space in an attempt to enlighten them?

Many writers too, were not writers in the old sense of the word. They could now sit in front of electronic machines which, when they pressed one of a hundred keys, would immediately spell out, at enormous speed, a whole paragraph or page embodying the writer's central thought and its surrounding qualifications. A master key permitted erasures and corrections and each key when depressed concluded its paragraph with suggestions for the next. It was possible with this machine, for a highly trained, quickly thinking 'writer' to prepare a competently written chapter for a practical text-book in a single day. These books were automatically printed and recorded and could be read or listened to. Half the books used by students and by the common 'reader' for enlightenment or entertainment were now prepared in this way, but there remained a number of old-fashioned writers and thinkers who still used a typewriter laboriously tapping out five hundred pages of typescript which finally emerged from the presses in the old manner. Poetry, more serious novels, works of criticism and philosophy remained highly individualized products in the old tradition.

In private life, oral contraception has long revolutionized the relations of the sexes and after a bitter struggle with the old religious forces, pre-marital intercourse has become an accepted fact. Church marriages have died out and marriage is now a civil contract in which both parties do not vow to remain together for better or worse for the rest of their lives, but accept the fact that two marriages in a lifetime has become a commonplace. It is now acknowledged that far too many people married their husbands or wives in the old days between the ages of eighteen and twenty-one when they were very immature, and later discovered large and widening differences of temperament, talent and interests, which seemed to falsify the whole basis of their marriage. People, it is now accepted, do not know their true potential at eighteen or twenty-one and husbands or wives selected within such a limited pool of experience may completely fail to satisfy the fully matured person of thirty or thirty-five who at last knows, for the first time, what he wants. Hence two marriages in a lifetime is now socially acceptable.

It was not realized until many experiments had been carried out just how the upbringing of children and adolescents in the

1960s irreparably split, in some cases, the two naturally interlocking spheres of sex and feeling. Until quite recently children
and adolescents were encouraged to develop feeling and affection
and simultaneously to repress sexuality; one was smiled, the
other frowned upon. This tended to split sex and feeling apart
with the result that when, in maturity, the young man or woman
was allowed—in marriage only—to give sex its head, he or she
found difficulty and in some cases great difficulty in integrating
the two. As Morton Hunt wrote all those years ago: 'This dis-
junction between affection and sex, maintained in the individual
for twenty or more years, is not easily repaired by the mere
ceremony of marriage; tensions, inhibitions and fears therefore
remain powerful pathological forces in the love life of a considerable number of adults.'[8] The now almost forgotten Kinsey
found that 'a large proportion of American males completed
the sex act in less than two minutes'[9] which was quite likely an
indication of guilty haste.

Today we have not only accepted the widespread habit of
pre-marital intercourse but have lost our revulsion for childish
sex-play and sexuality. We have also realized that an increased
expectation of life has lengthened the period when husband and
wife are expected to be entirely satisfactory to one another and
since this may now mean a span of fifty years, the temporary
intervention of another person in that time is no longer regarded
as the automatic prelude to divorce. Indeed, it is now seen as the
necessary condition for the survival of some marriages.

The tendency has grown for high I.Q.s to marry high I.Q.s
and the new form of popular romantic television play rings the
changes on the very beautiful young woman who falls hopelessly
in love with the brilliant scientist, and knowing her low I.Q.
may be a serious handicap to marriage, deliberately fakes a high
one. Intelligence now is more than a match for beauty as a
qualification for marriage, and a very low intelligence carries the
slur which was once associated with illegitimacy. The number of
children illegitimate in the old sense of the word has fallen away
sharply as oral contraception reached perfection, but the word
'illegitimate' is no longer valid. Children born before marriage
are automatically accepted by the community.

As the Christian sexual sanctions relaxed and the belief that
every foetus conceived was in some way endowed with an
immortal soul, waned, the resistance to eugenics diminished

and now a limited minority practise negative and positive eugenics. In the former group it is now legal to sterilize—with their consent—all those suffering from insanity and mental deficiency and this has helped to counter a trend very evident in 1850-1950 whereby the increase in mental deficiency by indiscriminate reproduction was put at ·2 per cent, but, as every geneticist knew, so many 'bad' genes were regressive in other-wise 'healthy' people that dealing with the self-evident ones did not have any very spectacular effect. In the positive sense there was a deliberate attempt among many people who conformed to the current ideal of Man and Woman, to marry someone of their own kind, but occasionally the laws of genetics continued to throw up unexpected results.

It is true that the time-honoured pangs of jealousy, possessive-ness, fanatical love and hate still have the power to break into and sometimes disrupt the new serenity which springs from the fuller realization of every individual in a harmonious society, but this is far less disturbing than in the past because a series of new drugs has been developed which makes it possible to treat any one of these conditions, in its more extreme form, as doctors treat normal illness. There is a new drug Stabiledrene which literally takes the sting out of jealousy, and another called Aid-Olescent, which can be taken in pill form by any very young girl who finds that her husband-to-be has deserted her or that her passionate love is utterly wasted. The agonies of unrequited love, the torment of infidelity, the anguish of the death of a loved person, each now has its special medical antidote and a whole field of emotional experience which was once liable to make a laughing-stock of personal progress, has been brought, to some extent, under control.

Even death itself is now not so inevitable as it was in the past. As Sir George Thomson wrote long ago in 1955: 'The whole business of old age is odd and little understood. Some primitive organisms which propagate by division are immortal apart from accidents. . . . There does not seem to be anything in the nature of the reproduction of tissue which demands its death; the cells of a chicken have been kept alive for a period far exceeding the normal life of the bird.'[10]

A curious anomaly became evident as a whole battery of new discoveries and treatments succeeded in extending the expecta-tion of life from seventy to ninety years. Many members of our present society are still reasonably active and healthy in their ninetieth year and research into hardening of the arteries is now approaching a climax where it may be possible to re-activate the vascular system, but far too many people who reach the age of a hundred do so at the cost of deafness, failing sight and heart conditions. As Sir George Thomson wrote: 'It is no good making everyone live to ninety if the last twenty years are decrepit. When one considers the very large differences in the age at which senility sets in, it does not seem at all a hopeless job to find ways of postponing it. It means learning a lot more about physiological processes, especially the more recondite ones. In the course of this work the mystery of cancer may be solved.'[11]

It has, indeed, been solved, and with it one of the greatest modern curses lifted from mankind. A remarkable discovery in physiology altered the old ideas about the way in which cells grow and divide in a healthy body, but although we can now check the gross multiplication of cells, we cannot yet give immortality to the properly healthy cell itself. Instead, the attack on the decrepitude which used to attend advanced age has become oblique. We have brought to a remarkable pitch of perfection the transplantation of separate organs and now, when a man of ninety is crippled by a weak heart, we can graft into his system a new and younger one, and if his kidneys have succumbed to ninety years of steady drainage he can be given a fresh, healthy, completely active kidney. Each hospital now has banks of living kidneys, hearts, eyes, retinas and a dozen other organs ready to be rushed to any patient, but it is tragic to reflect that the wealth of such available accessories is due to the still very high rate of road traffic deaths.

* * * *

Aeroplanes, space ships, sea-going ships and submarines—all these are now driven by nuclear energy, but the old-fashioned motor-car remains the chief means of transport driven by private individuals from door to door, and attempts to produce miniature reactors for cars proved a failure because the size and weight of the shield against toxic radiation were too massive for a small vehicle. Aeroplanes no longer have to cruise at dangerously high speeds along massive concrete runways. They take off vertically, by jet propulsion, and the initial part of any flight is like ascending into the heavens in a tremendously high-speed lift. Passengers avoid the long and tedious drive to an airport through traffic-choked streets, and leave instead from centralized air platforms, each group of platforms being planned at the centre of a group of residential towers. Submarines too now slip through the water at great depths carrying passengers on shorter journeys to relieve the congestion in the air, and once again Sir George Thomson's prophecies of sub-aquatic machines travelling at speeds of up to a hundred miles an hour have come true. As he then wrote: 'A submarine at depth produces practically no waves, and if it is properly designed its resistance need be very little more than "skin-friction". One is accustomed to think of a submerged submarine as slow, as almost all submarines have been till recently. But this is because of the difficulty of getting an engine which will produce high power and not consume oxygen. Nuclear power fills this need.'[12] Submarines are a small part of the nuclear-powered transport available. Giant nuclear-powered liners are now few in number and largely remain an indulgence for the rich who like to idle on the high seas, but whole fleets of specially designed cargo vessels still supplement the big air freighters.

There remain, of course, the rocket-ships capable of cruising about the immediate environs of our own solar system, which have opened up a new world of adventure for the young who think, talk and live space-travel and space-adventure, as our young ancestors once did aeroplanes.

The first man landed on the moon in 1970 and we now have a permanent colony of observers and scientists there who continuously investigate the routes to Venus. The moon can now be reached by rocket ship in two and a half days, but the first ship to reach and encircle Venus took a whole year for the return journey. Even now, no one has landed on Venus because it turned out to have an atmosphere charged with mysterious forces which we still have not clearly identified or countered. There is much talk today that within the next ten years we shall have reached a point where we can, if we choose, 'colonize' another planet and the imagination reels at the possibilities of other worlds more luxurious, more sympathetic to our new ideals of progress than the tired old earth, where whole new civilizations may be started, if they do not already exist.

It would be unwise to speak as if space-travel is now a

comfortable matter of cruising off into interstellar space according to earth-made time-tables and returning at pre-arranged points with any punctuality. We have witnessed tremendously exciting scenes at the moon launching platform, when a hundred young men, specially trained for several years in the enormous intricacies of space flight, soared off in these fantastically shaped space-ships, disappeared on journeys lasting three months and then, returning home, broke back into the earth's atmosphere at too high a speed and simply burnt up in one enormous incandescent flash which left nothing but a wisp of smoke and disintegrating fragments to mark the passage of ten years' work. The accident rate is still very high. The problem of showers of meteorites still has not been solved and many ships are simply blown to pieces without a single survivor. Most tragic and awe-inspiring is the case of the giant experimental ship which ventured further afield into interstellar space than any ship had been before and suddenly sent back a message—'We are out of control—out of control—Unknown Force sucking us into Zone 6'. Zone 6 was the beginning of the immense, uncharted, unknown loneliness which extended for billions of miles and even at enormous speeds like ten thousand miles an hour, would require a hundred years to traverse. The message was repeated unendingly for three days, growing steadily fainter and fainter, and then at last, it died to a whisper and faded into nothingness. It seemed impossible that a group of highly trained, highly educated, specially selected young men in a machine which represented the culmination of years of research, heartbreak and daring, should simply be drifting helplessly further and further into an unknown void where the night might last for five years, and nothing was there to hear, touch or see. Our psychologists have told us that the outcome for such a crew in such a position must be—since their concentrated food would last for at least a year—madness, and the imagination recoils from the last scenes which must have taken place in the ship.

*   *   *   *

The prospects which lie ahead for our new civilization are now awe-inspiring. Once upon a time, a handful of enlightened spirits realized that no matter where, or in what conditions, he or she was born, every man or woman on this earth had an equal right, with every other man and woman, to a condition called happiness. In the 1960s this seemed an illusory ideal. People whose material appetites for food, clothing, shelter and possessions were fully satisfied, people whose lives were buttressed against disasters in a network of securities, who were fulfilled professionally and privately, still experienced long periods of unhappiness. We had not found a means of overcoming the terrible penalties of emotional involvement or the dullness of repetitive and unsatisfying work. Now, these problems are coming, to some extent, under control, and where before we had a great literature of tragedy because life was a tragically harsh experience, we now have an equally profound and continuously developing literature of joy. We have found that suffering, as a means of building character, is undeniably salutary, but it was a great relief to modern philosophers to discover that joy too built a race of generous, responsive, confident and, not least, tough people who still found far too many conflicts in professional and private life to become soft or emasculated.

The question which continually recurs in scientific circles today is—What are the ultimate limits? 'If one considers the communities of ants, they have, we are told, most of the achievements of neolithic man. . . . Whether they "think" or not we cannot say. They are apt to run about at random when things go wrong but so do philosophers and Fellows of the Royal Society. Yet they have apparently stayed at this very high level for millions of years. . . . Shall we climb to our proper place in nature and settle there permanently? If so, where is it?'[13]

Sir George Thomson posed these questions seventy years ago. They are even more apt today. What once seemed our proper place in the evolutionary story has changed out of all recognition in the last hundred years, because we have so deeply interfered with our destiny that we are now deliberately trying to inject a law of progress into the aimless meanderings of nature. That is literally what is happening. We are trying to create the law of progress which we could not find in nature.

This is very evident in the new brain research. We have lately discovered new ways of activating areas in our own brains which, until now, seemed dead and useless. We are also breaking down the brain blockages created by wrong education, early conflicts and childhood indoctrinations, which seemed to cripple the free flow of thought and ideas in the maturity of so many people of the 1900s. It is reckoned that brain power, developed along these normal lines, has increased the intelligent response of the majority of people by ten per cent. But these are only the beginnings.

The liberation of human brain power is already accompanied by that of the giant computers. Whether these machines can be said to think or not is a matter of definition. Certainly these machines were capable, long ago, of learning by the human process of trial and error. Today we have gone far beyond the simple computers which work out and solve the very complicated mathematical problems confronting the modern physicists. Among the most advanced new machines are prediction machines which forecast with—as has been shown from experience—some degree of accuracy, the behaviour of people and events in a way which makes human planning a much more reliable instrument for re-shaping our own destiny. We can tell the effects of a certain piece of legislation simply by posing a series of questions which are fed into No. 10 of the Twenty Great Brains and we can predict—although with far less certainty—certain major events which lie ahead in history by supplying all the relevant data to Brain No. 6. A fully detailed answer from Brain No. 6 may take three months to mature because, despite thousands of circuits of immense complexity which are so much more reliable, lightning-quick and comprehensive than our own brains, the nature of the data is so detailed and extensive that it takes one month alone for complete assimilation of the problem by the Brain.

The most advanced brains of all have developed personalities of their own, and so immensely complex is their structure that not even the best electronic-geneticists can quite guarantee the limits of their behaviour. Of course they are inorganic; they are immobile; they are without feelings or emotion; they have to be fed like babies; but the element of indeterminacy which Heisenberg once formulated into a principle, is evident in a slightly sinister way in these new brains. We are reaching a stage where so many multiplying consequences of bringing together so many subtle circuits can only be calculated or shown by the Brain itself, and at this point it moves out of our immediate control into a self-determined world of its own.

The human mind is now inspired by future possibilities of a

kind which were once regarded as the wilder dreams of science-fiction writers. World government seems a certainty within the next fifty years unless we have another cataclysmic war. The decrepitude of old age will no longer trouble men in their hundredth year and new discoveries in the fundamental nature of the protein basis of life make it possible that one day we may achieve the dream of the old religions and become—immortal. The imagination quails at the philosophic problems which such a possibility creates and the day when death will only take place as the result of deliberate suicide or accident, will elevate our kind into a species of a different order from anything that has gone before. One marriage, one family, one career, one god may no longer be valid for such a person, but the responsibilities of immortal life may not be as terrifying as they would have been for our primitive counterparts in the 1960s. We know now, so much more about controlling pain, misery and even commonplace unhappiness, that the thought of indefinitely prolonging consciousness loses something of its old terror.

Immortal life remains a very remote dream, if not an impossibility, but life-spans of ninety healthy years are now a commonplace reality. The environment in which those years are lived has also undergone a radical change. We have modified the climate of the world by interfering with the two ice-caps and England, America and the greater part of Europe have now replaced winter with a prolonged and sunny spring.

There is no reason to suppose, our scientists tell us, that the earth will undergo any great catastrophe to make it uninhabitable in the next million years, but if it does, we now know that we can cruise off into space and colonize other planets. A new method of electrolysis has shown that we can artificially induce on a planet like Mars sufficient green vegetation to replace the missing oxygen in its atmosphere and this has opened up exciting possibilities of literally creating atmospheres suitable to homo sapiens on alien planets. As H. G. Wells wrote: 'So far and beyond the adventure may continue and our race survive. The impenetrable clouds that bound our life at last in every direction may hide innumerable trials and dangers, but there are no conclusive limitations even in their deeper shadows, and there are times and seasons, there are moods of exaltation—moments as it were of revelation—when the whole universe about us seems bright with the presence of as yet unimaginable things.'

There remains, in the heart of Man, many subjective problems which are not reconciled by the tremendous sweep of external potential. A new disease, mental and mysterious, which creates a state of ecstatic melancholy and is curiously contagious has troubled certain of the more brilliant groups among us. Psychologists tell us it is the result of stabilized happiness. Something in the human spirit cannot remain static. We are looking for the cure for this new and troublesome disease and such is our belief in the religion of progress that we are certain we shall find it, but, for the moment, a strange undercurrent of talk is much concerned with a topic flatly contradicted by all the available evidence. Amazingly, it is talk about whether there may not, one day, be an end to the brave music that is Man. . . .

Notes and Sources

Chapter 1

THE IDEA OF PROGRESS

1. J. B. Bury, *The Idea of Progress*, p. 293.

Chapter 2

MATERIAL PROGRESS

1. H. G. Wells, *Reshaping Man's Heritage*, p. 10.
2. Ibid. Major P. Grenville-Edge, 'Man's Lengthening Life', p. 83.
3. Ibid. L. J. Witts, 'The Conquest of the Germ', p. 53.
4. W. S. Davis, *Life on a Medieval Barony*, p. 281.
5. *Reshaping Man's Heritage*, L. J. Witts, 'The Banishment of Pain', p. 67.
6. S. J. Curtis, *History of Education in Great Britain*, p. 81.
7. Ibid. p. 102.
8. Ibid. p. 128.
9. *New Statesman*, 22 December, 1961.
10. W. Ashworth, *An Economic History of England, 1870-1939*, p. 200.

Chapter 3

PENAL PROGRESS

1. Sir James F. Stephen, *A History of the Criminal Law of England*, vol. 1, p. 9.
2. Ibid. p. 11.
3. *Digest* (Roman Law) xlviii, 3, 6.
4. *A History of the Criminal Law of England*, p. 44.
5. Ibid. p. 20.
6. Ibid. p. 19.
7. Ibid. p. 42.

Notes and sources

8. Quoted in *History of the Criminal Law of England*, p. 59.
9. Ibid.
10. Margery Fry, *Arms of the Law*, p. 37.
11. Sir Thomas Smith, *Commonwealth of England*, pp. 183-201.
12. *History of the Criminal Law of England*, vol. 1, p. 397.
13. Ibid. p. 398.
14. Ibid. p. 415.
15. Max Gruenhut, *Penal Reform*, pp. 30-1.
16. Ibid. p. 105.

Chapter 4

PROGRESS AND FREEDOM OF EXPRESSION

1. J. B. Bury, *A History of Freedom of Thought*, p. 13.
2. Ibid. p. 17.
3. Ibid. p. 18.
4. Ibid. p. 23.
5. Ibid. pp. 29-30.
6. Ibid. p. 32.
7. Gibbons's translation of the first edict of toleration issued in the eastern provinces (A.D. 311).
8. *A History of Freedom of Thought*, p. 41.
9. Ibid. p. 46.
10. Ibid. p. 54.
11. Ibid. p. 70.
12. *Encyclopaedia Britannica*, vol. 13, p. 186, 1959 edition.
13. Peter Benenson, *Persecution 1961*, p. 9.
14. Ibid. pp. 23-4.
15. Ibid. p. 84.
16. Ibid. p. 85.
17. Ibid. p. 43.

Chapter 5

PROGRESS AND WOMEN

1. Emil Reich, *Woman through the Ages*, vol. 1, p. 21.
2. Ibid. p. 27.
3. W. E. Gladstone, *Studies on Homer and the Homeric Age*, vol. II, p. 502.
4. *Woman through the Ages*, p. 72.
5. Thucydides, *History of the Peloponnesian War*, ii, 45.
6. *Woman through the Ages*, pp. 72-3.

7. James Donaldson, *Woman: her Position and Influence in Ancient Greece*, p. 51.
8. Charles Seltman, *Women in Antiquity*, p. 99.
9. H. D. F. Kitto, *The Greeks*, p. 221.
10. *Woman through the Ages*, vol. 1, p. 83.
11. *Woman: her Position and Influence*, p. 58.
12. Ibid.
13. Ibid. p. 80.
14. O. Kiefer, *Sexual Life in Ancient Rome*, trans. G. & H. Highet, pp. 22-3.
15. T. Livy, *The History of Rome*, trs. Rev. Canon Roberts, vol. 5, p. 45.
16. Ibid. pp. 46-7.
17. Ibid. p. 54.
18. *Woman through the Ages*, p. 125.
19. E. Westermarck, *Sociological Papers*, p. 150.
20. Ibid. p. 152.
21. Ibid. p. 153.
22. J. Langdon-Davies, *A Short History of Women*, p. 244.
23. *Histoire de la Civilisation en France*.
24. *A Short History of Women*, p. 273.
25. Ibid. p. 297.
26. W. S. Davis, *Life in Elizabethan Days*, pp. 91-2.
27. *A Short History of Women*, p. 90.
28. Ibid.
29. Lucy Hutchinson, *Memoirs of the Life of Colonel Hutchinson*.
30. G. M. Trevelyan, *England Under the Stuarts*, pp. 9-10.
31. S.P.D. ccclxxxv, 43. 8 March, 1638.
32. Alice Clark, *The Working Life of Women in the Seventeenth Century*, p. 87.
33. *English Historical Review*, vol. xiii, p. 522.
34. *The Working Life of Women*, p. 89.
35. Roger Fulford, *Votes for Women*, pp. 23-4.
36. Ibid. p. 71.
37. Mr and Mrs Hammond's *Town Labourer*.
38. *Votes for Women*, p. 156.
39. Ibid. p. 157.
40. Ibid. p. 299.

Chapter 6

MORAL PROGRESS

1. Morris Ginsberg, *Moral Progress*, p. 11.
2. W. E. H. Lecky, *A History of European Morals*, vol. II, p. 292.

3. Ibid.
4. L. T. Hobhouse, *Morals in Evolution*, p. 548.
5. Ibid. p. 550.
6. Thucydides, *History of the Peloponnesian War*, v., 105.
7. *Morals in Evolution*, p. 552.
8. Ibid. p. 555.
9. *A History of European Morals*, vol. I, p. 168.
10. Ibid.
11. Ibid.
12. *De Natura Deorum*, iii, 36.
13. *Encheiridion*, xlviii.
14. *A History of European Morals*, vol. I, p. 255.
15. Ibid. p. 261.
16. Ibid. p. 260.
17. Edward Westermarck, *The Origin and Development of the Moral Ideas*, vol. II, pp. 422-3.
18. Ibid. p. 425.
19. Ibid.
20. Havelock Ellis, *Studies in the Psychology of Sex*.
21. A move was afoot in 1961 not to remove the gaol sentence for women but to impose it on men as well.
22. R. V. Sampson, *Progress in the Age of Reason*, p. 244.
23. *Moral Progress*, p. 11.
24. Julian Huxley, *Evolutionary Ethics*, pp. 9-10.
25. C. H. Waddington, *The Ethical Animal*.
26. Julian Huxley, *The Humanist Frame*, p. 44.
27. W. D. Ross, *The Right and the Good*.
28. *Moral Progress*, p. 14.
29. Morris Ginsberg, *The Idea of Progress*, p. 66.
30. *Moral Progress*, p. 27.
31. Crane Brinton, *A History of Western Morals*, p. 421.

Chapter 7

PROGRESS AND RELIGION

1. Sigmund Freud, *Totem and Taboo*, pp. 76-7.
2. Ibid. p. 76.
3. Christopher Dawson, *Progress and Religion*.
4. Sir James Frazer, *The Golden Bough*, vol. 1, p. 67.
5. *Phaedrus*, p. 247.
6. *Symposium*, p. 211.

7.   A. J. Toynbee, *Civilization on Trial*, p. 13.
8.   Robert Graves and Joshua Podro, *The Nazarene Gospel Restored*, p. 40.
9.   Ibid. p. 41.
10. *Peri archon*, lib. ii, ch. iii, 4-5.
11. St Irenaeus, *Against Heresies*, v. 36, 1; iv, 37, 7.
12. *Progress and Religion*, p. 166.
13. Ibid.
14. Ibid. p. 181.
15. Ibid.
16. Ibid.
17. Ibid.
18. J. B. Bury, *The Idea of Progress*, p. 128.
19. John Baillie, *The Belief in Progress*, p. 117.
20. Ibid. p. 118.
21. Ibid.
22. Ibid. p. 119.
23. Ibid. p. 120.
24. Ibid. p. 122.
25. Ibid. p. 193.
26. Ibid. p. 200.
27. Ibid. p. 204.
28. Dodd, *History and the Gospel*, p. 168. Quoted in Baillie, p. 205.
29. Ibid. p. 170.
30. *The Belief in Progress*, p. 220.
31. Ibid. p. 233.
32. A. J. Toynbee, *Civilization on Trial*, p. 236.
33. Morris Ginsberg, *The Idea of Progress*, p. 60.
34. *Civilization on Trial*, p. 251.
35. Ginsberg, *The Idea of Progress*, pp. 64-5.
36. *New Statesman*, 22 December, 1961.
37. Ginsberg, *The Idea of Progress*, p. 8.
38. Dean Inge, *The Idea of Progress*, p. 21.
39. Edwyn Bevan, *The Kingdom of God and History* (1938 Conference Series), p. 66.
40. Sigmund Freud, *The Future of an Illusion*, p. 21.
41. Ibid. p. 22.
42. Ibid. p. 48.
43. *Progress and Religion*, p. 240.
44. Julian Huxley, *Religion without Revelation*, p. 7.
45. Pierre Teilhard de Chardin, *The Phenomenon of Man* (introduction by Julian Huxley), p. 18.
46. Ibid. p. 20.

Select Bibliography

John Baillie. *The Belief in Progress*. London, 1950.
Peter Benenson. *Persecution 1961*. London, 1961.
Crane Brinton. *A History of Western Morals*. 1959.
Vincent Brome. *H. G. Wells*. London, 1951.
J. B. Bury. *A History of Freedom of Thought*. 2nd ed. London, 1952.
    The Idea of Progress. London, 1920.
Pierre Charron. *De la Sagesse* (*Of Wisdom*). Rouen, 1623.
V. G. Childe. *Social Evolution*. London, 1951.
Alice Clark. *The Working Life of Women in the Seventeenth Century*.
    London, 1919.
Morris R. Cohen. *The Meaning of Human History*. London, 1947.
M. J. N. C. De Condorcet. *Esquisse d'un tableau historique des progrès
    de l'esprit humain* (*Sketch of a Historical Picture of the Progress of
    the Human Mind*). English trans. London, 1795.
S. J. Curtis. *History of Education in Great Britain*. 2nd ed. London,
    1950.
J. Langdon-Davies. *A Short History of Women*. London, 1927.
Christopher H. Dawson. *Progress and Religion*. London, 1929.
C. H. Dodd. *History and the Gospel*. London, 1938.
James Donaldson. *Woman: her Position and Influence in Ancient
    Greece*. London, 1907.
Sigmund Freud. *The Future of an Illusion*. London, 1928.
    Totem and Taboo. Trans. J. Strachey. London,
    1950.
Margery Fry. *Arms of the Law*. London, 1951.
Roger Fulford. *Votes for Women*. London, 1957.
Morris Ginsberg. *Essays in Sociology and Social Philosophy*, vol. I.
    London, 1956.
    The Idea of Progress—a Revaluation. London,
    1953.
    Moral Progress. London, 1944.
M. Glasgow. *The Subjection of Women and Tradition of Men*. New
    York, 1940.
Robert Graves and Joshua Podro. *The Nazarene Gospel Restored*.
    London, 1953.
M. Gruenhut. *Penal Reform: a Comparative Study*. London, 1948.

Select bibliography

L. T. Hobhouse. *Morals in Evolution*. London, 1906.
   Social Development. London, 1924.
   Social Evolution and Political Theory. New York, 1911.
Julian Huxley. *Evolutionary Ethics*. London, 1943.
   Religion without Revelation. London, 1941.
   ed. *The Humanist Frame*. London, 1962.
Julian Huxley, H. G. Wells, etc. *Re-shaping Man's Heritage*. London, 1944.
W. R. Inge. *The Idea of Progress*. London, 1920.
   The Price of Progress. London, 1937.
J. K. Ingram. *Outlines of the History of Religion*. London, 1900.
H. D. F. Kitto. *The Greeks*. London, 1951.
W. E. H. Lecky. *A History of European Morals*, 2 vols. London, 1911.
G. E. Lessing. *The Education of the Human Race*. Trans. F. W. Robertson. London, 1927.
T. Livius. *History of Rome*, 6 vols. London, 1921-4.
F. S. Marvin, ed. *Progress and History*. London, 1916.
A. G. Mason. *Women in the Golden Ages*. 1901.
P. J. Proudhon. *Philosophie du Progrès*. 1853.
Emil Reich. *Woman through the Ages*, 2 vols. London, 1908.
Bertrand Russell. *Has Man a Future?* London, 1962.
   A History of Western Philosophy. London, 1946.
R. V. Sampson. *Progress in the Age of Reason*. London, 1956.
G. Sorel. *Les Illusions du Progrès*. 1908.
Sir James F. Stephen. *A History of the Criminal Law of England*, 3 vols. London, 1883.
Sir George Thomson. *The Foreseeable Future*. London, 1955.
Pierre Tielhard de Chardin. *Phenomenon of Man* (intro. by Julian Huxley). Trans. Bernard Wall. London, 1959.
Alexis de Tocqueville. *De la Démocratie en Amérique*. Paris, 1835-40.
A. J. Toynbee. *Civilization on Trial*. London, 1948.
G. M. Trevelyan. *England Under the Stuarts*. London, 1946.
L. Weber. *Le Rythme du Progrès*. Paris, 1913.
E. A. Westermarck. *On the Position of Women in Early Civilizations*.
   Sociological Papers, vol. 1. London, 1905.
   The Origin and Development of the Moral Ideas, 2 vols. London, 1906.
A. N. Whitehead. *Religion in the Making*. London, 1926.
   Science and the Modern World. London, 1926.
T. Wright. *Womankind in Western Europe*. London, 1869.
Michael Young. *The Rise of the Meritocracy*. London, 1958.

INDEX

Index

Provinces, Roman, 36
Psychical progress, 11
Puberty, earlier, 137–8
Public schools, 29
Punishment: Anglo-Saxon, 40–1;
  18th-c. English, 24, 29, 47–8;
  Elizabethan, 23, 45; Roman,
  34–40, 124; in schools, 29
Puritanism, 103–5, 157

Racial prejudice, 51, 77–8, 142
Ranke, Leopold von, 199
Rationalism, 68–9, 158
Rayburn, Senator Sam, 192
Reade, Winwood, 24, 95
Reformation, 155–7, 186
Reich, Emil, 80, 81, 82, 84, 87,
  88, 92
Religion: dogma, attacks on, 67–9,
  72; future of, 171–3; and moral
  code, 124, 135; and mythology,
  147–9, 161; origins, 144–6; and
  scientific thought, 157–8, 161,
  167, 172
Religion and the Rise of Capitalism
  (Tawney), 188
Religion without Revelation
  (Huxley), 170
Religious persecution, 150, 153–4,
  166; Christianity and, 60–4;
  Roman, 59–62
Renaissance, 3–4, 64, 101, 186, 202
Renan, Ernest, 68, 69
Revolutionary movements, 186–9
Richardson, Samuel, 48
Rights of Man, The (Paine), 66–7,
  110
Rise of the Meritocracy, The
  (Young), 219
Robinson, Dr John, Bishop of
  Woolwich, 172
Roman Law, 34–40, 184
Romashkin, P., 196
Rome, 20–2; freedom of expres-
  sion, 58–61; government, 178–
  81, 184, 189, 211; and inter-

nationalism, 211, 216; legal
  system, 34–40, 50, 184;
  morality, 122–7, 129, 130; religion, 150–2; religious persecution, 59–62; Senate, 178–9,
  181; social divisions, 88, 89;
  women in, 88–93; working
  man in, 20–2
Ross, Sir David, 134, 135
Rousseau, Jean-Jacques, 187
Russell, Bertrand, 176, 177, 211,
  222–3, 225
Russia: criticism, suppression of,
  74, 75–7; economy, 214;
  government, 194–7; legal system, 52; opposition to America,
  211–12, 216; religion, attitude
  to, 165–6; and UNO, 214, 215
Russian Revolution, 187

Sacrifice, human, 118
Sacrilege, 39, 58
Saint-Pierre, Abbé de, 5, 158, 159
Saint-Simon, Comte de, 7, 8
Salvation, 3, 4, 135
Sampson, R. V., 130, 199, 200, 207
Samurai class, Wells's, 13–14
Sandwich, John Montagu, 4th
  Earl of, 71
Sartre, Jean-Paul, 16
Schapiro, Leonard, 165, 194,
  196–7
Scholasticism, 155
Science: and Christian teaching,
  68–9, 72; medieval, 3–4; mod-
  ern, beginnings of, 66; and
  religion, 157–8, 161, 167, 172;
  Renaissance and, 64
Science and the Modern World
  (Whitehead), 209
Seltman, Dr Charles, 84–5
Senate: American, 192; Roman,
  178–9, 181
Seneca, 93
Senility, postponement of, 232,
  237

259